Key Issues

THE SUBJECTION OF WOMEN
Contemporary Responses to John Stuart Mill

Key Issues

THE SUBJECTION OF WOMEN

Contemporary Responses to
JOHN STUART MILL

Edited and Introduced by
ANDREW PYLE
University of Bristol

THOEMMES PRESS

© Thoemmes Press 1995

Published in 1995 by
Thoemmes Press
11 Great George Street
Bristol BS1 5RR
England

ISBN
Paper : 1 85506 408 1
Cloth : 1 85506 409 X

The Subjection of Women :
Contemporary Responses to John Stuart Mill
Key Issues No. 6

British Library Cataloguing-in-Publication Data

A catalogue record of this title is available
from the British Library

Printed in Great Britain by Antony Rowe Ltd., Chippenham

CONTENTS

The reviews reprinted in this book have been taken from original copies and the different grammatical and stylistic arrangement of each has been preserved.

INTRODUCTION

Background

The *Subjection of Women*, although the work of a man, is one of the landmarks of British feminism.[1] It was written in 1861, not long after the death of Mill's beloved Harriet in 1858, but was not published until 1869. Why the long delay? The answer seems to have been that Mill waited until he thought the time was ripe. He served as MP for Westminster between 1865 and 1868, and proposed an amendment to the Reform Bill suggesting that the reference to the male sex be struck out of the electoral franchise. This was, he comments in his *Autobiography*, 'by far the most important, perhaps the only really important public service I performed in the capacity of a Member of Parliament'.[2] A petition was submitted to the House of Commons in 1866, and found as many as 73 backers, including eminent figures such as Disraeli and Salisbury.[3] Around the same time, Mill's stepdaughter Helen Taylor was active in the establishment of a society for the extension of the franchise to women. Mill himself was surprisingly optimistic about speedy success; in fact, another half-century would elapse before the final victory.

Interpretation of *The Subjection of Women* has unfortunately tended to become confused with assessment of Harriet Taylor and her influence on Mill. On this subject there is little that is new to say.[4] Mill's exaggerated estimate of Harriet's

1 J. S. Mill, *The Subjection of Women*, edited with a new introduction by Susan Moller Okin, Indianapolis, Hackett, 1988. See also J. S. Mill, *On Liberty and Other Essays*, ed. John Gray, Oxford, OUP, 1991.

2 J. S. Mill, *Autobiography* (Penguin Books, Harmondsworth, 1989), p. 222.

3 See Brian Harrison, *Separate Spheres: the Opposition to Women's Suffrage in Britain* (London, Croom Helm, 1978), p. 27. Among the prominent 'antis' were Gladstone and Queen Victoria.

4 Anne Mozley suggests that Mill's infatuation with Harriet clouded his brain, a charge accepted even by some of Mill's disciples. Bain, for example, thinks that the *Subjection* is full of 'exaggeration' and 'special pleading', due

talents and virtues has embarrassed many of his disciples, but affects the arguments not one jot. Mill tells us clearly in his *Autobiography* that his belief in the equality of women was not gained from Harriet; on the contrary, it was one of his earliest political convictions.[5] Meeting Harriet did, however, help to put some flesh on what had been, until then, 'little more than an abstract principle'. She also helped Mill to see how the subjection of women was linked to a wide variety of social evils – a key theme, of course, of the book.

The central contention of the work is stated with exemplary clarity on its first page. It is:

> That the principle which regulates the existing social relations between the two sexes – the legal subordination of one sex to the other – is wrong in itself, and now one of the chief hindrances to human improvement; and that it ought to be replaced by a principle of perfect equality, admitting no power or privilege on the one side, nor disability on the other.[6]

In support of this bold assertion Mill first argues, in Chapter One, that the subordinate status of women is not grounded in Nature. Chapter Two likens the position of the wife, in a Victorian household, to that of a domestic slave, and points to the demoralising effects of the master-slave relation on both parties. Chapter Three cites historical examples of what particular women have done to illustrate what women are capable of achieving. Chapter Four dwells upon the benefits – to individuals and to society – of female emancipation.

The present volume consists largely of reactions to *The Subjection of Women*, together with a small selection of the

no doubt to Harriet's influence. See Alexander Bain, *John Stuart Mill: A Criticism, with Personal Recollections* (London, Longmans, Green, & Co, 1882), pp. 130–31. Stefan Collini, in his introduction to Mill's *Essays on Equality, Law, and Education* (Vol. XXI of the *Collected Works*, published by the University of Toronto Press and Routledge Kegan Paul, Toronto and Buffalo, 1984, p. xxx), describes Harriet as a 'very clever, imaginative, passionate, intense, imperious, paranoid, unpleasant woman', but insists that Mill was already a committed feminist before he ever met her. For more details of the relationship, see F. A. Hayek, *John Stuart Mill and Harriet Taylor: their Correspondence and subsequent Marriage* (London, Routledge & Kegan Paul, 1951).

5   J. S. Mill, *Autobiography*, (ref. 2), p. 185.

6   J. S. Mill, *The Subjection of Women*, with a new introduction by Susan Moller Okin (Indianapolis, Hackett, 1988), p. 1.

ensuing controversial literature on the specific issue of political enfranchisement. We do however depart from our normal procedure by including two earlier pieces: a chapter of James Mill's famous *Essay on Government*, and Harriet Taylor's *Enfranchisement of Women*. The justification for this departure from precedent is straightforward. In the first place, these two individuals were far and away the two most important influences on John Stuart Mill's life and thought.[7] In the second place, much of Mill's argument is implicit in the former piece and explicit in the latter.

Like its companion volume *On Liberty*, the *Subjection* addresses a number of concrete legal and political issues in a manner that raises – often acutely – points and issues of philosophical principle. Let us seek, at the cost of some artificiality, to separate these issues.

Representative Government

James Mill's famous *Essay on Government*, written for the *Encyclopaedia Britannica* of 1820, marks an important turning-point in utilitarian thought. Jeremy Bentham had set out to reform the English Law, on the assumption that his utilitarian criterion ('does it promote the greatest happiness of the greatest number?') was obviously the touchstone of good legislation. The reception of his proposals for legal reform convinced him, however, that the British ruling class did not genuinely desire the greatest happiness of the greatest number, but were on the contrary protecting their own narrow vested interests. Government, at least in its existing form, was not the solution but part of the problem.[8]

This is the problem faced by James Mill in his *Essay*. How are we to ensure that the rulers act in the interest of the ruled? Monarchy and hereditary aristocracy manifestly fail the test: they provide no safeguard against the dominance of 'sinister interests'. Direct democracy may be simply unworkable in a

---

7   When Mill junior records his intellectual debts in the *Autobiography*, about 60% is devoted to these two central figures. See John Robson's introduction to the *Autobiography* (ref. 2), p. 13.

8   For the transformation of utilitarianism from a movement for legal reform into a school of political radicalism, see Leslie Stephen, *The English Utilitarians* (3 volumes, London, Duckworth, 1900; reprinted Bristol, Thoemmes, 1991), Volume 2.

large modern state. Representative government seems to
provide the only solution. But who should be allowed to vote
for the representatives? Must we allow all citizens the vote, or
would a subset of them suffice? The interests of children, says
Mill, are looked after by their parents; likewise, the interests of
'almost' all women are taken care of by their fathers or
husbands. With this casual aside, Mill senior dismisses the
issue of 'votes for women'.

The *Essay on Government* was the object of a savage attack,
in the *Edinburgh Review*, by the eminent Whig historian
Thomas Babington Macaulay. Most of Macaulay's polemic is
directed against Mill's methodology, but he also points out a
glaring inconsistency in Mill's position on votes for women.
Why, Macaulay asks scornfully, is Mill so confident that a
monarch *cannot* have the interests of his subjects at heart, but
that husbands and fathers *must* share the interests of their
wives and daughters? 'Without adducing one fact, without
taking the trouble to perplex the question by one sophism, he
placidly dogmatizes away the interests of one half of the human
race.'[9] Macaulay is not positively advocating votes for women
himself; he is merely pointing out that such a conclusion seems
to be the inevitable consequence of Mill's premises.

The younger generation of utilitarians, John Stuart Mill
included, accepted the force of this criticism, and argued that
the principles of the *Essay on Government* in fact entail more
radical conclusions than Mill senior had drawn. It is far from
absurd to suppose that women may have a special interest in
some piece of legislation; the only way to guarantee that this
interest will not be neglected is to admit them into the
franchise.[10] To suppose that the interests of women are best
served by their menfolk is naïve at best. Mill junior thus had a
principled reason for *not* proposing new laws regulating such
subjects as marriage and divorce. New legislation on such
topics, he insisted, should not even be attempted until the views
of women – whose interests are so vitally concerned – can be
represented. On this view, the political enfranchisement of

9   Thomas Babington Macaulay, 'Utilitarian Logic and Politics', *Edinburgh
    Review*, Vol. 49, March 1829, pp. 159-89. See especially pp. 177-8.
10 J. S. Mill tells us in his *Autobiography* that he always regarded his father's
    exclusion of women from the suffrage as 'as great an error as any of those
    against which the essay was directed' (p. 93), and adds that Macaulay's
    savage review 'gave me much to think about' (p. 127).

women becomes the primary goal, valuable not merely in itself but as a precondition of the adequate representation of women's interests in general.

How did the critics react to this fundamental utilitarian argument for the extension of the franchise to women? To the modern reader at least, their responses sound a little lame. The liberal Goldwin Smith repeats, rather surprisingly, the claim that the interests of wives are represented by their husbands, but seems not to address the obvious retort that (a) the coincidence of interests in a marriage is more an ideal than a fact, and (b) not all women are wives. Margaret Oliphant worries about the consequences for a marriage of political opposition between man and wife, but it is hard to see any weighty matter of political principle at stake here. William Dixon raises a deep worry for his male readers: since women are in the majority, he notes, their votes would outweigh those of men on any issue where the interests of the sexes are directly opposed. This, he sees, would involve a revolutionary shift in the balance of power, and is thus to be avoided as extremely dangerous.

None of these criticisms detracts from the force of the original argument, which is set out once more, with great force and clarity, by Millicent Garrett Fawcett. She lists no fewer than thirteen objections to women's suffrage, and subjects them to a withering critique. It is said, for example, that the interests of women are already represented. But the same was said of working men before 1867, and was not found acceptable. The same arguments can be re-applied to the new case. Are there no laws which press unjustly upon women? How, without a political voice, can women ensure that their interests are taken into account?

Preferences versus Interests

The argument so far has turned on the adequate representation of interests. But utilitarianism is often construed as being concerned with the satisfaction of people's subjective *preferences* rather than their interests. To assume that preferences and interests will always coincide would be dangerously naïve. What are we to say if our assessment of the interests of a given group diverges from the expressed preferences of its members? Have they all been brainwashed? Are they incapable of seeing

where their true interests lie? Or should we re-examine our
views about their interests?

Objections of this kind were levelled against Mill by James
Fitzjames Stephen, Anne Mozley, and William Dixon. The
existing generation of women, Stephen insists, do not mind
their subjection: 'The consciousness of this haunts Mr Mill
throughout the whole of his argument, and embarrasses him at
every turn.' Anne Mozley takes the argument further, castigat-
ing Mill for setting himself up as the self-appointed champion
of the rights of women without even stopping to ask whether
they want his help. Mill seems dissatisfied with his countrywomen as he finds them, a sure sign that he is disappointed by
their reception of his efforts on their behalf. He imagines
widespread discontent where it does not exist, generalising
from a limited experience of a few exceptional women. The
fact that ordinary women tend to be conservative in spirit
presents a problem for Mill; he has to regard such contented
females as 'artificial products', thus justifying overriding the
views of concrete people in the name of mere abstractions of his
own mind.

A similar objection is raised by Margaret Oliphant. According to Mill, every Victorian wife is - in law at least — no better
than a slave. But women don't recognise this picture as an
accurate representation of the married state. It is, says
Oliphant, just 'a gloomy image conjured up in the philosopher's study'. On a topic such as this, she continues, we can
contrast our own observations with the philosopher's theories.
The manifest discrepancy shows that Mill's judgment is
'sometimes warped by theory', not the product of impartial
enquiry. Real women, says Oliphant, look forward to the
married state as their proper goal, and do not regard the
marriage laws as an oppressive burden.

If Mill's utilitarianism were based simply on the maximal
satisfaction of existing preferences, this objection would - if its
basic premise is true - pose a fundamental problem.[11] Why
liberate the slaves, if they don't object to their condition? In
fact, however, Mill's utilitarianism is not of this crude kind. As
he explains in *On Liberty*, 'I regard utility as the ultimate
appeal on all ethical questions; but it must be utility in the

11 Much of the force of Julia Annas' critique of Mill ('Mill and the Subjection
of Women', *Philosophy*, Vol. 52, 1977, pp. 179-94) rests on this naïve
and indefensible interpretation of Mill's utilitarianism.

largest sense, grounded on the permanent interests of man as a progressive being'.[12] If many existing men, and no doubt some existing women too, actually prefer the status quo, this provides some positive grounds in its favour; but the 'permanent interests of man as a progressive being' may outweigh those grounds and require radical change.

Feminists could therefore provide a principled reason why existing preferences should be sacrificed in the name of long-term benefits. Alternatively, they can deny the premise of the conservative's argument, and insist that existing women are dissatisfied with their lot. Both responses are present in Harriet Taylor's *Enfranchisement*. It is said, she reports, that women do not seek emancipation, and reject the claims made on their behalf. But, she retorts, wouldn't the women in Turkish harems say the same? This suggests that she would be prepared to endorse measures for the emancipation of women, even if the majority of existing women were opposed to them. She also, however, points to the evidence from America of a growing number of women who clearly do resent their political subordination, and are not afraid to say so.

Frances Power Cobbe also addresses the same objection. The conservatives claim that women do not protest, but gladly accept the domination of the male sex. In the first place, retorts Cobbe, this is not entirely true – many women do protest. In the second place, we can be confident that more women *would* protest if not bribed and intimidated into silence. (She might have added a third class, women who suffer from existing arrangements but have too low a level of political consciousness to diagnose the source of their suffering.)

Millicent Garrett Fawcett regards this objection – that women do not want emancipation – as the most formidable of them all. It makes no difference, she sees, to the abstract justice of the case, but it clearly does affect practical politics. (Many an unjust law will remain on the statute books if no one demands its repeal.) Fawcett's reply to the conservatives is that many women are already petitioning parliament to obtain the vote, and that this demand is daily growing more powerful. As liberal principles come increasingly to dominate European political thought, she argues, the case for the emancipation of

[12] J. S. Mill, *On Liberty*, in *On Liberty in Focus*, edited by J. Gray and G. W. Smith (London, Routledge, 1991), p. 31.

women – in essence, just a straightforward corollary of those principles – will gradually come to appear irresistible. This, it may be conjectured, would have been Mill's own answer to the objection. Once liberal principles are established, no woman will accept that her inferior status can be due to a mere accident of birth. Resentment against the status quo can therefore be expected to spread.

Nature and Nurture

Another standard objection of the conservatives was, of course, their invocation of 'Nature' in support of patriarchy. Women, it is alleged, are different *by nature* from men, and this essential difference provides the grounds for their political subordination. Men are said to be naturally more physically robust, or more intellectually gifted, or just better suited to the rigours of public debate. Biology itself, according to some of the conservatives, gives the casting vote in favour of patriarchy.

Chapter One of the *Subjection* attempts to undermine this line of argument. Mill does not flatly deny that there are natural psychological differences between men and women, nor does he assert that observed gender differences are all cultural artefacts. His position is rather more subtle. In the absence of the right sorts of controlled experiments, he says, we can't know whether existing differences reflect 'nature' or 'nurture'. If a boy of sixteen shows more physical courage, say, than his sister, this *may* reflect innate gender differences; but equally, it *may* be a cultural artefact, reflecting only different education and expectations. If we wish to determine which of these hypotheses is correct, we would need to establish a science of *ethology*, that is, of the development of human character under varying environmental conditions.[13]

Unfortunately, the science of ethology is, Mill sees, conspicuous only by its absence. This is particularly manifest in the debate over the nature of women. Since the institution of patriarchy has been (almost) universal among humankind, we don't have the necessary 'control' group to check generalizations about the nature of women. If all observed women share

13 For Mill's views on the (hoped-for) science of ethology, see his *System of Logic*, Book 4, Chapter 4, in Ernest Nagel, ed., *John Stuart Mill's Philosophy of Scientific Method* (New York, Hafner, 1950), pp. 317-24. It is significant that Mill thinks that science must be deductive rather than merely observational.

some given trait of character, this may still be an artefact of an upbringing within a patriarchal culture.

It is sometimes claimed that Mill falls into two large inconsistencies in the *Subjection*. In the first place, it is alleged, his lists of female achievements in Chapter Three contradict his clear denial, in Chapter One, that we know anything of the nature or essence of woman.[14] This objection is just a mistake. Mill cites evidence of what women have achieved as evidence of what women *can* achieve; this serves only to exclude theories that would make women, by their very nature, incapable of (e.g.) political activity. Such anecdotal evidence provides the basis for no positive essentialist claim; but Mill was fully aware of the fact. In the second place, Mill is often accused of glibly endorsing conventional views about gender roles.[15] But such assumptions must be regarded as personal conjectures, not as part of Mill's political doctrine. He thus *guesses* that many women will remain content with the traditional role of wife and mother; but *insists* that all women must be free to choose the path of life best suited to their needs and talents. There is no inconsistency here.

Mill's abrupt and peremptory dismissal of the whole of human history as irrelevant to his argument was sure to evoke a storm of protest. The *Christian Observer* objects to this stratagem as tantamount to 'dismissing the teaching and experience of past ages as of no value in the discussion of the question', and re-emphasises the traditional doctrine of 'separate spheres'. Woman's function, we are reminded, is not inferior but complementary to man's; she is intended by Nature (that is, by God) as a 'help meet' for man, and her energies are best employed in her own proper sphere. Anne Mozley too admits a natural difference between men and women, claiming that women are less capable of profound and concentrated thought. There are exceptional cases, of course, but laws and institutions must be adapted to the norm rather than to the

---

[14]   Even Stefan Colloni, in his generally sympathetic introduction to Mill's *Essays on Equality, Laws, and Education* (ref. 4), thinks that Mill falls into inconsistencies here. See p. xxxiii.

[15]   This accusation can be found in several modern critics of Mill, notably in Susan Moller Okin's *Women in Western Political Thought* (Princeton University Press, Princeton, New Jersey, 1979), pp. 226–29. See also Zillah R. Eisenstein, *The Radical Future of Liberal Feminism* (Longman, New York & London, 1981), pp. 134–37.

xviii   The Subjection of Women

exception. Margaret Oliphant seeks to ground the doctrine of
separate spheres in biology. By nature, she insists, the man is
the bread-winner and the woman is the child-bearer, child-
rearer, and home-builder. Any theory which ignores these
biological facts does so at its peril.

Answers to these objections can be found in Harriet Taylor
and in Frances Power Cobbe. The 'proper sphere' for all human
beings, says Taylor, is 'the largest and the highest they are able
to attain to'. But to find this 'proper sphere' requires freedom of
choice. There need be no fear that women will usurp jobs they
are not capable of doing well; free competition on equal terms
will prevent this. What about motherhood? Not all women,
she replies, are mothers. And *if* there are professions genuinely
incompatible with motherhood, this will 'take care of itself'
without any involvement of law. (She clearly doesn't see that it
might be the business of the state to ensure equal opportunities
by, e.g., the provision of creches.)

In many ways, Frances Power Cobbe's response to the
conservatives is the most insightful of all. This is because she
grants them all their premises, and shows that their conclusions
still do not follow. Cobbe thinks that there are natural
differences of character between men and women – she even
admits that women may be intellectually inferior. She also
endorses traditional gender roles as part of God's grand design
for humankind. The division of labour within a marriage into
'external' and 'domestic' affairs strikes her as 'obvious', and
even as 'rightful'. In modern terms, she is anything but a radical
feminist. But, she insists, no political consequences flow from
these essentialist premises. It would be absurd to claim that all
women aspire naturally to be wives and mothers, and then to
try to coerce young women into marriage by denying them
alternatives.

Equality

Mill advocates a 'principle of perfect equality' for the relations
between the sexes, adding by way of explanation that this
principle admits 'no power or privilege on the one side, nor
disability on the other'. Given his explicit admission of
ignorance about the respective natures of men and women, we
cannot interpret this as an empirical thesis about equality of
powers or capacities. Rather, it has to be a normative claim

about equal rights – to be justified, presumably, by means of an indirect utilitarian argument. Unfortunately, the very word 'equality' seems to invite misunderstandings, and to generate muddle and confusion.

The most prominent of Mill's critics on this subject is James Fitzjames Stephen. For Stephen, the *Subjection of Women* is 'a work from which I dissent from the first sentence to the last'; its doctrine of equality is dismissed as 'unsound in every respect'. Differences of age and sex are, Stephen argues, so deep-seated that no system of laws can afford to ignore them. Mill admits, of course, that children must live in a state of dependence: to treat them as if they were adults would be 'infinitely worse than barbarism', and terribly cruel to the children themselves. But, Stephen continues, difference of sex is also a real inequality, and should as such be recognised by law. Men are not just physically stronger than women; they have greater 'intellectual force' and 'vigour of character'. Women are therefore in need of male protection; to regard them as equals is to do them a profound disservice.

Stephen does not address the obvious objections to his analogy between women and children. In the first place, all of us are children for much of our lives, so the legal minority of children is not incompatible with equality of all persons before the law. To justify treating children as legal minors one only needs to show that their interests are *better* protected by their parents than by the children themselves, and that the state of dependence may actually be necessary for them to arrive at full autonomy in due course. The situation of women is, rather obviously, parallel in neither respect.

What about the attempt to argue for different political rights from differences in physical or mental vigour? This is common ground for the conservatives, from the *Saturday Review* and the *Christian Observer* down to Anne Mozley, Sir Henry Taylor, and Fitzjames Stephen. But would any of them be prepared to follow this line of argument through to its conclusions? If political and legal rights are grounded in mere physical strength, shall we give two votes to blacksmiths and disenfranchise weedy clergymen? Are men to lose their rights as they become feeble in old age? Exactly the same points hold of mental vigour. The point is clearly grasped by Frances Power Cobbe and Millicent Garrett Fawcett. Cobbe, unimpressed by Mill's Chapter Three, grants the mental superiority of men, but sees that it is irrelevant to political questions concerning rights. Fawcett regards the question of the alleged intellectual inferiority of women as contentious, but – fortunately – irrelevant to her argument. Suppose, she asks, the Scots were proved to be intellectually superior to the English: 'Would the people of London be willing to relinquish their right to the franchise if it were proved to demonstration that on the average . . . they were intellectually inferior to the inhabitants of Edinburgh?' The question is obviously rhetorical, but it is worth pursuing it further and asking what extra conditions would have to be fulfilled for someone to be happy about ceding his or her rights to an intellectual superior. In the first place, one would have to be absolutely confident that this superior had one's interests at heart. In the second place, one would have to regard the exercise of one's political rights as having only a narrow and crudely instrumental value.

Justice or Expediency?

In much of this debate, questions of justice are contrasted with questions of expediency. Mill had of course attempted, in his *Utilitarianism*, to give an account of our intuitions of justice in utilitarian terms,[16] but this attempt scarcely resurfaces in the *Subjection*, where justice functions for the most part as a primitive term, and he constructs a twin-track argument for his position based equally on justice and on utility. In Chapter Four, for example, when seeking to show what good the adoption of his principles would do, he answers first in terms of placing the relations between the sexes on a footing of justice; then in terms of the advantages to society of this change. But do considerations of justice always coincide with considerations of expediency?

John Morley's contribution to the debate over the enfranchisement of women was to publish a translation of Condorcet's 'Plea for the Citizenship of Women'. The principles of the French Revolution, so long derided by English conservatives, at last get a public hearing in Britain, at least among the

16   J. S. Mill, *Utilitarianism*, in John Gray, ed., *On Liberty and Other Essays* (ref. 1), Chapter 5, 'On the Connection between Justice and Utility', pp. 176–201. Mill admits a psychological distinction between intuitions of justice and considerations of utility, but insists that the moral authority of the former intuitions must ultimately be grounded in the general good.

avant garde. Condorcet took the 'high road' throughout, arguing that the much-vaunted 'rights of man' *must*, in simple consistency, be extended equally to women. There are, he admitted, objections based on utility, but these cannot override the requirements of justice. After all, utility has been urged in defence of all manner of indefensible institutions and practices, e.g. chattel slavery.

The same high line is taken by Harriet Taylor at the beginning of the *Enfranchisement*. The equality of all citizens before the law is here presented as a simple requirement of justice. In the democratic USA, for example, no one can deny women their claims. 'All men are created equal' cannot, surely, refer only to white males? 'The contradiction between principle and practice cannot be explained away.' Later on in the same work, however, she adds utilitarian arguments to intuitive ones, attacking existing institutions as involving both an injustice against individuals and a loss of valuable talents to society as a whole. The patriarchal family, in particular, is denounced as a school of tyranny and a breeding-ground of anti-social vices, an argument Mill was to make much of in the *Subjection*.

But if 'abstract justice' and 'social expediency' are independent variables, providing the twin pillars of the feminist argument, what are Mill and Taylor going to say in the cases where they appear to pull in opposite directions? Sir Henry Taylor thinks it might be politically expedient to admit women to the suffrage, but rejects Mill's claim that it is required by justice. William Brighty Rands, on the other hand, thinks that justice requires the enfranchisement of women, insists that justice overrides utility, but is unhappy with the inevitable conclusion. To admit women to the suffrage at present would have, he sees, profoundly reactionary implications, and thus produce worse government rather than better. He ends rather lamely by admitting that if women demand the suffrage then they cannot in justice be denied it, but expressing the hope that they will not (yet) demand it.

In Goldwin Smith's article, 'Female Suffrage', this utilitarian case against votes for women appears in its full force, unfettered by any considerations of abstract right. Although Goldwin Smith was a liberal in his politics, and had even signed Mill's petition in support of female suffrage, experience of political life in the USA had caused him to change his mind.

Women, he argues, are reactionary, sentimental, and priest-ridden in their politics, and are always to be found on the conservative side in any pubic debate. To allow women the vote would lead to the restoration of the Bourbons in France, and to the prohibition of alcohol in the USA. The utilitarian case *against* votes for women is therefore a compelling one.

Goldwin Smith's article was seen as a desertion by his liberal friends, and provoked an immediate reply by the Irish economist John Elliot Cairnes, who argued on utilitarian lines that admission of women to the suffrage in Britain would not have the dreadful consequences that had been alleged. Once again, however, the final word had already been provided by Millicent Garrett Fawcett. There are some in the liberal camp, she notes, who fear that female suffrage would retard political and social reforms. But, she retorts, this is an argument against representative government, *not* against women's rights. Are women to be denied the vote on the grounds that they are likely to vote for conservative measures? Then you should, by the same reasoning, deny the vote to conservative men! If representative government is the best political system, then we must accept its logic; a 'representative' system in which the views of half the citizens are not represented is no better than 'a farce'.

Marriage

Turning now to more concrete and practical concerns, we must first discuss reactions to Mill's views on marriage. In English law, the Victorian patriarch still ruled his family as an absolute monarch: the wife had no right to her own property, no protection against marital rape, and no say in the education of her children. In a happy marriage, of course, the absolute legal power of the husband would not be exercised, and the wife would often get her way by persuasion. But not all marriages are successful, and the Victorian law gave wives almost no protection against the abuse of power by their husbands. Even in successful marriages, the existence of absolute power on one side and legal subjection on the other may have insidious effects. This is the burden of the argument in Harriet Taylor's *Enfranchisement*, and later in Mill's *Subjection*. It is note-worthy that Mill explicitly renounced, on the occasion of their marriage, all claim to absolute patriarchal powers.

The effect of patriarchy, according to Taylor and Mill, is to make men arbitrary and wilful, each a mini-tyrant in his own home, and to make women sycophantic and scheming, seeking to get their way by underhand means. Where there is no equality, there can be no respect; where there is no respect, there can be no true partnership.[17] In place of the traditional hierarchical picture of authority and submission, Mill offers a picture of a quasi-contractual relation between equals. In other contexts, he argues, this arrangement has not proved incompatible with effective decision-making. Only a relation of equals, he insists, can make marriage into a school of moral and civil virtues. This ideal conception of marriage is endorsed by the spinster Frances Power Cobbe, and by Millicent Garrett Fawcett, wife of Henry Fawcett, the blind professor of economics at Cambridge.

Mill clearly thinks that his ideal of marriage as a partnership of equals is compatible with the traditional division of labour between husband and wife. Harriet seems more radical in this regard, claiming that enforced domesticity is the reason why Victorian women are petty and trivial, incapable of taking an interest in public affairs, and often no better than a drag on the efforts of their husbands. (One thinks immediately of Rosamund Lydgate in George Eliot's *Middlemarch*.) This line of argument is taken up by Cairnes, who suggests that shared experience (e.g. in the workplace) may be a necessary condition for a good marriage, and that the confinement of women to the domestic sphere may thus have harmful social consequences. It is a striking feature of this debate that the advocates of feminism, male and female alike, are often frankly contemptuous of the vast majority of the women of their age.

Mills conception of marriage attracted a torrent of ridicule and abuse. He seems to regard it, says Goldwin Smith, as the union of two souls (accidentally male and female) 'in search of philosophical truth'. The *Christian Observer* accuses Mill of ignoring altogether 'the physical side of human nature', and treating men and women 'as if they were disembodied spirits'. Margaret Oliphant agrees, arguing that every young bride – even one schooled in Mill's principles – wants to serve and

---

17   The importance of marital friendship in the argument of the *Subjection* is emphasised by Mary Lyndon Shanley in her article, 'Marital Slavery and Friendship: John Stuart Mill's *The Subjection of Women*', *Political Theory*, Vol. 9, 1981, pp. 229–47.

minister to her husband. By nature, she insists, every wife is condemned to periods of dependence on the protection of her husband; any account of marriage which ignores these facts is 'a futile theory', based only on abstractions.

The *Christian Observer* also sought to add a supernatural support for patriarchy. Mill was generally willing, in his capacity as a public moralist, to make common cause with liberal Christians against their reactionary foes. But what if the great authorities of the Christian Church are explicitly in favour of patriarchy? Mill denies that Saint Paul's command, 'wives, obey your husbands' can be taken as an unqualified endorsement of the hierarchic principle. In his epistle to the Ephesians, our reviewer retorts, Paul is rather more explicit. Here he writes: 'Wives, submit yourselves unto your husbands as unto the Lord. For the husband is the head of the wife, even as Christ is the head of the Church; . . .'.[18] So much for Mill's claim that the equality he advocates is 'also the law of Christianity', unless he is prepared to dismiss Paul's opinion as un-Christian.

James Fitzjames Stephen raises a more fundamental objection. Mill assumes that equality is the only basis on which marriage can be a school of moral education; Stephen simply denies this. It is good for children to learn to submit to the superior wisdom of their parents; might it not be equally good for wives to submit to their husbands? Authority, Stephen argues, must be vested in a single head; all Mill's talk about contracts and negotiations is merely 'visionary'. In cases of disagreement, the wife ought to give way, as the first mate of a ship would give way to the captain. To resent this is the sign of a base and mutinous disposition. Mill will ask, of course, whether the superior (parent, captain, husband) is required to give reasons for his orders. If reasons are given, and appreciated, there is no need of commands; if no reasons are offered and blind obedience is demanded of the inferior, the moral evils of arbitrary power and subjection are as apparent as before.

In the history of our legal system there has been a gradual transition, Stephen admits, from *status* (fixed by birth) to *contract* (freely entered into), but this need not represent progress. The existence of a contract does not, Stephen insists,

18   Epistle to the Ephesians, Chapter 5, Verses 22–23.

entail any real equality: contract is still compatible with authority on the one side and submission on the other, and with extremes of wealth and poverty. The will of the stronger party will inevitably determine' the nature and terms of the contract. But this entails that, in a society governed according to Mill's principles, women would find themselves in a very vulnerable position. They would lose the protection that their current status affords them, and become indeed 'men's slaves and drudges'. The same objection is made by Anne Mozley, who thinks that Mill's book will serve a useful purpose, if only negatively, that is by teaching that 'meddling with the marriage laws is dealing with edge tools'. Existing marriage laws, she reminds her readers, serve to protect women against male exploitation.

Divorce

If marriage is a contract rather than a sacrament, does it not follow that it should be terminable at will? As it stands, of course, it is meant to be 'till death do us part', but would any rational being enter into a contractual relationship on such strict terms? From Mill's liberal principles it seems to follow, according to the critics, that the terms of the contract should be relaxed to make divorce and remarriage available more or less on demand. But what, they ask, would be the effects of this on public morality?

The *Saturday Review* was, throughout this period, a prominent voice in the opposition to the emancipation of women. Its reviewer notes that Mill has failed conspicuously to discuss divorce and remarriage, and expresses fears about the 'demoralising' effects of such measures, especially on female modesty. Anne Mozley too points out that Mill's principles would permit separation and divorce on 'frivolous' grounds. Mill, she notes, seeks to evade the difficult issue of divorce, but allows separation more or less on demand; this will have 'hideous' consequences for morals. It would also increase the vulnerability of the wife: if a married couple separate at fifty, she asks rhetorically, which partner would have the better prospects?

Sir Henry Taylor repeats the same charge: that Mill had run away from the difficult subject of divorce rather than spell out the shocking consequences of his own principles. Fitzjames

Stephen agrees: if marriage is a contract between equals, he argues, it may be dissolved at pleasure. 'The advocates of women's rights are exceedingly shy of stating this plainly.' But if this were granted, says Stephen, it would indeed make wives the slaves of their husbands. Even Sheldon Amos, a generally sympathetic critic, takes Mill to task for evading this problem.

In discussing Mill's views on this question, we must distinguish between his private opinions – which tended to be extremely radical[19] – and what he allowed to appear in print. He had mentioned the subject in On Liberty, where he had cited – without endorsing – the opinion of Baron Wilhelm von Humboldt that divorce should be available on demand. As it stands, Mill comments, this opinion is too simple to be defensible: some compensation may be due to a deserted spouse, and some provision must be made for the needs of children. Humboldt's view nevertheless provides a valuable starting-point for detailed discussion of the implications of liberal principles in this disputed domain.

In the Subjection, Mill justifies his omission of the subject of divorce by a manoeuvre that seemed disingenuous to many of his critics, but may be more principled than it appears. What he says is that his first priority is the political enfranchisement of women. Legislation about marriage and divorce, he argues, touches so profoundly the interests of women that it would be presumptuous folly for MPs to try to tamper with it until the views of women themselves can be heard. In the profound social revolution that Mill envisages, votes for women must come first, since it is a necessary precondition of progress in other areas.

Education

The issue of female education is intimately connected with questions about women's nature and their supposed vocation for the married state. The conservative view was, of course, that every woman is intended 'by nature' for the traditional role of wife and mother. If this is so, then giving her an academic or professional education will seem like a waste of valuable resources, and may actually make her less capable of fulfilling

---

19   In a letter of 1855 to an unidentified correspondent, Mill advocates 'entire freedom on both sides to dissolve this like any other partnership'. See Collected Works, (ref. 4), Vol. XIV, p. 500.

her traditional role. Goldwin Smith, for example, suggests that educated women might, from a biological point of view, make worse mothers.

Unfortunately for the conservatives, the numbers of the sexes didn't add up. To put it crudely, there were too many women, surplus to the marital requirements of the males in a monogamous society. If all women were intended by God for marriage, it seemed that He had got His sums wrong. In reply to the claim that the family was woman's 'proper sphere', Millicent Garrett Fawcett points out that Britain had about one million more women than men. What to do with all these surplus women posed a serious social problem, and caused some rethinking even among those who were basically opposed to female emancipation. Margaret Oliphant, for example, takes a traditional view of marriage, but notes the existence of a growing class of single women wanting access to educational institutions. Although a woman cannot, she thinks, combine a marriage with a career, and most will choose the former, this is irrelevant to these single women. It seems to be only prejudice that prevents them from becoming doctors, lawyers, and politicians, and thus using their energies and abilities for the public good. Goldwin Smith also notes the existence of a large number of unmarried women seeking to make a living, and requires that 'every facility ought in justice to be afforded to them' to do so.

Sir Henry Taylor discusses in some detail the lifting of legal restrictions on the entry of women into the professions. Only custom and sentiment, he says, stand in the way of the admission of women to the priesthood, but custom and sentiment are not altogether to be despised. As for medicine, there would be 'stumbling blocks' (mixed education, shocking dissection rooms), but the existence of qualified women would be a significant advantage in some areas. It is only in the case of the law that Taylor sees, rather curiously, a 'special unfitness' of women for the profession. Could a young woman, he asks, go through a course of legal studies, in the company of the male law students, without demoralisation?

The answer to this objection is provided by William Brighty Rands. Rands is convinced that there is a stable and permanent 'type' of femininity, and even endorses the traditional view that the role of woman is to beautify life. He insists, however, that no one can deny to women 'perfect freedom of vocation and of culture'. My personal ideals may revolt against the idea of women doctors and lawyers, he admits, but this is no *argument* for their legal exclusion from those professions. Those critics who accuse Mill of timidity in accepting traditional sex roles seem to have missed this crucial distinction between principles and sentiments.

What one misses in these discussions is any adequate discussion of the more radical feminist case, sketched by Harriet Taylor in the *Enfranchisement*, that equal educational opportunities are a simple requirement of justice. On this view, we shouldn't ask whether an educated woman will make a better wife, or whether the social capital invested in her education will be wasted. Education is her right as a rational being; it is entirely up to her what use she makes of it. None of our feminists seems prepared to rest their entire case on such an appeal to intuition, eschewing all considerations of utility. Instead they argue, with Millicent Garrett Fawcett, that education is socially desirable alike for married and unmarried women. Here Mill's elevated conception of marriage as a partnership of equals will buttress the utilitarian leg of the argument. In a household of educated people, husband, wife and children can all be 'improved' by conversation; where only the husband has any knowledge of the world, he will inevitably come to despise his wife, often with tragic consequences.

Property

One part of Mill's case met with almost universal approval, even from conservative critics. This was his polemic against the legal incapacity of married women to own property, and even to have a right to the proceeds of their own labour. Under English law as it then stood, the wife was effectively a minor under the guardianship of her husband: what was hers was his, but not of course *vice versa*. It was evident to all that this legal doctrine led to monstrous injustices, and had to be reformed. The Married Women's Property Bill was only a few years away.[20]

None of Mill's critics defend the existing law. The judge Fitzjames Stephen admits the existence of some 'abuses' in need

20   For dates and details of the legislation, see Lee Holcombe, *Wives and Property: Reform of the Married Women's Property Law in Nineteenth-Century England* (Oxford, Martin Robinson, 1983).

of correction, and advocates piecemeal legal reforms. Margaret Oliphant thinks a Married Woman's Property Bill urgently required. Goldwin Smith describes the existing law as a mere 'survival' from an earlier age, but adds that it can be set aside without radical political changes. Henry Taylor thinks that married women should have a right to own property, but adds that this measure will probably only help well-off women and not the wives of the poor.

The critics all insist, however, that such piecemeal legal reforms carry no revolutionary implications. Bringing a greater degree of equity into the affairs of the household does not, Fitzjames Stephen insists, involve accepting the preposterous doctrine of equality. Henry Taylor agrees: the passage of a Married Women's Property Act would not entail, he insists, that the husband ceases to be 'paramount' within his own home. But is the distinction between equity and equality as clear as these men think? One of the ways the Victorian paterfamilias maintained his authority was, clearly, by the power of the purse. Take this weapon away, and the balance of power within many marriages (wherever the wife either possesses property of her own or is capable of earning in her own right) changes markedly. This will, of course, give the feminists another argument for the importance of women's education: it increases the options and hence the bargaining power of even those women who choose the traditional role of wife and mother.

Notes on the Contributors

James Mill (1773–1836), father of John Stuart, was a Scotsman who moved to London in 1802, where he scraped a living through writing and journalism, until his monumental *History of India* (1818) earned him a well-paid job in the East India Company. He also became the driving force behind the utilitarian movement, helping to found the Political Economy Club and the radical *Westminster Review*. His *Essay on Government*, written for the *Encyclopaedia Britannica* of 1820, became a text-book for the radicals.

Harriet Taylor (1807–58) was, of course, the great love of John Stuart Mill's life. Mill's own account of their relationship can be found in his *Autobiography*, but his view of her talents and virtues seems exaggerated, and does not coincide with the reports of others. They met in 1830, and quickly became devoted (Platonic) friends – not an easy position for a married woman to sustain. Her husband having died in July 1849, Mill and Harriet were eventually married in April 1851. From then until her death they worked closely together, and Mill insisted that the works of this period (including *On Liberty*) were as much hers as his. There is no doubt that her arguments and ideas, as expressed in the *Enfranchisement* and elsewhere, played a crucial role in the writing of the *Subjection*.

William Hepworth Dixon (1821–79) was born in Manchester, of a Puritan family. Although called to the bar in London in 1854, he never practised, but made a living by writing and journalism. As well as editing the *Athenaeum* (1853–69) he also wrote biographies, histories, and works on travel.

Frances Power Cobbe (1822–1904) was born in Dublin, the daughter of a well-off landlord and magistrate. As a girl, she had a crisis of faith, and lapsed briefly into agnosticism. Her father's death left her a small private income which enabled her to engage in philanthropic work, to travel, and to write. In her writings, she was a committed advocate of women's rights, with a particular interest in the education of girls. She was also one of the earliest campaigners against vivisection and for the more humane treatment of animals.

Anne Mozley (1809–91) was the sister of J. B. Mozley (Professor of Divinity at Oxford) and Thomas Mozley (a prominent high-church divine). She never married, but took charge of the household of her brother Thomas. She published volumes of poetry, wrote for the *Saturday Review* and for *Blackwood's*, reviewing such works as George Eliot's *Adam Bede*, and edited, in later life, the letters of J. B. Mozley and of Cardinal Newman.

Margaret Oliphant (1828–97) was born near Musselburgh in Scotland to a family who were partisans of the Scottish Free Church. She came to London around 1851, and married her cousin Francis Oliphant, an artist, in 1852. His death in 1859 left her with a burden of debt and three children to support. The burden was intensified when she also found herself looking after the three children of her widowed brother. Thereafter, her life was one of 'slavery to her pen', producing a string of popular novels for Blackwood's, plus works on Cervantes and Dante, and a mass of reviews.

Sheldon Amos (1835–86) graduated BA from Clare College Cambridge in 1859, and was called to the London bar in 1862. In 1869 he accepted the Chair of Jurisprudence at University College London, a post he resigned for reasons of health ten years later. After travelling for a while, he settled in Alexandria shortly before the British occupation of 1882. On the ensuing reorganization of the Egyptian judiciary he was appointed judge of the Court of Appeal. During his period in London he wrote for the radical *Westminster* on such issues as the emancipation of women and the Contagious Diseases Acts.

Sir Henry Taylor (1800–1886) was born in Durham, the younger son of an impoverished squire. He was largely self-educated, and squandered a number of career opportunities before establishing himself as a clerk in the Colonial Office and as a poet and dramatist, whose *Philip van Artevelde* was a great success on the London stage. In literature, he considered himself a disciple of Wordsworth and Southey. He was knighted in 1869 for his many years of service to the Colonial Office.

William Brighty Rands (1823–82) wrote under the pseudonyms of Henry Holbeach and Matthew Browne. As the son of a Chelsea shopkeeper he had little formal education, but worked in a warehouse, on the stage, as a clerk, and as a reporter in the House of Commons. In between sessions of Parliament, he wrote masses of prose and verse, contributing articles to the *Illustrated Times* under the heading of 'The Literary Lounger'. He achieved his greatest fame, however, as a writer of children's verse, becoming known as 'the laureate of the nursery'.

Millicent Garrett Fawcett (1847–1929) was one of the giants of the women's suffrage movement. She had little formal schooling herself, and saw at first hand the educational disadvantages of women when her sister Elizabeth was unable to train as a doctor. In 1867 Millicent married Henry Fawcett, blind professor of economics at Cambridge and MP for Brighton. John Stuart Mill was a close friend of the couple, who soon found themselves campaigning, at Cambridge, for the establishment of women's colleges. In 1867 she became a member of the first women's suffrage committee; despite opposition and ridicule, she fought on for another fifty years, until success had eventually been achieved.

Sir James Fitzjames Stephen (1829–94) was educated at Eton and Trinity College Cambridge, where he took his BA in 1851. Called to the bar in 1854, he supplemented his earnings by journalism, writing for the *Pall Mall Gazette* and the *Saturday Review*. In 1869 he succeeded Maine as legal member of council in India, where he spent the next three years trying to codify its laws. *Liberty, Equality, Fraternity* is a collection of essays from the *Pall Mall Gazette*, attacking popular but in his view misconceived notions. Stephen derived authoritarian conclusions from utilitarian premises, and thought that the later Mill had 'gone soft' and abandoned his Benthamite principles. On Stephen's return to England he became a judge in 1879 and a baronet in 1891.

Goldwin Smith (1823–1910) was born in Reading and educated at Eton and Oxford, graduating BA (1845) and MA (1848). In 1846 he accepted the Stowell Professorship of Law at University College Oxford, a post he sought to combine with a legal career in London. He was called to the bar in 1850, but found the practice of the law less congenial than academic life. During the 1850s and 1860s he was active in the political life of the university (attacking clerical power) and of the country (advocating the anti-imperialist, free trade policies of the Manchester School). The suicide of his father in 1867 left Smith wealthy but deeply disturbed. Refusing the liberals' offer of a safe seat in Parliament, he quit Oxford in 1868 and emigrated to the USA, where he became the first Professor of English at Cornell University. Later he moved to Toronto, where he made himself unpopular by denouncing imperialism and supporting the 'Canada First' movement, which aimed to emancipate the colony from British rule.

John Elliot Cairnes (1823–75) was the son of an Irish brewer. He was sent to school at Chester, but was considered a dull boy and sent back to his parents' home at Drogheda. He later persuaded his father to send him to Trinity College Dublin, where he gained his BA in 1848, his MA in 1854, and where he won a competition for the Whately Professorship of Political Economy in 1856. In 1859 he became Professor of Political Economy and Jurisprudence at Queens College, Galway. In 1865 he moved to London, becoming Professor of Economics at UCL in the following year. He was friendly with John Stuart Mill (whose economic views he largely followed) and with Henry Fawcett. His *Political Essays* appeared in 1873, as did a volume of *Essays on Political Economy*.

WHAT IS REQUIRED IN THE ELECTIVE BODY TO SECURE THE REQUISITE PROPERTIES IN THE REPRESENTATIVE BODY
[James Mill]

Having considered the means which are capable of being employed for identifying the interest of the representatives, when chosen, with that of the persons who choose them, it remains that we endeavor to bring to view the principles which ought to guide in determining who the persons are by whom the act of choosing ought to be performed.

It is most evident that upon this question everything depends. It can be of no consequence to insure, by shortness of duration, a conformity between the conduct of the representatives and the will of those who appoint them, if those who appoint them have an interest opposite to that of the community, because those who choose will, according to the principles of human nature, make choice of such persons as will act according to their wishes. As this is a direct inference from the very principle on which government itself is founded, we assume it as indisputable.

We have seen already that if one man has power over others placed in his hands, he will make use of it for an evil purpose – for the purpose of rendering those other men the abject instruments of his will. If we, then, suppose that one man has the power of choosing the representatives of the people, it follows that he will choose men who will use their power as representatives for the promotion of this his sinister interest.

We have likewise seen that, when a few men have power given them over others, they will make use of it exactly for the same ends and to the same extent as the one man. It equally follows that, if a small number of men have the choice of the representatives, such representatives will be chosen as will promote the interests of that small number by reducing, if possible, the rest of the community to be the abject and helpless slaves of their will.

In all these cases, it is obvious and indisputable that all the benefits of the representative system are lost. The representative system is, in that case, only an operose and clumsy machinery for doing that which might as well be done without it – reducing the community to subjection under the *one* or the *few*.

When we say the "few," it is seen that, in this case, it is of no importance whether we mean a few hundreds, or a few thousands, or even many thousands. The operation of the sinister interest is the same, and the fate is the same of all that part of the community over whom the power is exercised. A numerous aristocracy has never been found to be less oppressive than an aristocracy confined to a few.

The general conclusion, therefore, which is evidently established is this, that the benefits of the representative system are lost in all cases in which the interests of the choosing body are not the same with those of the community.

It is very evident that, if the community itself were the choosing body, the interest of the community and that of the choosing body would be the same. The question is whether that of any portion of the community, if erected into the choosing body, would remain the same?

One thing is pretty clear, that all those individuals whose interests are indisputably included in those of other individuals may be struck off without inconvenience. In this light may be viewed all children, up to a certain age, whose interests are involved in those of their parents. In this light, also, women may be regarded, the interest of almost all of whom is involved either in that of their fathers or in that of their husbands.

Having ascertained that an interest identical with that of the whole community is to be found in the aggregate males of an age to be regarded as *sui juris*, who may be regarded as the natural representatives of the whole population, we have to go on and inquire whether this requisite quality may not be found in some less number, some aliquot part of that body.

As degrees of mental qualities are not easily ascertained, outward and visible signs must be taken to distinguish, for this purpose, one part of these males from another. Applicable signs of this description appear to be three: years, property, profession or mode of life.

According to the first of these means of distinction, a portion of the males, to any degree limited, may be taken by prescribing an advanced period of life at which the power of voting for a representative should commence. According to the second, the elective body may be limited by allowing a vote to those only who possess a certain amount of property or of income. According to the third, it may be limited by allowing a vote only to such persons as belong to certain professions or certain connections and interests. What we have to inquire is, if the interest of the number, limited and set apart, upon any of those principles, as the organ of choice for a body of representatives, will be the same with the interest of the community?

With respect to the first principle of selection, that of age, it would appear that a considerable latitude may be taken without inconvenience. Suppose the age of forty were prescribed as that at which the right of suffrage should commence; scarcely any laws could be made for the benefit of all the men of forty which would not be laws for the benefit of all the rest of the community.

The great principle of security here is that the men of forty have a deep interest in the welfare of the younger men, for otherwise it might be objected, with perfect truth, that, if decisive power were placed in the hands of men of forty years of age, they would have an interest, just as any other detached portion of the community, in pursuing that career which we have already described – for reducing the rest of the community to the state of abject slaves. But the great majority of old men have sons, whose interest they regard as an essential part of their own. This is the law of human nature. There is, therefore, no great danger that, in such an arrangement as this, the interests of the young would be greatly sacrificed to those of the old.

We come next to the inquiry, whether the interest of a body of electors, constituted by the possession of a certain amount of property or income, would be the same with the interest of the community?

It will not be disputed that, if the qualification were raised so high that only a few hundreds possessed it, the case would be exactly the same with that of the consignment of the electoral suffrage to an aristocracy. This we have already considered and have seen that it differs in form rather than substance from a

simple aristocracy. We have likewise seen that it alters not the
case in regard to the community, whether the aristocracy be
some hundreds or many thousands. One thing is, therefore,
completely ascertained, that a pecuniary qualification, unless it
were very low, would only create an aristocratical government
and produce all the evils which we have shown to belong to
that organ of misrule.

This question, however, deserves to be a little more minutely
considered. Let us next take the opposite extreme. Let us
suppose that the qualification is very low, so low as to include
the great majority of the people. It would not be easy for the
people who have very little property to separate their interests
from those of the people who have none. It is not the interest of
those who have little property to give undue advantages to the
possession of property, which those who have the great
portions of it would turn against themselves.

It may, therefore, be said that there would be no evil in a low
qualification. It can hardly be said, however, on the other
hand, that there would be any good, for if the whole mass of
the people who have some property would make a good choice,
it will hardly be pretended that, added to them, the comparatively small number of those who have none, and whose
minds are naturally and almost necessarily governed by the
minds of those who have, would be able to make the choice a
bad one.

We have ascertained, therefore, two points. We have
ascertained that a very low qualification is of no use, as
affording no security for a good choice beyond that which
would exist if no pecuniary qualification was required. We
have likewise ascertained that a qualification so high as to
constitute an aristocracy of wealth, though it were a very
numerous one, would leave the community without protection
and exposed to all the evils of unbridged power. The only
question, therefore, is whether, between these extremes, there
is any qualification which would remove the right of suffrage
from the people of small or of no property, and yet constitute
an elective body, the interest of which would be identical with
that of the community?

It is not easy to find any satisfactory principle to guide us in
our researches and to tell us where we should fix. The
qualification must either be such as to embrace the majority of
the population or something less than the majority. Suppose, in

the first place, that it embraces the majority, the question is whether the majority would have an interest in oppressing those who, upon this supposition, would be deprived of political power? If we reduce the calculation to its elements, we shall see that the interest which they would have of this deplorable kind, though it would be something, would not be very great. Each man of the majority, if the majority were constituted the governing body, would have something less than the benefit of oppressing a single man. If the majority were twice as great as the minority, each man of the majority would only have one-half the benefit of oppressing a single man. In that case, the benefits of good government, accruing to all, might be expected to overbalance to the several members of such an elective body the benefits of misrule peculiar to themselves. Good government would, therefore, have a tolerable security. Suppose, in the second place, that the qualification did not admit a body of electors so large as the majority; in that case, taking again the calculation in its elements, we shall see that each man would have a benefit equal to that derived from the oppression of more than one man, and that, in proportion as the elective body constituted a smaller and smaller minority, the benefit of misrule to the elective body would be increased and bad government would be insured.

It seems hardly necessary to carry the analysis of the pecuniary qualification as the principle for choosing an elective body any further.

We have only remaining the third plan for constituting an elective body. According to the scheme in question, the best elective body is that which consists of certain classes, professions, or fraternities. The notion is that, when these fraternities or bodies are represented, the community itself is represented. The way in which, according to the patrons of this theory, the effect is brought about is this: Though it is perfectly true that each of these fraternities would profit by misrule and have the strongest interest in promoting it, yet, if three or four such fraternities are appointed to act in conjunction, they will not profit by misrule and will have an interest in nothing but good government.

This theory of representation we shall not attempt to trace further back than the year 1793. In the debate on the motion of Mr. (now Earl) Grey for a reform in the system of representation, on the 6th of May of that year, Mr. Jenkinson, the present Earl of Liverpool, brought forward this theory of representation, and urged it in opposition to all idea of reform in the British House of Commons, in terms as clear and distinct as those in which it has recently been clothed by leading men on both sides of that House. We shall transcribe the passage from the speech of Mr. Jenkinson, omitting, for the sake of abbreviation, all those expressions which are unnecessary for conveying a knowledge of the plan and of the reasons upon which it was founded:

> Supposing it agreed (he said) that the House of Commons is meant to be a legislative body, representing all descriptions of men in the country, he supposed every person would agree that the landed interest ought to have the preponderant weight. The landed interest was, in fact, the *stamina* of the country. In the second place, in a commercial country like this, the manufacturing and commercial interest ought to have a considerable weight, secondary to the landed interest, but secondary to the landed interest only. But was this all that was necessary? There were other descriptions of people, which, to distinguish them from those already mentioned, he should style professional people, and whom he considered as absolutely necessary to the composition of a House of Commons. By "professional people" he meant those members of the House of Commons who wished to raise themselves to the great offices of the State; those that were in the army, those that were in the navy, those that were in the law.

He then, as a reason for desiring to have those whom he calls "professional people" in the composition of the House of Commons, gives it as a fact that country gentlemen and merchants seldom desire, and seldom have motives for desiring, to be ministers and other great officers of state. These ministers and officers, however, ought to be made out of the House of Commons. Therefore, you ought to have "professional people" of whom to make them. Nor was this all:

> There was another reason why these persons were absolutely necessary. We were constantly in the habit of discussing in that House all the important concerns of the State. It was necessary, therefore, that there should be persons in the practice of debating such questions.

There was a third reason which, to his mind, was stronger than all the rest. Suppose that in that House there were only country gentlemen, they would not then be the representatives of the nation, but of the landholders. Suppose there were in that House only commercial persons, they would not be the representatives of the nation, but of the commercial interest of the nation. Suppose the landed and commercial interest could both find their way into the House, the landed interest would be able, if it had nothing but the commercial interest to combat with, to prevent that interest from having its due weight in the constitution. All descriptions of persons in the country would thus, in fact, be at the mercy of the land-holders.

He adds,

the professional persons are, then, what makes this House the representatives of the people. They have collectively no *esprit de corps*, and prevent any *esprit de corps* from affecting the proceedings of the House. Neither the landed nor commercial interest can materially affect each other, and the interests of the different professions of the country are fairly considered. The Honorable gentleman (Mr. Grey) and the petition on this table rather proposed uniformity of election. His ideas were the reverse – that the modes of election ought to be as varied as possible, because, if there was but one mode of election, there would, generally speaking, be but one description of persons in that House, and by a varied mode of election only could that variety be secured.

There is great vagueness undoubtedly in the language here employed, and abundant wavering and uncertainty in the ideas. But the ideas regarding this theory appear in the same half-formed state in every speech and writing in which we have seen it adduced. The mist, indeed, by which it has been kept surrounded alone creates the difficulty, because it cannot be known precisely how anything is good or bad till it is precisely known what it is.

According to the ideas of Lord Liverpool, the landholders ought to be represented; the merchants and manufacturers ought to be represented; the officers of the army and navy ought to be represented; and the practitioners of the law ought to be represented. Other patrons of the scheme have added that literary men ought to be represented. And these, we believe, are almost all the fraternities which have been named for this purpose by any of the advocates of representation by clubs. To insure the choice of representatives of the landholders, landholders must be the choosers; to insure the choice of representatives of the merchants and manufacturers, merchants and manufacturers must be the choosers; and so with respect to the other fraternities, whether few or many. Thus it must be at least in *substance*, whatever the form under which the visible acts may be performed. According to the scheme in question, these several fraternities are represented *directly*, the rest of the community is *not* represented directly, but it will be said by the patrons of the scheme that it is represented *virtually*, which, in this case, answers the same purpose.

From what has already been ascertained, it will appear certain that each of these fraternities has its sinister interest and will be led to seek the benefit of misrule if it is able to obtain it. This is frankly and distinctly avowed by Lord Liverpool. And by those by whom it is not avowed, it seems impossible to suppose that it should be disputed.

Let us now, then, observe the very principle upon which this theory must be supported. Three or four or five or more clubs of men have unlimited power over the whole community put into their hands. These clubs have, each and all of them, an interest, an interest the same with that which governs all other rulers in misgovernment – in converting the persons and properties of the rest of the community wholly to their own benefit. Having this interest, says the theory, they will not make use of it but will use all their powers for the benefit of the community. Unless this proposition can be supported, the theory is one of the shallowest by which the pretenders to political wisdom have ever exposed themselves.

Let us resume the proposition. Three or four or five fraternities of men, composing a small part of the community, have all the powers of government placed in their hands. If they oppose and contend with one another, they will be unable to convert these powers to their own benefit. If they agree, they will be able to convert them wholly to their own benefit and to do with the rest of the community just what they please. The patrons of this system of representation assume that these fraternities will be sure to take that course which is *contrary* to their interest. The course which is *according* to their interest appears as if it had never presented itself to their imaginations!

There being two courses which the clubs may pursue, one contrary to their interest, the other agreeable to it, the patrons of the club system must prove, they must place it beyond all doubt, that the clubs will follow the first course, and not follow the second; if not, the world will laugh at a theory which is founded upon a direct contradiction of one of the fundamental principles of human nature.

In supposing that clubs or societies of men are governed, like men individually, by their interests, we are surely following a pretty complete experience. In the idea that a certain number of those clubs can unite to pursue a common interest, there is surely nothing more extraordinary than that as many individuals should unite to pursue a common interest. Lord Liverpool talks of an *esprit de corps* belonging to a class of landholders made up of the different bodies of landholders in every county in the kingdom. He talks of an *esprit de corps* in a class of merchants and manufacturers made up of the different bodies of merchants and manufacturers in the several great towns and manufacturing districts in the kingdom. What, then, is meant by an *esprit de corps*? Nothing else but a union for the pursuit of a common interest. To the several clubs supposed in the present theory, a common interest is created by the very circumstance of their composing the representing and represented bodies. Unless the patrons of this theory can prove to us, contrary to all experience, that a common interest cannot create an *esprit de corps* in men in combinations as well as in men individually, we are under the necessity of believing that an *esprit de corps* would be formed in the classes separated from the rest of the community for the purposes of representation; that they would pursue their common interest and inflict all the evils upon the rest of the community to which the pursuit of that interest would lead.

It is not included in the idea of this union for the pursuit of a common interest that the clubs or sets of persons appropriated to the business of representation should totally harmonize. There would, no doubt, be a great mixture of agreement and disagreement among them. But there would, if experience is any guide, or if the general laws of human nature have any power, be sufficient agreement to prevent their losing sight of the common interest; in other words, for insuring all that abuse of power which is useful to the parties by whom it is exercised.

The real effect of this motley representation, therefore, would only be to create a motley aristocracy, and, of course, to insure that kind of misgovernment which it is the nature of aristocracy to produce, and to produce equally whether it is a uniform or a variegated aristocracy, whether an aristocracy all of landowners, or an aristocracy in part landowners, in part merchants and manufacturers, in part officers of the army and navy, and in part lawyers.

We have now, therefore, examined the principles of the representative system and have found in it all that is necessary to constitute a security for good government. We have seen in what manner it is possible to prevent in the representatives the rise of an interest different from that of the parties who choose them – namely, by giving them little time, not dependent upon the will of those parties. We have likewise seen in what manner identity of interest may be insured between the electoral body and the rest of the community. We have, therefore, discovered the means by which identity of interest may be insured between the representatives and the community at large. We have, by consequence, obtained an organ of government which possesses that quality without which there can be no good government.

THE ENFRANCHISEMENT OF WOMEN
[Harriet Taylor]

Art. I. - *The New York Tribune for Europe*. October 29th, 1850

Most of our readers will probably learn from these pages for the first time, that there has arisen in the United States, and in the most civilized and enlightened portion of them, an organised agitation on a new question – new, not to thinkers, nor to any one by whom the principles of free and popular government are felt as well as acknowledged, but new, and even unheard of, as a subject for public meetings and practical political action. This question is, the enfranchisement of women; their admission, in law and in fact, to equality in all rights, political, civil, and social, with the male citizens of the community.

It will add to the surprise with which many will receive this intelligence, that the agitation which has commenced is not a pleading by male writers and orators *for* women, those who are professedly to be benefitted remaining either indifferent or ostensibly hostile: it is a political movement, practical in its objects, carried on in a form which denotes an intention to persevere. And it is a movement not merely *for* women, but *by* them. Its first public manifestation appears to have been a Convention of Women, held in the State of Ohio, in the spring of 1850. Of this meeting we have seen no report. On the 23rd and 24th of October last, a succession of public meetings was held at Worcester, in Massachusetts, under the name of a "Women's Rights Convention," of which the president was a woman, and nearly all the chief speakers women; numerously reinforced, however, by men, among whom were some of the most distinguished leaders in the kindred cause of negro emancipation. A general and four special committees were nominated, for the purpose of carrying on the undertaking until the next annual meeting.

According to the report in the New York Tribune, above a

thousand persons were present throughout, and "if a larger place could have been had, many thousands more would have attended." The place was described as "crowded from the beginning with attentive and interested listeners." In regard to the quality of the speaking, the proceedings bear an advantageous comparison with those of any popular movement with which we are acquainted, either in this country or in America. Very rarely in the oratory of public meetings is the part of verbiage and declamation so small, that of calm good sense and reason so considerable. The result of the Convention was in every respect encouraging to those by whom it was summoned: and it is probably destined to inaugurate one of the most important of the movements towards political and social reform, which are the best characteristic of the present age.

That the promoters of this new agitation take their stand on principles, and do not fear to declare these in their widest extent, without time-serving or compromise, will be seen from the resolutions adopted by the Convention, part of which we transcribe:–

> "*Resolved* – That every human being, of full age, and resident for a proper length of time on the soil of the nation, who is required to obey the law, is entitled to a voice in its enactment; that every such person, whose property or labour is taxed for the support of the government, is entitled to a direct share in such government; therefore

> "*Resolved* – That women are entitled to the right of suffrage, and to be considered eligible to office, . . . and that every party which claims to represent the humanity, the civilization, and the progress of the age, is bound to inscribe on its banners, equality before the law, without distinction of sex or colour.

> "*Resolved* – That civil and political rights acknowledge no sex, and therefore the word "male" should be struck from every State Constitution.

> "*Resolved* – That, since the prospect of honourable and useful employment in after life is the best stimulus to the use of educational advantages, and since the best education is that we give ourselves, in the struggles, employments, and discipline of life; therefore it is impossible that women should make full use of the instruction already accorded to

them, or that their career should do justice to their faculties, until the avenues to the various civil and professional employments are thrown open to them.

"*Resolved* - That every effort to educate women, without according to them their rights, and arousing their conscience by the weight of their responsibilities, is futile, and a waste of labour.

"*Resolved* - That the laws of property, as affecting married persons, demand a thorough revisal, so that all rights be equal between them; that the wife have, during life, an equal control over the property gained by their mutual toil and sacrifices, and be heir to her husband precisely to that extent that he is heir to her, and entitled at her death to dispose by will of the same share of the joint property as he is."

The following is a brief summary of the principal demands:-

"1. *Education* in primary and high schools, universities, medical, legal, and theological institutions.

"2. *Partnership* in the labours and gains, risks and remunerations, of productive industry.

"3. *A coequal share* in the formation and administration of laws - municipal, state, and national - through legislative assemblies, courts, and executive offices."

It would be difficult to put so much true, just, and reasonable meaning into a style so little calculated to recommend it as that of some of the resolutions. But whatever objection may be made to some of the expressions, none, in our opinion, can be made to the demands themselves. As a question of justice, the case seems to us too clear for dispute. As one of expediency, the more thoroughly it is examined the stronger it will appear.

That women have as good a claim as men have, in point of personal right, to the suffrage, or to a place in the jury-box, it would be difficult for anyone to deny. It cannot certainly be denied by the United States of America, as a people or as a community. Their democratic institutions rest avowedly on the inherent right of everyone to a voice in the government. Their Declaration of Independence, framed by the men who are still their great constitutional authorities - that document which has been from the first, and is now, the acknowledged basis of their polity, commences with this express statement:-

"We hold these truths to be self-evident: that all men are created equal; that they are endowed by their Creator with certain inalienable rights; that among these are life, liberty, and the pursuit of happiness; that to secure these rights, governments are instituted among men, deriving their just powers from the consent of the governed."

We do not imagine that any American democrat will evade the force of these expressions by the dishonest or ignorant subterfuge, that "men," in this memorable document, does not stand for human beings, but for one sex only; that "life, liberty, and the pursuit of happiness" are "inalienable rights' of only one moiety of the human species; and that "the governed," whose consent is affirmed to be the only source of just power, are meant for that half of mankind only, who, in relation to the other, have hitherto assumed the character of *governors*. The contradiction between principle and practice cannot be explained away. A like dereliction of the fundamental maxims of their political creed has been committed by the Americans in the flagrant instance of the negroes; of this they are learning to recognise the turpitude. After a struggle which, by many of its incidents, deserves the name of heroic, the abolitionists are now so strong in numbers and in influence that they hold the balance of parties in the United States. It was fitting that the men whose names will remain associated with the extirpation, from the democratic soil of America, of the aristocracy of colour, should be among the originators, for America and for the rest of the world, of the first collective protest against the aristocracy of sex; a distinction as accidental as that of colour, and fully as irrelevant to all questions of government.

Not only to the democracy of America, the claim of women to civil and political equality makes an irresistible appeal, but also to those radicals and chartists in the British islands, and democrats on the Continent, who claim what is called universal suffrage as an inherent right, unjustly and oppressively withheld from them. For with what truth or rationality could the suffrage be termed universal, while half the human species remain excluded from it? To declare that a voice in the government is the right of all, and demand it only for a part – the part, namely, to which the claimant himself belongs – is to renounce even the appearance of principle. The chartist who denies the suffrage to women, is a chartist only because he is not a lord; he is one of those levellers who would level only down to themselves.

Even those who do not look upon a voice in the government as a matter of personal right, nor profess principles which require that it should be extended to all, have usually traditional maxims of political justice with which it is impossible to reconcile the exclusion of all women from the common rights of citizenship. It is an axiom of English freedom that taxation and representation should be co-extensive. Even under the laws which give the wife's property to the husband, there are many unmarried women who pay taxes. It is one of the fundamental doctrines of the British constitution, that all persons should be tried by their peers: yet women, whenever tried, are tried by male judges and a male jury. To foreigners the law accords the privilege of claiming that half the jury should be composed of themselves; not so to women. Apart from maxims of detail, which represent local and national rather than universal ideas; it is an acknowledged dictate of justice to make no degrading distinctions without necessity. In all things the presumption ought to be on the side of equality. A reason must be given why anything should be permitted to one person and interdicted to another. But when that which is interdicted includes nearly everything which those to whom it is permitted most prize, and to be deprived of which they feel to be most insulting; when not only political liberty but personal freedom of action is the prerogative of a caste; when even in the exercise of industry, almost all employments which task the higher faculties in an important field, which lead to distinction, riches, or even pecuniary independence, are fenced round as the exclusive domain of the predominant section, scarcely any doors being left open to the dependent class, except such as all who can enter elsewhere disdainfully pass by; the miserable expediencies which are advanced as excuses for so grossly partial a dispensation, would not be sufficient, even if they were real, to render it other than a flagrant injustice. While, far from being expedient, we are firmly convinced that the division of mankind into two castes, one born to rule over the other, is in this case, as in all cases, an unqualified mischief; a source of perversion and demoralization, both to the favoured class and to those at whose expense they are favoured; producing none of the good which it is the custom to ascribe to it, and forming a bar, almost insuperable while it lasts, to any really vital improvement, either in the character or in the social condition of the human race.

These propositions it is now our purpose to maintain. But before entering on them, we would endeavour to dispel the preliminary objections which, in the minds of persons to whom the subject is new, are apt to prevent a real and conscientious examination of it. The chief of these obstacles is that most formidable one, custom. Women never have had equal rights with men. The claim in their behalf, of the common rights of mankind, is looked upon as barred by universal practice. This strongest of prejudices, the prejudice against what is new and unknown, has, indeed, in an age of changes like the present, lost much of its force; it if had not, there would be little hope of prevailing against it. Over three-fourths of the habitable world, even at this day, the answer, "it has always been so," closes all discussion. But it is the boast of modern Europeans, and of their American kindred, that they know and do many things which their forefathers neither knew nor did; and it is perhaps the most unquestionable point of superiority in the present above former ages, that habit is not now the tyrant it formerly was over opinions and modes of action, and that the worship of custom is a declining idolatry. An uncustomary thought, on a subject which touches the greater interests of life, still startles when first presented; but if it can be kept before the mind until the impression of strangeness wears off, it obtains a hearing, and as rational a consideration as the intellect of the hearer is accustomed to bestow on any other subject.

In the present case, the prejudice of custom is doubtless on the unjust side. Great thinkers, indeed, at different times, from Plato to Condorcet, besides some of the most eminent names of the present age, have made emphatic protests in favour of the equality of women. And there have been voluntary societies, religious or secular, of which the Society of Friends is the most known, by whom that principle was recognised. But there has been no political community or nation in which, by law, and usage, women have not been in a state of political and civil inferiority. In the ancient world the same fact was alleged, with equal truth, in behalf of slavery. It might have been alleged in favour of the mitigated form of slavery, serfdom, all through the middle ages. It was urged against freedom of industry, freedom of conscience, freedom of the press; none of these liberties were thought compatible with a well-ordered state, until they had proved their possibility by actually existing as facts. That an institution or a practice is customary is no presumption of its goodness, when any other sufficient cause can be assigned for its existence. There is no difficulty in understanding why the subjection of women has been a custom. No other explanation is needed than physical force.

That those who were physically weaker should have been made legally inferior, is quite conformable to the mode in which the world has been governed. Until very lately, the rule of physical strength was the general law of human affairs. Throughout history, the nations, races, classes, which found themselves the strongest, either in muscles, in riches, or in military discipline, have conquered and held in subjection the rest. If, even in the most improved nations, the law of the sword is at last discountenanced as unworthy, it is only since the calumniated eighteenth century. Wars of conquest have only ceased since democratic revolutions began. The world is very young, and has but just begun to cast off injustice. It is only now getting rid of negro slavery. It is only now getting rid of monarchical despotism. It is only now getting rid of hereditary feudal nobility. It is only now getting rid of disabilities on the ground of religion. It is only beginning to treat any *men* as citizens, except the rich and a favoured portion of the middle class. Can we wonder that it has not yet done as much for women? As society was constituted until the last few generations, inequality was its very basis; association grounded on equal rights scarcely existed; to be equals was to be enemies; two persons could hardly co-operate in anything, or meet in any amicable relation, without the law's appointing that one of them should be the superior of the other. Mankind have outgrown this state, and all things now tend to substitute, as the general principle of human relations, a just equality, instead of the dominion of the strongest. But of all relations, that between men and women being the nearest and most intimate, and connected with the greatest number of strong emotions, was sure to be the last to throw off the old rule and receive the new: for in proportion to the strength of a feeling, is the tenacity with which it clings to the forms and circumstances with which it has even accidentally become associated.

When a prejudice, which has any hold on the feelings, finds itself reduced to the unpleasant necessity of assigning reasons, it thinks it has done enough when it has re-asserted the very point in dispute, in phrases which appeal to the pre-existing feeling. Thus, many persons think they have sufficiently justified the restrictions on women's field of action, when they have said that the pursuits from which women are excluded are *unfeminine*, and that the *proper sphere* of women is not politics or publicity, but private and domestic life.

We deny the right of any portion of the species to decide for another portion, or any individual for another individual, what is and what is not their "proper sphere." The proper sphere for all human beings is the largest and highest which they are able to attain to. What this is, cannot be ascertained, without complete liberty of choice. The speakers at the Convention in America have therefore done wisely and right, in refusing to entertain the question of the peculiar aptitudes either of women or of men, or the limits within which this or that occupation may be supposed to be more adapted to the one or to the other. They justly maintain, that these questions can only be satisfactorily answered by perfect freedom. Let every occupation be open to all, without favour or discouragement to any, and employments will fall into the hands of those men or women who are found by experience to be most capable of worthily exercising them. There need be no fear that women will take out of the hands of men any occupation which men perform better than they. Each individual will prove his or her capacities, in the only way in which capacities can be proved – by trial; and the world will have the benefit of the best faculties of all its inhabitants. But to interfere beforehand by an arbitrary limit, and declare that whatever be the genius, talent, energy, or force of mind of an individual of a certain sex or class, those faculties shall not be exerted, or shall be exerted only in some few of the many modes in which others are permitted to use theirs, is not only an injustice to the individual, and a detriment to society, which loses what it can ill spare, but is also the most effectual mode of providing that, in the sex or class so fettered, the qualities which are not permitted to be exercised shall not exist.

We shall follow the very proper example of the Convention, in not entering into the question of the alleged differences in physical or mental qualities between the sexes; not because we have nothing to say, but because we have too much; to discuss this one point tolerably would need all the space we have to bestow on the entire subject.[1] But if those who assert that the "proper sphere" for women is the domestic, mean by this that they have not shown themselves qualified for any other, the assertion evinces great ignorance of life and of history. Women have shown fitness for the highest social functions, exactly in proportion as they have been admitted to them. By a curious anomaly, though ineligible to even the lowest offices of state, they are in some countries admitted to the highest of all, the regal; and if there is any one function for which they have shown a decided vocation, it is that of reigning. Not to go back to ancient history, we look in vain for abler or firmer rulers than Elizabeth; than Isabella of Castile; than Maria Teresa; than Catherine of Russia; than Blanche, mother of Louis IX. of France; than Jeanne d'Albret, mother of Henri Quatre. There are few kings on record who contended with more difficult circumstances, or overcame them more triumphantly, than these. Even in semi-barbarous Asia, princesses who have never been seen by men, other than those of their own family, or ever spoken with them unless from behind a curtain, have as regents, during the minority of their sons, exhibited many of the most brilliant examples of just and vigorous administration. In the middle ages, when the distance between the upper and lower ranks was greater than even between women and men, and the women of the privileged class, however subject to tyranny from the men of the same class, were at a less distance below them than any one else was, and often in their

---

[1] An excellent passage on this part of the subject, from one of Sydney Smith's contributions to the 'Edinburgh Review,' we will not refrain from quoting:- "A great deal has been said of the original difference of capacity between men and women, as if women were more quick and men more judicious - as if women were more remarkable for delicacy of association, and men for stronger powers of attention. All this, we confess, appears to us very fanciful. That there is a difference in the understandings of the men and the women we every day meet with, everybody, we suppose, must perceive; but there is none surely which may not be accounted for by the difference of circumstances in which they have been placed, without referring to any conjectural difference of original conformation of mind. As long as boys and girls run about in the dirt, and trundle hoops together, they are both precisely alike. If you catch up one-half of these creatures, and train them to a particular set of actions and opinions, and the other half to a perfectly opposite set, of course their understandings will differ, as one or the other sort of occupations has called this or that talent into action. There is surely no occasion to go into any deeper or more abstruse reasoning, in order to explain so very simple a phenomenon." - *Sydney Smith's Works*, vol. i. p. 200.

absence represented them in their functions and authority –
numbers of heroic chatelaines, like Jeanne de Montfort, or the
great Countess of Derby as late even as the time of Charles I.,
distinguished themselves not only by their political but their
military capacity. In the centuries immediately before and after
the Reformation, ladies of royal houses, as diplomatists, as
governors of provinces, or as the confidential advisers of kings,
equalled the first statesmen of their time: and the treaty of
Cambray, which gave peace to Europe, was negociated in
conferences where no other person was present, by the aunt of
the Emperor Charles the Fifth, and the mother of Francis the
First.

Concerning the fitness, then, of women for politics, there
can be no question: but the dispute is more likely to turn upon
the fitness of politics for women. When the reasons alleged for
excluding women from active life in all its higher departments,
are stripped of their garb of declamatory phrases, and reduced
to the simple expression of a meaning, they seem to be mainly
three: the incompatibility of active life with maternity, and
with the cares of a household; secondly, its alleged hardening
effect on the character; and thirdly, the inexpediency of making
an addition to the already excessive pressure of competition in
every kind of professional or lucrative employment.

The first, the maternity argument, is usually laid most stress
upon: although (it needs hardly be said) this reason, if it be
one, can apply only to mothers. It is neither necessary nor just
to make imperative on women that they shall be either mothers
or nothing; or that if they have been mothers once, they shall
be nothing else during the whole remainder of their lives.
Neither women nor men need any law to exclude them from an
occupation, if they have undertaken another which is
incompatible with it. No one proposes to exclude the male sex
from Parliament because a man may be a soldier or sailor in
active service, or a merchant whose business requires all his
time and energies. Nine-tenths of the occupations of men
exclude the *de facto* from public life, as effectually as if they
were excluded by law; but that is no reason for making laws to
exclude even the nine-tenths, much less the remaining tenth.
The reason of the case is the same for women as for men. There
is no need to make provision by law that a woman shall not
carry on the active details of a household, or of the education
of children, and at the same time practise a profession or be

elected to parliament. Where incompatibility is real, it will take care of itself: but there is gross injustice in making the incompatibility a pretence for the exclusion of those in whose case it does not exist. And these, if they were free to choose, would be a very large proportion. The maternity argument deserts its supporters in the case of single women, a large and increasing class of the population; a fact which, it is not irrelevant to remark, by tending to diminish the excessive competition of numbers, is calculated to assist greatly the prosperity of all. There is no inherent reason or necessity that all women should voluntarily choose to devote their lives to one animal function and its consequences. Numbers of women are wives and mothers only because there is no other career open to them, no other occupation for their feelings or their activities. Every improvement in their education, and enlargement of their faculties – everything which renders them more qualified for any other mode of life, increases the number of those to whom it is an injury and an oppression to be denied the choice. To say that women must be excluded from active life because maternity disqualifies them for it, is in fact to say, that every other career should be forbidden them in order that maternity may be their only resource.

But secondly, it is urged, that to give the same freedom of occupation to women as to men, would be an injurious addition to the crowd of competitors, by whom the avenues to almost all kinds of employment are choked up, and its remuneration depressed. This argument, it is to be observed, does not reach the political question. It gives no excuse for withholding from women the rights of citizenship. The suffrage, the jury-box, admission to the legislature and to office, it does not touch. It bears only on the industrial branch of the subject. Allowing it, then, in an economical point of view, its full force; assuming that to lay open to women the employments now monopolized by men, would tend, like the breaking down of other monopolies, to lower the rate of remuneration in those employments; let us consider what is the amount of this civil consequence, and what the compensation for it. The worst ever asserted, much worse than is at all likely to be realized, is that if women competed with men, a man and a woman could not together earn more than is now earned by the man alone. Let us make this supposition, the most unfavourable supposition possible: the joint income of the two would be the same as before, while the woman would be raised from the position of a servant to that of a partner. Even if every woman, as matters now stand, had a claim on some man for support, how infinitely preferable is it that part of the income should be of the woman's earning, even if the aggregate sum were but little increased by it, rather than that she should be compelled to stand aside in order that men may be the sole earners, and the sole dispensers of what is earned. Even under the present laws respecting the property of women,[2] a woman who contributes materially to the support of the family, cannot be treated in the same contemptuously tyrannical manner as one who, however she may toil as a domestic drudge, is a dependent on the man for subsistence. As for the depression of wages by increase of competition, remedies will be found for it in time. Palliatives might be applied immediately; for instance, a more rigid exclusion of children from industrial employment, during the years in which they ought to be working only to strengthen their bodies and minds for after life. Children are necessarily dependent, and under the power of others; and their labour, being not for themselves but for the gain of their parents, is a proper subject for legislative regulation. With respect to the future, we neither believe that improvident multiplication, and the consequent excessive difficulty of gaining a subsistence, will always continue, nor that the division of mankind into capitalists and hired labourers, and the regulation of the reward of labourers mainly by demand and supply, will be for ever, or even much longer, the rule of the world. But so long as competition is the general law of human life, it is tyranny to shut out one half of the competitors. All who have attained the age of self-government, have an equal claim to be permitted to sell whatever kind of useful labour they are capable of, for the price which it will bring.

The third objection to the admission of women to political or professional life, its alleged hardening tendency, belongs to an age now past, and is scarcely to be comprehended by people of the present time. There are still, however, persons who say that

2   The truly horrible effects of the present state of the law among the lowest of the working population, is exhibited in those cases of hideous maltreatment of their wives by working men, with which every newspaper, every police report, teems. Wretches unfit to have the smallest authority over any living think, have a helpless women for their household slave. These excesses could not exist if women both earned, and had the right to possess, a part of the income of the family.

the world and its avocations render men selfish and unfeeling; that the struggles, rivalries and collisions of business and of politics make them harsh and unamiable; that if half the species must unavoidably be given up to these things, it is the more necessary that the other half should be kept free from them; that to preserve women from the bad influences of the world, is the only chance of preventing men from being wholly given up to them.

There would have been plausibility in this argument when the world was still in the age of violence; when life was full of physical conflict, and every man had to redress his injuries or those of others, by the sword or by the strength of his arm. Women, like priests, by being exempted from such responsibilities, and from some part of the accompanying dangers, may have been enabled to exercise a beneficial influence. But in the present condition of human life, we do not know where those hardening influences are to be found, to which men are subject and from which women are at present exempt. Individuals now-a-days are seldom called upon to fight hand to hand, even with peaceful weapons; personal enmities and rivalities count for little in worldly transactions; the general pressure of circumstances, not the adverse will of individuals, is the obstacle men now have to make head against. That pressure, when excessive, breaks the spirit, and cramps and sours the feelings, but not less of women than of men, since they suffer certainly not less from its evils. There are still quarrels and dislikes, but the sources of them are changed. The feudal chief once found his bitterest enemy in his powerful neighbour, the minister or courtier in his rival for place; but opposition of interest in active life, as a cause of personal animosity, is out of date; the enmities of the present day arise not from great things but small, from what people say of one another, more than from what they do; and if there are hatred, malice, and all uncharitableness, they are to be found among women fully as much as among men. In the present state of civilization, the notion of guarding women from the hardening influences of the world, could only be realized by secluding them from society altogether. The common duties of common life, as at present constituted, are incompatible with any other softness in women than weakness. Surely weak minds in weak bodies must ere long cease to be even supposed to be either attractive or amiable.

But, in truth, none of these arguments and considerations touch the foundations of the subject. The real question is, whether it is right and expedient that one-half of the human race should pass through life in a state of forced subordination to the other half.. If the best state of human society is that of being divided into two parts, one consisting of persons with a will and a substantive existence, the other of humble companions to these persons, attached, each of them to one, for the purpose of bringing up *his* children, and making *his* home pleasant to him; if this is the place assigned to women, it is but kindness to educate them for this; to make them believe that the greatest good fortune which can befal them, is to be chosen by some man for this purpose; and that every other career which the world deems happy or honourable is closed to them by the law, not of social institutions, but of nature and destiny.

When, however, we ask why the existence of one-half the species should be merely ancillary to that of the other – why each woman should be a mere appendage to a man, allowed to have no interests of her own, that there may by nothing to compete in her mind with his interests and his pleasure; the only reason which can be given is, that men like it. It is agreeable to them that men should live for their own sake, women for the sake of men: and the qualities and conduct in subjects which are agreeable to rulers, they succeed for a long time in making the subjects themselves consider as their appropriate virtues. Helvetius has met with much obloquy for asserting, that persons usually mean by virtues the qualities which are useful or convenient to themselves. How truly this is said of mankind in general, and how wonderfully the ideas of virtue set afloat by the powerful, are caught and imbibed by those under their dominion, is exemplified by the manner in which the world were once persuaded that the supreme virtue of subjects was loyalty to kings, and are still persuaded that the paramount virtue of womanhood is loyalty to men. Under a nominal recognition of a moral code common to both, in practice self-will and self-assertion form the type of what are designated as manly virtues, while abnegation of self, patience, resignation, and submission to power, unless when resistance is commanded by other interests than their own, have been stamped by general consent as pre-eminently the duties and graces required of women. The meaning being merely, that power makes itself the centre of moral obligation, and that a man likes to have his own will, but does not like that his domestic companion should have a will different from his.

We are far from pretending that in modern and civilized times, no reciprocity of obligation is acknowledged on the part of the stronger. Such an assertion would be very wide of the truth. But even this reciprocity, which has disarmed tyranny, at least in the higher and middle classes, of its most revolting features, yet when combined with the original evil of the dependent condition of women, has introduced in its turn serious evils.

In the beginning, and among tribes which are still in a primitive condition, women were and are the slaves of men for the purposes of toil. All the hard bodily labour devolves on them. The Australian savage is idle, while women painfully dig up the roots on which he lives. An American Indian, when he has killed a deer, leaves it, and sends a woman to carry it home. In a state somewhat more advanced, as in Asia, women were and are the slaves of men for the purposes of sensuality. In Europe there early succeeded a third and milder dominion, secured not by blows, nor by locks and bars, but by sedulous inculcation on the mind; feeling also of kindness, and ideas of duty, such as a superior owes to inferiors under his protection, became more and more involved in the relation. But it did not for many ages become a relation of companionship, even between unequals; the lives of the two persons were apart. The wife was part of the furniture of home, of the resting-place to which the man returned from business or pleasure. His occupations were, as they still are, among men; his pleasures and excitements also were, for the most part, among men – among his equals. He was a patriarch and a despot within four walls, and irresponsible power had its effect, greater or less according to his disposition, in rendering him domineering, exacting, self-worshipping, when not capriciously or brutally tyrannical. But if the moral part of his nature suffered, it was not necessarily so, in the same degree, with the intellectual or the active portion. He might have as much vigour of mind and energy of character as his nature enabled him, and as the circumstances of his times allowed. He might write the 'Paradise Lost,' or win the battle of Marengo. This was the condition of the Greeks and Romans, and of the moderns until a recent date. Their relations with their domestic subordinates occupied a mere corner, though a cherished one, of their lives.

Their education as men, the formation of their character and faculties, depended mainly on a different class of influences.

It is otherwise now. The progress of improvement has imposed on all possessors of power, and of domestic power among the rest, an increased and increasing sense of correlative obligation. No man now thinks that his wife has no claim upon his actions but such as he may accord to her. All men of any conscience believe that their duty to their wives is one of the most binding of their obligations. Nor is it supposed to consist solely in protection, which, in the present state of civilization, women have almost ceased to need: it involves care for their happiness and consideration of their wishes, with a not unfrequent sacrifice of their own to them. The power of husbands has reached the stage which the power of kings had arrived at, when opinion did not yet question the rightfulness of arbitrary power, but in theory, and to a certain extent in practice, condemned the selfish use of it. This improvement in the moral sentiments of mankind, and increased sense of the consideration due by every man to those who have no one but himself to look to, has tended to make home more and more the centre of interest, and domestic circumstances and society a larger and larger part of life, and of its pursuits and pleasures. The tendency has been strengthened by the changes of tastes and manners which have so remarkably distinguished the last two or three generations. In days not far distant, men found their excitement and filled up their time in violent bodily exercises, noisy merriment, and intemperance. They have now, in all but the very poorest classes, lost their inclination for these things, and for the coarser pleasures generally; they have now scarcely any tastes but those which they have in common with women, and, for the first time in the world, men and women are really companions. A most beneficial change, if the companionship were between equals; but being between unequals, it produces, what good observers have noticed, though without perceiving its cause, a progressive deterioration among men in what had hitherto been considered the masculine excellences. Those who are so careful that women should not become men, do not see that men are becoming, what they have decided that women should be – are falling into the feebleness which they have so long cultivated in their companions. Those who are associated in their lives, tend to become assimilated in character. In the present closeness of association between the sexes, men cannot retain manliness unless women acquire it.

There is hardly any situation more unfavourable to the maintenance of elevation of character or force of intellect, than to live in the society, and seek by preference the sympathy, of inferiors in mental endowments. Why is it that we constantly see in life so much of intellectual and moral promise followed by such inadequate performance, but because the aspirant has compared himself only with those below himself, and has not sought improvement or stimulus from measuring himself with his equals or superiors. In the present state of social life, this is becoming the general condition of men. They care less and less for any sympathies, and are less and less under any personal influences, but those of the domestic roof. Not to be misunderstood, it is necessary that we should distinctly disclaim the belief, that women are even now inferior in intellect to men. There are women who are the equals in intellect of any men who ever lived: and comparing ordinary women with ordinary men, the varied though petty details which compose the occupation of most women, call forth probably as much of mental ability, as the uniform routine of the pursuits which are the habitual occupation of a large majority of men. It is from nothing in the faculties themselves, but from the petty subjects and interests on which alone they are exercised, that the companionship of women, such as their present circumstances make them so often exercises a dis-solvent influence on high faculties and aspirations in men. If one of the two has no knowledge and no care about the great ideas and purposes which dignify life, or about any of its practical concerns save personal interests and personal vanities, her conscious, and still more her unconscious influence, will, except in rare cases, reduce to a secondary place in his mind, if not entirely extinguish, those interests which she cannot or does not share.

Our argument here brings us into collision with what may be termed the moderate reformers of the education of women; a sort of persons who cross the path of improvement on all great questions; those who would maintain the old bad principles, mitigating their consequences. These say, that women should be, not slaves, nor servants, but companions; and educated for that office: (they do not say that men should be educated to be the companions of women). But since uncultivated women are

not suitable companions for cultivated men, and a man who
feels interest in things above and beyond the family circle
wishes that his companion should sympathize with him in that
interest, they therefore say, let women improve their understanding and taste, acquire general knowledge, cultivate
poetry, art, even coquet with science, and some stretch their
liberality so far as to say, inform themselves on politics; not as
pursuits, but sufficiently to feel an interest in the subjects, and
to be capable of holding a conversation on them with the
husband, or at least of understanding and imbibing his
wisdom. Very agreeable to him, no doubt, but unfortunately
the reverse of improving. It is from having intellectual
communion only with those to whom they can lay down the
law, that so few men continue to advance in wisdom beyond
the first stages. The most eminent men cease to improve, if they
associate only with disciples. When they have overtopped those
who immediately surround them, if they wish for further
growth, they must seek for others of their own stature to
consort with. The mental companionship which is improving,
is communion between active minds, not mere contact between
an active mind and a passive. This inestimable advantage is
even now enjoyed, when a strong-minded man and a strong-
minded woman are, by a rare chance, united: and would be
had far oftener, if education took the same pains to form
strong-minded women which it takes to prevent them from
being formed. The modern, and what are regarded as the
improved and enlightened modes of education of women,
abjure, as far as words go, an education of mere show, and
profess to aim at solid instruction, but mean by that
expression, superficial information on solid subjects. Except
accomplishments, which are now generally regarded as to be
taught well if taught at all, nothing is taught to women
thoroughly. Small portions only of what it is attempted to
teach thoroughly to boys, are the whole of what it is intended
or desired to teach to women. What makes intelligent beings is
the power of thought: the stimuli which call forth that power
are the interest and dignity of thought itself, and a field for its
practical application. Both motives are cut off from those who
are told from infancy that thought, and all its greater
applications, are other people's business, while theirs is to
make themselves agreeable to other people. High mental
powers in women will be but an exceptional accident, until

every career is open to them, and until they, as well as men, are educated for themselves and for the world – not one sex for the other.

In what we have said on the effect of the inferior position of women, combined with the present constitution of married life, we have thus far had in view only the most favourable cases, those in which there is some real approach to that union and blending of characters and of lives, which the theory of the relation contemplates as its ideal standard. But if we look to the great majority of cases, the effect of women's legal inferiority on the character both of women and of men must be painted in far darker colours. We do not speak here of the grosser brutalities, not of the man's power to seize on the woman's earnings, or compel her to live with him against her will. We do not address ourselves to any one who requires to have it proved that these things should be remedied. We suppose average cases, in which there is neither complete union nor complete disunion of feelings and of character; and we affirm that in such cases the influence of the dependence on the woman's side, is demoralizing to the character of both.

The common opinion is, that whatever may be the case with the intellectual, the moral influence of women over men is almost always salutary. It is, we are often told, the great counteractive of selfishness. However the case may be as to personal influence, the influence of the position tends eminently to promote selfishness. The most insignificant of men, the man who can obtain influence or consideration nowhere else, finds one place where he is chief and head. There is one person, often greatly his superior in understanding, how is obliged to consult him, and whom he is not obliged to consult. He is judge, magistrate, ruler, over their joint concerns; arbiter of all differences between them. The justice or conscience to which her appeal must be made, is his justice and conscience: it is his to hold the balance and adjust the scales between his own claims or wishes and those of another. His is now the only tribunal, in civilized life, in which the same person is judge and party. A generous mind, in such a situation, makes the balance incline against its own side and gives the other not less, but more, than a fair equality; and thus the weaker side may be enabled to turn the very fact of dependence into an instrument of power, and in default of justice, take an ungenerous advantage of generosity; rendering the unjust power, to those who make an unselfish use of it, a torment and a burthen. But how is it when average men are invested with this power, without reciprocity and without responsibility? Give such a man the idea that he is first in law and in opinion – that to will is his part, and hers to submit; it is absurd to suppose that this idea merely glides over his mind, without sinking into it, or having any effect on his feelings and practice. The propensity to make himself the first object of consideration, and others at most the second, is not so rare as to be wanting where everything seems purposely arranged for permitting its indulgence. If there is any self-will in the man, he becomes either the conscious or unconscious despot of his household. The wife, indeed, often succeeds in gaining her objects, but it is by some of the many various forms of indirectness and management.

Thus the position is corrupting equally to both; in the one it produces the vices of power, in the other those of artifice. Women, in their present physical and moral state, having stronger impulses, would naturally be franker and more direct than men yet all the old saws and traditions represent them as artful and dissembling. Why? Because their only way to their objects is by indirect paths. In all countries where women have strong wishes and active minds, this consequence is inevitable: and if it is less conspicuous in England than in some other places, it is because Englishwomen, saving occasional exceptions, have ceased to have either strong wishes or active minds.

We are not now speaking of cases in which there is anything deserving the name of strong affection on both sides. That, where it exists, is too powerful a principle not to modify greatly the bad influences of the situation; it seldom, however, destroys them entirely. Much oftener the bad influences are too strong for the affection, and destroy it. The highest order of durable and happy attachments would be a hundred times more frequent than they are, if the affection which the two sexes sought from one another were that genuine friendship, which only exists between equals in privileges as in faculties. But with regard to what is commonly called affection in married life – the habitual and almost mechanical feeling of kindliness, and pleasure in each other's society, which generally grows up between persons who constantly live together, unless there is actual dislike – there is nothing in this to contradict or qualify the mischievous influence of the unequal relation. Such feelings often exist between a sultan and his favourites, between a master and his servants; they are merely examples of the pliability of human nature, which accommodates itself in some degree even to the worst circumstances, and the commonest natures always the most easily.

With respect to the influence personally exercised by women over men, it, no doubt, renders them less harsh and brutal; in ruder times, it was often the only softening influence to which they were accessible. But the assertion, that the wife's influence renders the man less selfish, contains, as things now are, fully as much error as truth. Selfishness towards the wife herself, and towards those in whom she is interested, the children, though favoured by their dependence, the wife's influence, no doubt, tends to counteract. But the general effect on him of her character, so long as her interests are concentrated in the family tends but to substitute for individual selfishness a family selfishness, wearing an amiable guise, and putting on the mask of duty. How rarely is the wife's influence on the side of public virtue: how rarely does it do otherwise than discourage any effort of principle by which the private interests or worldly vanities of the family can be expected to suffer. Public spirit, sense of duty towards the public good, is of all virtues, as women are now educated and situated, the most rarely to be found among them; they have seldom even, what in men is often a partial substitute for public spirit, a sense of personal honour connected with any public duty. Many a man, whom no money or personal flattery would have bought, has bartered his political opinions against a title or invitations for his wife; and a still greater number are made mere hunters after the puerile vanities of society, because their wives value them. As for opinions; in Catholic countries, the wife's influence is another name for that of the priest: he gives her, in the hopes and emotions connected with a future life, a consolation for the sufferings and disappointments which are her ordinary lot in this. Elsewhere, her weight is thrown into the scale either of the most common-place, or of the most outwardly prosperous opinions: either those by which censure will be escaped, or by which worldly advancement is likeliest to be procured. In England, the wife's influence is usually on the illiberal and anti-popular side: this is generally the gaining side for personal interest and vanity; and what to her is the democracy or liberalism in which she has no part – which leaves her the Pariah it found her? The man himself, when he marries, usually declines into Conservatism; begins to sympathize with the holders of power, more than with its victims, and thinks it his part to be on the side of authority. As to mental progress, except those vulgarer attainments by which vanity or ambition are promoted, there is generally an end to it in a man who marries a woman mentally his inferior; unless, indeed, he is unhappy in marriage, or becomes indifferent. From a man of twenty-five or thirty, after he is married, an experienced observer seldom expects any further progress in mind or feelings. It is rare that the progress already made is maintained. Any spark of the *mens divinior* which might otherwise have spread and become a flame, seldom survives for any length of time unextinguished. For a mind which learns to be satisfied with what it already is – which does not incessantly look forward to a degree of improvement not yet reached – becomes relaxed, self-indulgent, and loses the spring and the tension which maintain it even at the point already attained. And there is no fact in human nature to which experience bears more invariable testimony than to this – that all social or sympathetic influences which do not raise up, pull down; if they do not tend to stimulate and exalt the mind, they tend to vulgarize it.

For the interest, therefore, not only of women but of men, and of human improvement in the widest sense, the emancipation of women, which the modern world often boasts of having effected, and for which credit is sometimes given to civilization, and sometimes to Christianity, cannot stop where it is. If it were either necessary or just that one portion of mankind should remain mentally and spiritually only half developed, the development of the other portion ought to have been made, as far as possible, independent of their influence. Instead of this, they have become the most intimate, and it may now be said, the only intimate associates of those to whom yet they are sedulously kept inferior; and have been raised just high enough to drag the others down to themselves.

We have left behind a host of vulgar objections, either as not worthy of an answer, or an answered by the general course of our remarks. A few words, however, must be said on one plea, which in England is made much use of for giving an unselfish air to the upholding of selfish privileges, and which, with unobserving, unreflecting people, passes for much more than it is worth. Women, it is said, do not desire – do not seek, what is called their emancipation. On the contrary, they generally

disown such claims when made in their behalf, and fall with
acharnement upon any one of themselves who identifies herself
with their common cause.

Supposing the fact to be true in the fullest extent ever
asserted, if it proves that European women ought to remain as
they are, it proves exactly the same with respect to Asiatic
women; for they too, instead of murmuring at their seclusion,
and at the restraint imposed upon them, pride themselves on it,
and are astonished at the effrontery of women who receive
visits from male acquaintances, and are seen in the streets
unveiled. Habits of submission make men as well as women
servile-minded. The vast population of Asia do not desire or
value, probably would not accept, political liberty, nor the
savages of the forest, civilization; which does not prove that
either of those things is undesirable for them, or that they will
not, at some future time, enjoy it. Custom hardens human
beings to any kind of degradation, by deadening the part of
their nature which would resist it. And the case of women is, in
this respect, even a peculiar one, for no other inferior caste that
we have heard of, have been taught to regard their degradation
as their honour. The argument, however, implies a secret
consciousness that the alleged preference of women for their
dependent state is merely apparent, and arises from their being
allowed no choice; for if the preference be natural, there can be
no necessity for enforcing it by law. To make laws compelling
people to follow their inclination, has not hitherto been
thought necessary by any legislator. The plea that women do
not desire any change, is the same that has been urged, times
out of mind, against the proposal of abolishing any social evil –
"there is no complaint;" which is generally not true, and when
true, only so because there is not that hope of success, without
which complaint seldom makes itself audible to unwilling ears.
How does the objector know that women do not desire
equality and freedom? He never knew a woman who did not,
or would not, desire it for herself individually. It would be very
simple to suppose, that if they do desire it they will say so.
Their position is like that of the tenants or labourers who vote
against their own political interests to please their landlords or
employers; with the unique addition that submission is
inculcated on them from childhood, as the peculiar attraction
and grace of their character. They are taught to think, that to
repel actively even an admitted injustice done to themselves, is

somewhat unfeminine, and had better be left to some male friend or protector. To be accused of rebelling against anything which admits of being called an ordinance of society, they are taught to regard as an imputation of a serious offence, to say the least, against the proprieties of their sex. It requires unusual moral courage as well as disinterestedness in a woman, to express opinions favourable to women's enfranchisement, until, at least, there is some prospect of obtaining it. The comfort of her individual life, and her social consideration, usually depend on the good will of those who hold the undue power; and to possessors of power any complaint, however bitter, of the misuse of it, is a less flagrant act of insubordination than to protest against the power itself. The professions of women in this matter remind us of the state offenders of old, who, on the point of execution, used to protest their love and devotion to the sovereign by whose unjust mandate they suffered. Griselda herself might be matched from the speeches put by Shakspeare into the mouths of male victims of kingly caprice and tyranny; the Duke of Buckingham, for example, in 'Henry the Eighth,' and even Wolsey. The literary class of women, especially in England, are ostentatious in disclaiming the desire for equality or citizenship, and proclaiming their complete satisfaction with the place which society assigns to them; exercising in this, as in many other respects, a most noxious influence over the feelings and opinions of men, who unsuspectingly accept the servilities of toadyism as concessions to the force of truth, not considering that it is the personal interest of these women to profess whatever opinions they expect will be agreeable to men. It is not among men of talent, sprung from the people, and patronized and flattered by the aristocracy, that we look for the leaders of a democratic movement. Successful literary women are just as unlikely to prefer the cause of women to their own social consideration. They depend on men's opinion for their literary as well as for their feminine successes; and such is their bad opinion of men, that they believe there is not more than one in ten thousand who does not dislike and fear strength, sincerity, or high spirit in a woman. They are therefore anxious to earn pardon and toleration for whatever of these qualities their writings may exhibit on other subjects, by a studied display of submission on this: that they may give no occasion for vulgar men to say (what nothing will prevent vulgar men from saying), that learning makes women unfeminine, and that literary ladies are likely to be bad wives.

But enough of this; especially as the fact which affords the occasion for this notice, makes it impossible any longer to assert the universal acquiescence of women (saving individual exceptions) in their dependent condition. In the United States at least, there are women, seemingly numerous, and now organised for action on the public mind, who demand equality in the fullest acceptation of the word, and demand it by a straightforward appeal to men's sense of justice, not plead for it with a timid deprecation of their displeasure.

Like other popular movements, however, this may be seriously retarded by the blunders of its adherents. Tried by the ordinary standard of public meetings, the speeches at the Convention are remarkable for the preponderance of the rational over the declamatory element; but there are some exceptions; and things to which it is impossible to attach any rational meaning, have found their way into the resolutions. Thus, the resolution which sets forth the claims made in behalf of women, after claiming equality in education, in industrial pursuits, and in political rights, enumerates as a fourth head of demand something under the name of "social and spiritual union," and "a medium of expressing the highest moral and spiritual views of justice," with other similar verbiage, serving only to mar the simplicity and rationality of other demands: resembling those who would weakly attempt to combine nominal equality between men and women, with enforced distinctions in their privileges and functions. What is wanted for women is equal rights, equal admission to all social privileges; not a position apart, a sort of sentimental priest-hood. To this, the only just and rational principle, both the resolutions and the speeches, for the most part, adhere. They contain so little which is akin to the nonsensical paragraph in question, that we suspect it not to be the work of the same hands as most of the other resolutions. The strength of the cause lies in the support of those who are influenced by reason and principle; and to attempt to recommend it by sentimentalities, absurd in reason, and inconsistent with the principle on which the movement is founded, is to place a good cause on a level with a bad one.

There are indications that the example of America will be followed on this side of the Atlantic; and the first step has been taken in that part of England where every serious movement in the direction of political progress has its commencement – the manufacturing districts of the North. On the 13th of February 1851, a petition of women, agreed to by a public meeting at Sheffield, and claiming the elective franchise, was presented to the House of Lords by the Earl of Carlisle.

THE SUBJECTION OF WOMEN[1]

The first fruits of Mr. Mill's retirement from Parliament are to be found in the essay whose title we quote, which will be studied by his more ardent followers with enthusiasm, and by all his readers with interest. It displays in a high degree many of the qualities for which he is distinguished – the power of logical arrangement, the capacity for compressing into a few pages the essence of a long train of thought, and a fulness and weightiness of style, giving dignity to many reflections which in other writers might appear to be commonplace. It shows in an equal degree a quality for which inattentive readers would not, until lately, have given him credit – an almost passionate enthusiasm in the cause which he advocates. People who knew Mr. Mill only from his *Logic* or his *Political Economy* generally failed to recognise the hints, which might be occasionally detected even in those writings, of a certain fervour of temperament which we do not expect to find in a philosophical speculator. Everybody has now had the opportunity of observing it in his political career. The zeal with which he attacked Governor Eyre, and proposed a revolutionary scheme of Irish reform, must have convinced those who disagreed with him that the last fault with which he could be plausibly taxed was that of a cold-blooded indifference to human interests. It is only fair to say that no man is more ready to denounce in the most generous spirit anything which in his opinion savours of injustice, and to throw himself, regardless of consequences, against every kind of social or political tyranny. He may be very wrong in his opinions, but at least his faults are due to an exaggerated generosity; they are not the faults of a mean or cynical nature, but of one which forgets even logic in its hatred of oppression. If any new proof was wanting of this tendency, he has given it in his present essay. Many men in talking of women's rights show, not merely a

---

[1] *The Subjection of Women.* By John Stuart Mill, London: Longmans & Co. 1869.

dislike to the eccentricities of their advocates, but a certain
jealousy of the claim of equality of those whom they hold to be
inferior beings. They admit with reluctance any proofs of
feminine intellect, and manage to make their compliments as
insulting as their abuse. From this fault at least Mr. Mill is as
free as it is possible for a man to be. He seems at times to be
anxious to establish rather the superiority than the equality of
those whom he describes as our "slaves"; and we may therefore
assume that women have found in him an advocate whose zeal
is equal to his ability, great as that undoubtedly is, and have
consequently the very best face put upon their pretensions.

Mr. Mill is not one of those writers whose argument can be
compressed into a sentence or two. It would of course be easy
to sum up in a few phrases a compendious account of his
opinions and to supply an equally compendious refutation. In
fact, however, we must admit that his essay fails chiefly on the
side of insufficiently developing his theory; and it will therefore
be fairer, without affecting to compress once more what is
already so closely packed, to indicate as shortly as we can the
general nature of his argument and to point out the omissions
which, in our opinion, take away some of its force. The essay,
then, is divided into four chapters. The first is intended to rebut
the general presumption against the truth of his theories; the
second points out what are the particular social arrangements
of which he complains; the third is designed to prove the
capacity of women for profiting by the proposed changes; and
the final chapter is an answer to the question, what definite
good results are to be anticipated? The purpose of the whole
essay is summed up in the first page, where the author
announces his intention of explaining the grounds of an
opinion which he has held with constantly increasing strength
of conviction:-

> That the principle which regulates the existing social
> relations between the two sexes – the legal subordination of
> one sex to the other – is wrong in itself, and now one of the
> chief hindrances to human improvement; and that it ought to
> be replaced by a principle of perfect equality, admitting no
> power or privilege on the one side, nor disability on the
> other.

The first chapter, after dwelling on the difficulties of attacking
a position resting on so many prejudices and associations that

the burden of proof is thrown upon the advocate, instead of the assailant, of an equality which in all other cases would have a general presumption in its favour, proceeds to argue that experience is really in his favour. Not only, he argues, has there never been an experiment of any other than the existing system, but such inferences as we can draw from history are in favour of a change. In all other cases, there has been a gradual transition from compulsory to voluntary arrangements. In old times society was founded, to an extent which we can scarcely realize, upon the law of superior strength. Nobody, except philosophers or saints, saw anything wrong in the principle. By very slow degrees slavery was gradually abolished, though within the last forty years Englishmen might buy and sell human beings, and within the century might kidnap them, carry them off, and work them to death. Women, however, are still slaves by law; and if in some respects better off than ordinary slaves, in others their position is even worse. The dependence of women on men is, in short, a relic of barbarous times; it has "not lost the taint of its brutal origin"; and, standing alone amongst modern ideas on all others but this most important point, it is as though "a gigantic dolmen occupied the site of St. Paul's and received daily worship, whilst the surrounding Christian churches were only resorted to on fasts and festivals." The argument that the distinction rests upon a difference in the nature of men and women is, it is urged, irrelevant, because the nature of women is the artificial product of this very subjection. It is a parallel to the argument that, because a cottier deeply in arrears to his landlord is not industrious, therefore the Irish are "naturally" idle. As a matter of fact we know little philosophically as to the nature of women, and few men know much about more than one side of the nature of one or two women. If, however, they are disqualified by nature from any employments, we may trust to free competition to find it out. We do not make laws to provide that only strong-armed men shall be blacksmiths; we leave it to the weak-armed men to find out by experience that they can do better elsewhere.

The presumption against equality of the sexes being thus rebutted, what are the evils due to a neglect of the principle? The most prominent evil, according to Mr. Mill, is the state of the marriage-law. A husband has absolute rights over the person and property of his wife. "She can do no act whatever

but by his permission, at least tacit. She can acquire no
property but for him; the instant it becomes hers, even if by
inheritance, it becomes *ipso facto* his." The system of
settlements only evades this partly, and only in the case of the
richer classes. The husband alone has legal rights over the
children. And from this state the woman has no power of
withdrawing herself. Mr. Mill remarks that the consideration of the propriety of divorce is foreign to his purpose; but
that, if the present system is permitted to continue, the only
alleviation possible would be to allow a woman to change her
master; and that alleviation is forbidden. Of course many,
indeed most, men do not push their rights to extremes; and
women have a resource in what Mr. Mill calls "the power of
the scold, or the shrewish sanction"; but, as it is, a tyranny
exists the results of which, besides great misery to
individuals, are summed up in the phrase that "the family is
the school of despotism, in which the virtues of despotism,
but also its vices, are largely nourished." There is of course
no difficult in showing, by the ordinary reasoning, that
arbitrary power causes many evils, even if in a majority of
cases it is moderately exercised, and, in many, exercised with
all possible wisdom and benevolence. The argument, however, to which Mr. Mill is chiefly concerned to reply is the
obvious one that when two people ride a horse, one must sit
behind. When two people are intimately connected, one must
have the deciding voice. In answer to this, he says that
voluntary partnerships do not necessarily imply that one
partner is to have the entire control; although such a
principle would be less dangerous in cases where the union
may be dissolved at will. He admits that men will, as a rule,
take the largest share in supporting the family, and will so far
have the more potential voice; but he thinks that these
matters may be left to voluntary arrangement in each case;
and that, as in practice some sort of compromise is amicably
affected, except in unfavourable cases, the law might
correspond to the facts. Matters, he says, are not improved
by making the husband a despot whose concessions may be
recalled at pleasure and without warning. Meanwhile the
effect of the present law, even where no advantage is taken of
it, is, he contents, to encourage the husband to hug himself in
the consciousness of his power, and the more decidedly in
proportion to his unfitness for its exercise.

The third chapter, after shortly noticing the claims of women to the suffrage, deals chiefly with the question of the supposed inferiority of the feminine intellect. It is a curious consideration, says Mr. Mill in one of those skilful turns of argument for which he has so great a talent, "that the only things which the existing law excludes women from doing are the things which they have proved that they are able to do." There is no law, that is to say, against women writing poems or composing music, but there is a law forbidding them to take part in politics. Now Mr. Mill regards it as certain that women are able to govern, and, in some respects, peculiarly well qualified for government. To prove this, he refers to such cases as Queen Elizabeth and Margaret of Austria, and he denounces the argument, or the "bad joke," that women govern better than men, because under women men govern, and under men women. We cannot enter into so wide a question, but there is something to be said for Turgot's form of the remark, that no woman ever chose a woman for her Prime Minister. Queen Elizabeth is a commonplace instance, but students of history may doubt whether the glory of her reign would properly fall to her or to such Ministers as Cecil and Walsingham. To this Mr. Mill replies, that women at least have a capacity for selection the best Ministers; and he goes into a long argument, showing that the various feminine qualities – intuitive perception, quickness of apprehension, versatility, and so forth – eminently fit women for government. To say the truth, this strikes us as one of the weakest parts of his book, for the very reason which he has explained elsewhere, that we possess as yet no philosophical analysis of the distinctive character of the sexes. It is easy by an *à priori* method to prove that any talent whatever is likely to be useful in government; and Mr. Mill omits the one quality which is after all the most essential, and in which women are supposed, at least, to be inferior. The governor must, above all things, be able to govern – that is to say, he must be strong; and no special pleading will evade the importance of this quality. It does not, of course, follow that women should be entirely excluded from all departments of public business. Turning to other talents, Mr. Mill labours to prove that, although no woman has hitherto attained the first rank in any intellectual or scientific department, the opportunities of women have hitherto been so small that we have no right to expect such a result. The want of feminine musical composers, which is the chief difficulty of his case, is accounted for by pointing to the difference between amateurs and professionals and the want of any thorough training of women in the higher branches of the art, especially in Germany and Italy – the only two countries that have produced great composers. Further, he remarks upon the time spent by women on frivolous pursuits, saying that whatever a woman does is done at odd times, and on the degree in which love of fame is discouraged as positively unfeminine. This whole chapter, though able, is of necessity occupied with a rather hypothetical argument, and betrays an eagerness to make the most of every point which detracts from Mr. Mill's usual appearance of candour.

The final chapter is, we think, more eloquent and less open to dispute than the remainder of the book. Its purpose is to insist upon the advantages to be anticipated from the elevation of women to an equality with men; the doubling of the mass of available faculties; the removal of a sense of injustice; the improvement in the tone of public opinion, so far as it depends upon women; the more intelligent direction of charity; the encouragement to wives to aid their husband's aspirations, instead of bringing him into bondage to Mrs. Grundy; the improvement of the happiness of married life when men and women can regard each other as equals, and mutually assist in each other's labours. These and other topics of a similar character are insisted upon shortly but forcibly, with Mr. Mill's usual skill in investing threadbare subjects with a certain interest and novelty. All we need say is, that most of the proposed benefits would result from an improvement of the feminine intellect rather than from an alteration in the legal position of women.

We have thus followed Mr. Mill through an argument which deals, as will be seen, with a vast variety of subjects, in some of which no one can do more than make a probable conjecture. Up to a certain point most people would sympathize with him; but it may be that he would be very little thankful for their going nine miles in his company unless they are prepared to proceed for the tenth. Thus it is difficult to put too strongly the importance of raising in every way the standard of the feminine intelligence, and of enabling women to choose lives full of great interests, instead of a hopeless round of frivolity. We may admit, too, that women, when their cultivation approaches the masculine standard, may develop talents not at present suspected, and even that they may share or appropriate to themselves some fields of labour from which they are now excluded. Indeed, if one circumstance were altered, Mr. Mill's whole argument would be not merely powerful, but absolutely conclusive. If women were simply men in a different dress, only distinguished by certain peculiarities of temperament and by varieties of physical constitution, the present restrictions would be utterly indefensible. By all means, we should say, throw down all barriers, remove all invidious privileges, and leave free competition to distribute the functions of life indifferently. But women are not men, and that undeniable truth reminds us that Mr. Mill has neglected one fact, which, to say the least, has a considerable bearing upon marriage laws. He has discussed marriage with scarcely any reference to its effect upon sexual morality. He has therefore neglected to answer the strongest argument that can be brought against him. We may grant that it is desirable that women should have the widest possible scope for the faculties they possess; it is to be hoped that those faculties may turn out to be as great as Mr. Mill can possibly suppose; but it is also important, in an equal degree, that the standard of feminine purity should not be lowered. There is, it may be, much unfairness in the present state of our social arrangements, but at least they secure this important point, that women as a rule are far more moral in some respects than men of the same class. The family, says Mr. Mill, is the school of despotism; but it is also the school of certain virtues of modesty and purity which are of the highest importance to the interests of mankind. A Mahommedan, it might be replied, would urge the same argument in favour of the complete seclusion of women; he would be wrong, we admit, in enforcing extravagant precautions, but it does not follow that no precautions are necessary against one of the most powerful of human instincts. Conservatives may be extreme in their opposition to all relaxation of discipline; but they are not only excusable, but are amply justified, in looking with great carefulness at any tampering with existing laws. It might be the height of folly to admit Eastern women at once to the freedom of intercourse which we can safely indulge in European countries; and the fact upon which Mr. Mill insists so forcibly, that the feminine nature is so much the product of artificial regulations, may suggest the serious danger of acting rashly in altering them suddenly. Mr. Mill, for example, guards himself against pronouncing upon the propriety of divorce "in the sense involving the liberty of re-marriage." He would, however, apparently allow an indefinite facility of separation – which, indeed, follows almost logically from his premisses. Complete equality of rights would be meaningless unless the partners could separate on any hopeless divergence of opinion. In the American States, whose example is quoted in favour of the separation of property, the power of divorce has been generally carried to an extreme; and, if not a necessary, it is at least a highly probable, consequence of the proposed principle. It is therefore strictly relevant to inquire what are the probable results of a system which, at first sight at least, is highly prejudicial to sexual morality. Not only may it be fairly maintained that an unlimited power of divorce is likely to be demoralizing, but it would also appear to be in many ways conducive to tyranny. Mr. Mill takes no notice of the circumstance which materially mitigates the "slavery" of women. If the wife is the slave of her husband, he is at least bound to have only one slave. This implies a certain reciprocity of no little importance. The husband gives up a right the use of which would generally tell to his advantage. When two people live together on such intimate terms, it will be a general result, not of positive law, but of the nature of the case, that one will be chiefly dependent on the other; and in most cases the ruler would, for obvious reasons, be the strongest and the best able to shift for himself. If the husband could dismiss his wife at pleasure, or make her so uncomfortable as to be forced into assenting to separation, a new weapon of oppression would be put into his hands. The woman is, and is likely to remain, as Mr. Mill admits, far more dependent than the man on her family and household life; if the man could break it up at his pleasure, he would have a mode of coercion which probably would be even more efficient in many cases than those which the law now puts into his hand. The indissolubility of the marriage tie, except under certain defined circumstances, acts as a protection to the weaker partner in the concern, and Mr. Mill's theories obviously tend to weaken this bond, though it may be doubtful to what extent he would go. We do not state this as a conclusive answer to all Mr. Mill's complaints, some of which, indeed, appear to have a very sound foundation;

but it is a view of the case which he cannot avoid simply by refusing to pronounce upon the question of divorce.

The same omission tells also against the argument for the free admission of women to professions. Admitting in the fullest way that women might admirably discharge many functions from which they are at present excluded, it does not follow that a breaking down of all existing limitations would of necessity cure more evils than it would cause. That women should be mingled with men in all the employments of life may be desirable if we look at it merely from the point of view of the utilization of all existing talents. But the moral question is also one of supreme importance, and it is that upon which the simple principles of free trade and open competition fail to throw any light. The weak-armed, as he truly says, will not be blacksmiths, even if the forges are left open to everybody to enter; women will, on the same principle, only take to those trades where they can make money; but it does not follow that they will avoid trades which are demoralizing, though not unprofitable. As a fact, we have been compelled to exclude them by legislation from duties by which they could earn money to the prejudice of the public morality; and there is no presumption in favour of leaving such questions merely to the play of the market. If women are to be doctors, lawyers, and preachers, according to their tastes, it may probably be necessary to enforce regulations against certain obvious dangers as much as in the case of mines or field-labour. If women are now hot-house plants, as Mr. Mill says, we must be very cautious how we suddenly plant them in the open air. It is the general indifference of the advocates of women's rights to these obvious considerations which tends as much as anything else to prejudice sensible people against them, and we can only regret that Mr. Mill's book, though full of eloquence, of generous feeling, and in many places of views which appear to be sound as well as striking, should be exposed to the same objection. We do not know, as he says, very much about the nature of women as it might be manifested under a system of absolute equality; but we do know this, that men and women differ very profoundly, and that the relation between the sexes is one with which.it is exceedingly dangerous to play tricks without much consideration and a careful feeling of the way.

THE SUBJECTION OF WOMEN

Lady Morgan began it. In that story of the fair sex called 'Woman and Her Master,' the witty and brilliant Irish lady raised the cry for female rights into a literary question. Poets and philanthropists followed suit, until the author of 'Ion' was able to carry a first remedial measure through the three estates. That measure – passed, of poetic right, in a female reign – is known as Serjeant Talfourd's Act. Since the Third year of Victoria – when our Courts first recognized some part of a mother's right in her own children – the position of woman before the law has been accepted as a Parliamentary question.

In Mr. Mill's hands, the question takes a wider range than was ever imagined by the Irish wit and the English poet. Mr. Mill asks for political equality, where they would have been content with legal justice. He extends into public life an argument which they had confined to private life.

The cause brought up for trial by the late Member for Westminster is one that might be expected to stir the deepest passions of our race. Subjection of women is the law of every clime; and, if it be wrong, the whole world is wrong. Has nature given this law to man and woman when they come together, that there shall be in every house one head, and that this head shall be the highest male? We look around, and find it the universal fact. This order of masculine precedence and responsibility is not the rule of one nation and of one time only, but of every country and of every age. It is the rule of a Pawnee wigwam and of an English home. It was once the rule of Babylon; it is now the rule of Boston. But whether we call it right or not right, we shall find it co-extensive with organized society, all but co-extensive with organized life. If there be exceptions to such a rule, they are few and far away. The female bee is said to reign, the female spider to possess the superior size and strength; but the tale of masculine domination is so constant that those who think it a law of nature, for which no reason need be sought, can certainly fall back on a vast and striking array of facts. A challenge to try the cause afresh is, therefore, certain to provoke the anger of thoughtless men.

What is still worse, the sex for which Mr. Mill does battle will hardly smile upon their knight. A few sad and thoughtful women may praise and love him, seeing the goodness of his work, and knowing how much it costs him in fame and power; but the brighter portion of the sex will either laugh at his wise words or pass them by as idle wind. All happy women are conservative in spirit; and a great majority of women, it may be hoped, are happy in their lot. They think too much of men. In their eyes, a lover is a hero, a husband is a god. Female rights! Such rights as they wish for, they have got; for all desires of the female heart begin and end in love. A woman who has won her husband's heart has gained the only prize on earth for which she cares. Why should a happy wife excite her nerves about the crotchets of Eliza Farnham and Cora Hatch? To her a vote is useless, seeing that she feels no separate interest and finds no independent light. The lady who said she was "too fond of being taken care of" to make a noise about her abstract rights, was no indifferent sample of her sex.

Thus a plea for woman's equality with man, even though it be put in sober form and phrase, is not unlikely to be denounced in male quarters as a portent, while it is welcomed in female circles as a jest.

Yet the points brought up for trial are worth a good deal of thought; more perhaps on the part of men than on that of women; and for this reason, if for no other, that they shed the light of philosophy on such efforts as have recently been made to amend our common law, not only in the old world but in the new. If Justice Talfourd led the way in this reform, Mr. Shaw Lefevre, Mr. Jacob Bright, Sir Charles Dilke, and many more are following in his wake. In a few months the property of married women will be placed on a new footing; a few months later, women may be voting in all municipal elections. These efforts to discharge a debt long due from the sterner to the softer sex should be studied in connexion with the whole facts of the case, and especially with what have been proved to be fair and useful arrangements in the United States.

We could have wished that Mr. Mill had not mixed up in one general view the two essentially distinct branches of his subject. Woman's wrongs are of two kinds – public and private – political and personal; and much advantage would be gained by treating them apart. Equity is one thing: Equality is another. The sentiment on which Equity can be claimed for women is different from that on which Equality can be claimed for them. A man would be ashamed to refuse his wife justice, who would feel no scruple in refusing to give her power. Even those advocates of reform who say that these two classes of female wrongs arise from a common source – the abuse of power in men – must see that they have their differing times and seasons, and that any attempt to force them on together will delay the second and defeat the first.

The day for Equity has come; the day for Equality has not come. Many States in the American Union have freed their women from the old fetters in which they were bound by the common law; but no State in the Union has yet adopted the platform of female suffrage, – not even Kansas, which has given votes to Negroes and Shawnees, and which, in respect to liberal opinion, is probably the most forward State on earth. A party in England – weak in number, but strong in purpose – is ready to follow in the track prepared for them by our American kinsfolk, as fast and far as they can see that the road is safe. But this party is cautious. It like to see its way. It will not leap in the dark. In the present state of public opinion, this party is honestly, and not unreasonably, afraid of female suffrage. The question of that suffrage is no simple thing. In claiming a full share of public power for women, Mr. Mill is preparing for us the greatest revolution ever yet effected on this planet. Once upon a time, some people fancy, the earth suddenly changed its axis of rotation; if it ever did so, that was a change in the physical sphere which might be compared with what is proposed to be done in the moral sphere. Mr. Mill is working towards no less radical a change than a transfer of the whole government of the world to women!

Of course, he avoids presenting his case in any such words, and probably the facts have not offered themselves to his observation in any such way. But may not cautious men fear that this result would follow the adoption of his ideas? He proposes in the name of a just law that the male and female shall have equal rights and powers. He implies that all such rights and powers would be exercised in a just society in accordance with the general will. He would allow, as we take him, the vote of a majority to be the only expression of that general will. In fact, under his system of free and equal government, the majority would have its way; and while the lesser number would have a claim to be heard, the final answer that must be given to every argument would be a vote of the stronger side. Now, in this empire, as we know to our grief, the woman's party is numerically stronger than the man's. The males are fewer than the females, – not only in the Three Kingdoms, but in every part of them. The difference in numbers is about a million; and an act of Parliament which should call the female population to political power would give them, not a share in the government, but the whole. No fact is clearer. Under an equal franchise for male and female, the women would possess a working majority of votes in every county, and probably in every town.

Not a word need be said here on the right or wrong of female suffrage. What is of use just now is to notice such facts as are likely to disturb the judgment of prudent men. Many persons, we may be sure, would shrink from the public perils of such a change who would lend a ready hand in removing the domestic grievance. Hence we regret to have these future pretensions of the sex urged to the peril of nearer and clearer claims. Even those advocates who say that a woman's right to public power is just as good as her right to personal justice, cannot deny that the personal emancipation must precede the political change.

When we come to the special question of Equity, we have to point out a necessary flaw, or what seems to be a necessary flaw, in Mr. Mill's argument. The whole plea proceeds upon exceptional facts. The cause is not that of woman, but of women; not that of the female sex, but of certain females who have fallen out of line. This flaw is common to all the advocates of this reform, from Mrs. Farnham to Mr. Mill. They think of woman rather as a partner than as a wife. They forget the part which affection plays as the universal leveller. They are the bondsmen of law, and of the phrases which hold good in law. Baron and feme, the master and his woman – there is a pretty phrase, cries Lady Morgan! Yet under this legal term, millions of happy women have lived and died, not knowing that they were slaves. In fact, these writers talk of law, and forget the law of Love. They treat of the contracts which surround our family life, and omit that element of sympathy which makes them one. Legal subordination! The truly married pair knows no law but that of confidence, and pines for no equality but that of love.

To feel the case truly – in its broad expanse, and with its close limitations – we must begin by seeing that all these wails are droned, and all these sermons preached, on behalf of a class and in the name of our failures – on the part of those hapless women to whom have fallen the blanks of life. Where love reigns there is no need for law. Had it been otherwise – had the baron been a "master" to his "woman" – the seeming wrongs of the sex could not have been maintained so long. A bad law may last for centuries if no one puts it to the proof. Blackstone speaks of our English law as highly favourable to the female sex, and he uses this language in the very same sentence in which he says the common law gives a man power to beat his wife. It was precisely because men did not habitually beat their wives that the law remained in the Statute-book. Where penalties are extreme, we may be sure the crime to which they refer is rare. On a tablet in the British Museum we find some laws of very ancient times, in which it is enacted that if a husband is false to his wife, he shall be fined half a maneh in silver; and that if a wife is false to her husband, she shall be cast into the river and drowned. What does the law imply? That infidelity on the part of men was common; that on the part of women it was rare. By the old English law, if a man killed his wife it was simple murder; if a woman killed her husband, it was petty treason. In the first case, the man was hung; in the second case, the woman was burnt to death. This crime of husband-murder was in early times all but unknown. There is no name for such a crime in our language. Patricide, fratricide, regicide we have; but the particular crime of husband-killing never had in English a distinctive name. These penalties inflicted by the law on female offenders, like the disabilities of which complaint is now made, existed only because they touched the wretched few, and not the general body of their sex. Clarissa could see no injury to herself in Moll Flanders being stripped to the waist and flogged down the Strand.

Yet these unhappy ones – if few in number – deserve some pity and demand some justice. The harsher features of the common law have been removed, no doubt, and the two sexes stand to-day on a nearer level than they stood of old. We have abolished the distinction of quality in the crime of wife-killing and husband-killing. We have ceased to call the same offence felony in one sex and treason in the other sex. We have given up the practice of burning women alive. We have put an end to the male benefit of "clergy," by which, in cases of simple larceny, a woman would be hung when a man (being able to read) was only branded and imprisoned. But we have a great deal more to do before the law of England can be accepted as a satisfactory statement of the relations which ought to exist between man and wife in a Christian land.

The claim of an English married woman to a safer standing in the family order is not to be denied, hardly to be postponed, by any man who keeps his eyes upon to the light of science. After all that wits have said and statesmen have done, her standing in that order is the worst feature of our civilization – the standing of a married English lady being lower than that of any other female who is not a slave. In some respects, it is lower than that of the ordinary woman who *is* a slave. The favourite of a Turkish Effendi, of a Syrian Bey, lives in a better position before the law than any English wife.

As Mr. Mill puts his case, a married woman is "the actual bond-servant" of her husband. At the altar, she vows a life-long service to her lord, and the law compels her to keep that vow. She can do nothing without his leave. She can hold no property of her own; in which respect she is denied a right that was possessed by a Roman slave. A father, it is true, may make provision for his daughter by a settlement of his money; but even that father cannot give the money to his child. He must leave it to some *man* for her use. Even when this other man has paid the money to her, the law will not treat it as her own. So soon as it comes into her hands, the husband may take it from her – either seize it by force or gain it by wile; yet she can neither punish him for his theft nor recover from him that which was her father's gift. As against her husband a wife has no rights. "No slave is a slave to the same lengths, and in so full a sense of the word, as a wife is." If she has children, they are her husband's, not hers. She has no separate rights over them. Even when her husband dies she does not become their legal guardian, unless he makes her so by will. He may use her badly, he may rob her, he may break her heart; yet she will have no right to complain against him. Only when a husband adds adultery to his other wrongs can a wife obtain the right to quit his house. The legal power of an English husband to do wrong in what concerns his wife is so grossly out of keeping with the moral sense, that we need not wonder at more civilized nations actually thinking we can sell our wives at the market-cross for a pot of ale.

Now, it is well to know that this abominable state of things exists in England only. In France and Italy a woman has some legal rights. In those countries she can enter into trade, she can acquire property, she can sue and be sued, she can be lodged in prison for debt. But in no Christian land is a woman so well off before the law as she is in Turkey, Egypt, and Mohammedan India. In the East a wife has a dozen rights of which her fairer sisters never dream. She retains her name. She keeps her property. All the rights which belong to her as her father's child are hers through life. Her husband must support her in accordance with her rank. Appeal against ill-usage is always open to her. If her husband parts from her, he must restore to her every para of her fortune. Yet some of the men who object to Mr. Lefevre's Bill presume to talk of the East as a barbarous portion of the world!

In the United States they have done something to amend these monstrous provisions of the old English law – more, indeed, than Mr. Mill appears to be aware. In some of the Southern States – such as Texas and Louisiana, which follow the Spanish and French Codes – the old common law of England is unknown; and, in the States where it once prevailed under our colonial judges, it has been greatly modified in recent years. In no part of America is Mr. Mill's description of an Englishwoman applicable. Though much remains to be done in that country, no wife is there a "chattel" and a "slave." But a wise amendment of our common law, she has attained to something like equality with a Persian and a Turkish wife, at least so far as regards her proprietorial rights. For example, in the State of New York it is now the law that "the real and personal property of any female which she may own at the time of marriage, and the fruits, issues, and profits thereof, shall not be subject to the disposal of her husband nor be liable for his debts, and shall continue her sole and separate property as if she were a single woman." In the State of Pennsylvania it is now the law that "every species and description of property, whether consisting of real, personal, or mixed, which may be owned by any single woman, shall continue to be the property of such woman as well after her marriage as before." In the State of Massachusetts there is a similar law; and in the State of California women lose none of their rights on becoming wives.

In the young Western States generally, substantial justice has been done to women in the State Codes. Wisconsin, Iowa, and Illinois lead the way in liberality of spirit. Kentucky is not far behind. Below the line of the Potomac things are a little worse; but even in the old slave States the married women stand on a higher level than they do in Great Britain. Even the State of Alabama secures to her women the property which they may own before the nuptial knot is tied.

But the American Courts, we are glad to say, go further in the rectification of woman's wrongs than the simple maintenance of her right to that which is her own in the way of house and land. They regard her as something else than a proprietor. They take note of her as a human being, and cover her person as well as her goods with the protection of public law. To wit, in every State of New England (with one exception) the seduction of a woman is punished as a crime; and this is the law in several of the Western States. Seduction with promise of marriage is treated as a grave offence, even in New York. It is severely punished in Ohio and Pennsylvania. Generally, this offence is sternly treated by the American law; and the Canadians, stirred into action by a recent crime, which the law condemned and the public sentiment approved – the shooting of a seducer, – are making efforts to bring their law into line with the popular conscience, as it is in the United States.

Adultery, again, is a crime in most of the States. In every part of New England the man taken in adultery is sent to jail and branded with public odium; not as a trespasser on some *other man's* estate, who has deprived him of a daughter's "service," or of a wife's "society," – and therefore done an injury to *him*, – but as a scoundrel, who has done the most fearful wrong to the woman whom he has led astray, and probably destroyed for life.

In this direction there should be no scruple in pushing forward. Here, at least, we may very safely strive to Americanize our institutions.

THE SUBJECTION OF WOMEN
[Frances Power Cobbe]

The Subjection of Women. By John Stuart Mill. London: Longmans. 1869.

The Taj-mahal has often been described as the fairest monument in the world of a husband's love for his departed wife. Colonel Sleeman tells us of a lady who, after visiting it, wished that she might die, if only somebody would build her such a tomb. We have always imagined that this Eastern trophy of affection had an English counterpart, built of better things than bronze and marble; and that, in the unwearied advocacy of the claims of women by one of the greatest thinkers of our time, we beheld the worthiest monument of a noble conjugal friendship, the continuation by the survivor of the work of the beloved companion long withdrawn from earth. That such sacred feelings have blended with Mr. Mill's steady enthusiasm we still believe; but from the opening sentence of the present book we learn that the adoption of his task took place yet earlier than we had supposed. His present opinion, he says, was formed "from the very earliest period when I had formed any opinions at all on social and political matters;" and instead of being weakened or modified, it has constantly grown stronger by the progress of reflection and the experience of life.

This "opinion," bravely stated in the next phrase, and calmly argued out in a long consecutive chain of reasoning throughout the book, is one which will startle many even of those who have given Mr. Mill credit for accumulating the very worst heresies hitherto known, moral, religious and political, in his single person. "We always knew he was a dangerous free-thinker" (we hear them say), "but truly this new doctrine out-herods Herod. Where are we drifting, when such subversive ideas can be unblushingly enunciated by a man of reputation? Truly, in all seriousness, we believe we are drifting a great way from the old moorings. Churches and systems of representation have been undergoing revolutions, and now the change threatens to come not only to our doors, but within them, and into the inmost recesses of our domestic life.

In one of the delicious old German stories collected by the brothers Grimm, there is a tale, called Frederick and Catherine, wherein the heroine, being desired by her husband to lock the door of their house when they are setting out on a journey, thinks she does a great deal better by taking the door off its hinges and carrying it on her back. Having also to carry some nuts and some vinegar, she ingeniously fastens them to the door, by way of alleviation; and staggers under her load, till, overpowered with fatigue, she stops to think how she can lighten it. "It must be the vinegar," says the poor fool; and straightway pours her vinegar away, drop by drop. But the door remains as heavy as ever. "Then it can only be the nuts," she cries; and so she lets them fall one by one on the road. Still her burden is unbearable. "Perhaps, after all, who knows but it may be the door?" So the door is thrown down, and the trouble removed. Very much in this way it would seem that women and their friends, for some years back, have been pondering what it could possibly be which weighed so heavily on them and made them such poor creatures. One detail after another has been canvassed, – the law which enabled husbands to beat their wives, the law which forbade women to testify against their husbands, the divorce laws, the common law regarding the property of married women, the obstructions to education and to entering professions, the refusal of the municipal and political franchise. "It must be the vinegar!" "It must be the nuts!" The vinegar has been a good deal of it poured away, and the nuts seem in process of scattering. But the weight is not lifted yet. And now comes Mr. Stuart Mill, saying composedly, "My dear, it is the door which causes your suffering; get rid of that, and all will be well."

> "The principle which regulates the existing social relations between the two sexes – the legal subordination of one sex to the other – is wrong in itself, and now one of the chief hindrances of human improvement. It ought to be replaced by a system of perfect equality, admitting no power or privilege on the one side, nor disability on the other."[1]

[1] P. 1.

Such is the thesis of Mr. Mill's book; a tolerably daring one, we think it will on all hands be admitted to be. So daring, that before we have time to consider how he will defend it, we are inclined to think, How he will be abused for this! What an avalanche of sarcasms and rebukes and jokes will be flung at him as he stands to be pilloried by those "sworn tormentors" of women and their knights, the Saturday Review and the Pall Mall Gazette! Think of "Paterfamilias" in the *Times*! Think of the probable Blackwood and possible Quarterly! Think of the High-church sermons on the marriage vow of obedience! Think of the Low-church lectures on texts culled at pleasure from Solomon who had a thousand wives, and from Paul who had none! Think – but we really can only think of Mr. Mill as of that African nation described by Herodotus, who went to war with the south wind, and the wind blew and covered them with the sand of the desert. The philosopher has gone forth to encounter the fierce simoom of prejudice, and if he be not blown upon with a vengeance, it will be a miracle indeed.

Having thrown down his gauntlet, our knight proceeds to ride round the course; and it must be confessed that he makes a tolerably clear sweep of it. In the present paper we shall try to follow him so as to do him the best justice in our power, namely, to give him not our praises, but a fair sketch of his argument, in as far as such close calm logic, such well-linked arguments, and sledge-hammer periods, are capable of being condensed or described by weaker hands. It is very generous of Mr. Mill to admit the mental equality of women; but it would have done our souls good to have seen a woman's name on the title-page of such a book, or even to know any woman who was thoroughly capable of reviewing it. But then, per contra, how many men can write like Mr. Mill?

It is not without knowing what sort of dragons he has to contend against, that our author has set out on his arduous expedition. *Logic*, he thinks, is all on his own side, but *Feeling* is all, or nearly all, against him, and to attack Feeling with the weapons of Logic is extremely like cutting a fog with a hatchet. You may slash and hew right and left, and only wish for more resistance, if it were but of a man of straw to be knocked down. But when you drop your axe, the fog will be there quite undisturbed, and close round you, blinding your eyes and choking your lungs precisely as before. Nay, somehow, people cling to their prejudices with peculiar fondness when they are threatened with being exploded by reason. We are persuaded that the Baal-worshipers had quite a "Revival" after that scene in which Elijah confuted them in so aggravating a manner. Is not this a deep bit of that science for which some scholar should find us the proper name, but which we shall beg leave for the moment to call human-nature-ology?

"So long as an opinion is strongly rooted in the feelings, it gains rather than loses in stability by having a preponderating weight of argument against it. For, if it were accepted as the result of argument, the refutation of the argument might shake the solidity of the conviction; but when it rests solely on feeling, the worse it fares in argumentative contest, the more persuaded its adherents are, that *their feelings must have some deeper ground which the arguments do not reach.*"

In truth, it is not only natural, but in a certain sense right, for people to hesitate to surrender long-received opinions at the first summons. The understandings of the majority would need, as Mr. Mill himself says, to be much better cultivated, before they can be asked to place such reliance on their own power of estimating arguments as to give up practical principles in which they have been born and bred, at the first attack which they are not capable of logically resisting. There are fools at both ends of the scales of credulity; and the fool who too soon changes his opinion upon the graver matters of life, is a more dangerous fool than he who doggedly sticks to what he has been taught, after reasonable confutation. The Philistine is a better, or at least a safer citizen of the commonwealth, than the unstable politician who lurches from side to side with every roll of the ship of state, and makes it well nigh impossible to trim the craft with such shifting ballast. But the reliance on customary opinion, when confuted by argument, ought to have its limit; and that limit ought to be reached soon when it can be shewn that the customary opinion has obviously arisen from any false and perverted sources - i.e. when there is proof that it is not natural sentiment, or (if Mr. Mill would grant us the word) intuition, but prejudice *pur et simple*. Custom may be either a venerable old gentleman deserving of all attention, or a disreputable old villain, to be dealt with on the principles of the Habitual Criminals Bill, and judged guilty till he prove his innocence. Mr. Mill consents to let his success hinge on the preliminary proof that the customary opinion which he opposes (namely, that of the rightful subordination of women to men), is the natural result of causes notoriously at work for ages, warping the consciences of men in the direction of their passions. In a word, he answers those who maintain that trees are most properly developed when their branches are all on one side, by shewing them the quarter whence a sea-blast constantly blows on them and forces them to grow awry.

It is of course not very difficult to shew how long it is in any community before the strong begin to feel that the weak have any rights as against them. Greece and Rome called themselves free, and lauded Liberty in every note of poetry, while the great majority of men were miserable slaves who might be killed and tortured with absolute impunity. To this day, few nations – nay, not even all professed moral philosophers – recognize that brutes have claims to mercy at our hands. "Non è Cristiano," settles all appeals for pity towards horses and dogs throughout Italy and the Levant; and more than one English divine has laid down the principle, that we are called on to refrain from uselessly torturing them, not for their sakes, but our own. Despotisms of all kinds justify themselves always to the despot; and multitudes even of those who are degraded by enduring it, hug the yoke. But no tyranny of king over subject, master over slave, has ever had so many roots of vitality as the rule over women by men. "It comes home to the person and hearth of every male head of a family, and of everyone who looks forward to being so. The clodhopper exercises, or is to exercise, his share of the power equally with the highest nobleman. And the case is that in which the desire of power is strongest; for every one desires power most over those who are nearest to him, and in whom any independence of his authority is oftenest likely to interfere with his individual preferences."[2] Other tyrannies are got rid of by the combination of the sufferers; but in the case of women such combination is impossible, and moreover "each individual of the subject class is in a chronic state of bribery and intimidation combined." Do people say it is "natural" that males should rule females? The law of force always seems the most natural of all things *to the strong*. "Conquering races hold it to be nature's own dictate

2   P. 19.

that the feebler and unwarlike races should submit to the braver and manlier." "Unnatural" generally means "uncustomary," and nothing more.

Again, is it said that women themselves gladly accept the domination of the stronger sex? It is answered, that, in the first place, multitudes of them do nothing of the kind, but protest against it with all their small means of making themselves heard; and, in the second place, as above said, they are not only intimidated into silence, but bribed to submission. "The masters of women want more than simple obedience," and the whole education afforded to women tends to check independence and nourish submission.

"If it had been made the object of the life of every young plebeian to find personal favour in the eyes of some patrician, if domestication with him and a share of his affections had been held out as the prize to which he should aspire, and if when the prize had been obtained he had been shut out by a wall of brass from all interests not centering in him, – would not plebeians and patricians have been as broadly distinguished at this day as men and women are, and would not all but a thinker here and there have believed the distinction to be an unalterable fact of human nature?"

These and similar considerations prove, as Mr. Mill believes, that the supposed consciousness of the rightful subordination of one sex to the other, is the result of long-maintained and universal conquest constantly witnessed, and therefore confounded with a law of nature. A Chinese, in like manner, we suppose, might decide that compressed feet were a natural type of refined womanhood, and that it was an indefeasible instinct of the "eternal fitness of things" which makes Chinese mothers cram their babies' toes into iron shoes.

Whatever may be thought of the final conclusions of our author, it will hardly be denied that in these opening pages he has placed the *origin* of female subjection in a new light; and maintained not unsuccessfully his challenge to prove the common belief in its justice to rest on very ignoble grounds. Whether there be other arguments in its favour beside those of such popular feeling, he examines in detail as he proceeds.

The laws which determine the influence of circumstance on character, ought to form a very important branch of psychology, and not till some attempt has been made at ascertaining them, is there room for anybody to dogmatize about what are, or are not, the natural differences between men and women. M. Victor Hugo, by way of illustrating the horrors of aristocracy, has recently described in a slightly apocryphal manner how children used to be distorted in their growth to make agreeable toys for the "nobility, clergy and gentry" of former times. In China, he assures us, they used to be put in porcelain jars, expressly made to order; so that a mandarin had nothing to do but to sketch the ins and outs which his fancy suggested as a variety of the received undulations of the human form, and in the course of a few years he received a man precisely of the required shape and size. We have of course no doubt of the absolute truth of these wonderful anecdotes. But inasmuch as the children experimented upon by those sculptors of humanity discovered by M. Hugo could not fairly be described "natural," neither can the characters and abilities of creatures manipulated as women are, fairly come under that designation. Even if we were to confine ourselves to the training of a single girl, and treat her as an isolated being, there would be much in her physical and moral treatment to remind us of the Porcelain Jar system of education. She may freely grow, and even swell to abnormal proportions in the regions of the heart; but the head has but a small chance of expansion, and the whole base is weak and ricketty in the extreme. Nothing can be more misleading, however, than to think of the training of human creatures or of animals as if it reached only the individuals immediately subjected to it. We recognize familiarly how the offspring of a trained dog, or of a cat taught to be peculiarly trustful, inherit the parents' qualities; and it is absurd to suppose that the same thing does not take place in the human race in the vast though obscure field of our instinctive tendencies and antipathies, facilities and disabilities. Dr. Darwin describes how rabbits when tamed gradually go on through generations increasing in general bulk as they are well fed, but growing more stupid and having proportionally smaller and smaller brains as there is no need for them to exert even the small intelligence of rabbinical existence in the construction of holes and the escape from weasels. Finally it comes to pass that the daughter of a hundred (not exactly high-born, but) hutch-born rabbits is twice as heavy as her ancestress was when "wild in woods that noble savage ran;" but her brain actually weighs several ounces less. Whether Mr.

Darwin intended it, we dare not surmise, but did he not in these interesting observations furnish us with a very parable in the manner of Æsop concerning the development of women in an artificial and hutch-like state of existence? "Oh, but," it will be said, "inherited qualities must run in both male and female lines alike. The male offspring and the female will share them equally." I reply, that of course they will, *if both are kept all their lives in the hutch.* But if all the young male rabbits are taken out as soon as they are weaned, and permitted to get their own living among the gorse and the turnips, while the young females are kept close in the "sacred shelter of the home," and supplied with unsought-for cabbage-leaves, the result will certainly be manifest in that day when they are both brought up for philosophical examination, roast or boiled, as the case may be. The brother bred in the open air will have a "game flavour," while the sister will resemble her forbears, so bitterly satirized by Boileau (the Saturday Reviewer of the Siécle of Louis XIV.),

"Qui, dès leur tendre enfance élevés dans Paris,
Sentait encore le chou dont ils furent nourris."

Mr. Mill does not touch on this part of the subject, but presses on to urge that we are yet wholly in the dark as to what women could, or could not, do were freedom given to them, and that

"There are no means of finding what either one person or many can do but by trying; and no means by which any one else can discover for women what it is for their happiness to do or leave undone. One thing we may be certain of – that what is contrary to woman's nature to do, they never will be made to do by simply giving their natures free play. The anxiety of mankind to interfere on behalf of nature, for fear lest nature should not succeed in effecting its purpose, is an altogether unnecessary solicitude. What women by nature cannot do, it is quite superfluous to forbid them from doing. What they can do, but not so well as the men who are their competitors, competition suffices to exclude them from, since nobody asks for protective duties and bounties in favour of women; it is only asked that the present bounties and protective duties in favour of men should be recalled."[3]

---

[3]   P. 49.

The double absurdity of the case comes out when we consider that women are at once supposed to be so exclusively and passionately desirous of being wives and mothers, that they are all sensible of being complete failures in life when they do not become so; and that a sour and embittered, or at best mournful and resigned, aspect is the appropriate expression for an old maid; while all the time, if other vocations besides matrimony be thrown open to them, there is imminent danger to the community of a general rush of women away from the hitherto all-inviting bowers of connubial felicity, into offices and chambers, consulting-rooms and hospitals. Instead of seven women taking hold of the skirts of one man, it is dreaded that seven men will then endeavour to seize the (much abbreviated) skirts of one woman; and Mr. Greg's somewhat impertinent question, "Why are Women Redundant?" will be answered by a brisk denial of his major proposition, and a cheerful chorus of feminine voices,

"We've got our work to do!"

Perhaps, in sober earnest, it would be extremely well for both husbands and wives if women were generally allowed the option of some other course of life beside matrimony, and did not always stand in the market-place idle till some man hired them. If Mr. B., who fondly believes he is chosen exclusively for his own irresistible attractions, were to know all the motives of weariness of an aimless life, fear of solitary age, narrowness of circumstances, and hopelessness of finding remunerative employment, which combine to turn the balance against dislike of his person and contempt for his vanity, he would probably think that, after all, it would have been better for both parties had Miss A. had some other choice beside Hobson's open to her as a career. Of course the simple and obvious fact is, that, as marriage is undoubtedly the Creator's plan for his creatures, so it is presumably the form of life most conducive to happiness for the majority of them. Nor can there ever be any change in this broad principle, unless in the case of human legislation adding such arbitrary conditions to the natural bond of mutual faith and love as shall make it intolerably irksome to either sex, and outbalance the felicity God meant to attach to it. Let marriage be as simple as possible, and as little clogged with onerous and irrelevant conditions, and the greater number of men and women will always prefer it either to celibacy or to those temporary unions which claim to be still more natural, but are in truth much less so, – seeing that all human love (as distinguished from brute passion) spontaneously desires to eternize its union with the one beloved, and the vow of mutual and perpetual fidelity alone fulfils this sacred instinct. On the other hand, if anything could have been ingeniously devised to deter one sex from the natural desire of marriage, it would be the conditions arbitrarily attached to it by man-made laws all over the world. Every man in effect says to the woman whom he invites to wed him, *not*,

"Oh come with me and be my love,"

but –

"Oh come with me and be my slave."

"I will treat you with the utmost kindness and consideration, but still *that* will be our real legal relation, which I can enforce at any time if I please." It is not very wonderful that some women decline the tempting invitation; or that many men, who know what it signifies, think it highly desirable to shut every door behind those women who might be induced to back out of such engagements into other modes of life.

Mr. Mill thinks that the fact is, that the men who oppose the opening of professions to women are not afraid lest women should be unwilling to marry, but "lest they should insist that marriage should be on equal conditions; lest all women of spirit and capacity should prefer doing almost anything else rather than marry, when marrying is giving themselves a master, and a master too of all their earthly possessions." He proceeds further to point out that, according to such policy, all that has been done towards giving women education has been a mistake. With all deference we would submit, however, that this accusation of far-sighted policy can at most apply but to a few men. The truth to us seems rather to be, that all men whose natures are either egotistic or despotic, – all men who desire to absorb their wives' whole interests to themselves, – all, in short, who are not capable of rising to a very pure and noble love, which shall combine the mutuality of friendship with the tenderness of conjugal passion, – instinctively and without any reflection at all, dislike everything in a woman which has a tendency to give her a standpoint outside of themselves, a

power of being happy and self-sufficing through her own gifts
and pursuits. The more obvious is the gift, the more
honourable and brilliant the career opened to a woman, the
more distasteful it is to a man of the character we have
described. Why is it that actresses, singers and ballet-dancers,
are the exceptionally favoured and remunerated of all female
artists, and alone make brilliant marriages? Is it not obvious
that it is because their arts are all mere appeals to men's
personal admiration, and thus gratifications of their vanity
instead of mortifications of it? Men of superior class and
fortune by dozens bestow their wealth and their coronets on
women who have violated every article in the code of
bienséances of their order, as well as the natural laws of
personal dignity. But which of them desires to be the husband
of the most modest and amiable of female painters, novelists
and sculptors? Running over our memory the brilliant list for
the last hundred years of good and gifted women, from the
days of Madame de Staël and Angelina Kauffman and Mrs.
Hemans, to those of our own day, we do not remember one
whose romances, or pictures, or poems, have proved such an
attraction as would have been the art of standing on the tips of
her toes and swinging her legs at right angles; not one who has
married a single degree above the station of her birth; and a
remarkably large number who, having married in their own or
a lower rank, have been treated with peculiar cruelty by their
husbands. Not even such absolutely feminine gifts as those of
poor L. E. L., Mrs. Norton, Mrs. Hemans and Mrs.
Jamieson, saved them from extremest misery in marriage. In
the present generation the greatest female painter of France and
sculptress of America are allowed to pursue their vocations
"in maiden meditations fancy free." We do not hear of *them*
being pursued (even with all the wealth their gifts command,
and all the charm of their characters) by such adoring swains as
follow a Patti or even a Schneider with proposals of marriage.
Thus we need to go deeper than Mr. Mill has done to get at the
root of the matter. There is a notion more profoundly planted
in the minds of the common sort of men than even that of their
rightful despotism over women. It is the notion (too readily
accepted by many women also) that a perfect marriage does not
mean a marriage wherein two persons are each the first in the
world to one another; but a marriage wherein the woman is
absorbed in the man, and the man is absorbed in - himself.

In his second chapter, Mr. Mill traces historically the condition of married women up to the present day, and discusses the existing law of England on the subject.

> "Because the various enormities of earlier times have fallen into disuse, men suppose that all is now as it should be in regard to the marriage contract, and we are continually told that civilization and Christianity have restored to the woman her just rights. Meanwhile the wife is the actual bond-servant of her husband; not less so, as far as legal obligation goes, than slaves commonly so called."

He has (till Mr. Lefevre and Mr. Gurney's Bill become law) the absolute right over her property and earnings, unless she happen to be protected by a settlement. He has a right over her person which even a slave who loathed her master for his vices and his cruelty might resist, but which a wife cannot resist. And, lastly, he has a right over her children.

> "They are by law *his* children. He alone has any legal rights over them. Not one act can she do towards them except by delegation from him. Even after he is dead she is not their legal guardian, unless he by will has made her so." (Mr. Mill might have added, that even when the husband does constitute his widow sole guardian of their children, she cannot again by testament appoint her successor.) "This is her legal state. And from this she has no means of withdrawing herself. If she leave her husband, she can take nothing with her, neither her children nor anything which is rightfully her own. If he choose, he can compel her to return by law or by physical force. It is only legal separation by a decree of a court of justice, which entitles her to live apart, . . . and this is even yet only given in cases of the extreme of cruelty or wrong."

Nor is the case one of temporary suffering only. The lot once cast, a wife's misery, if she have a bad husband, is all but irremediable. Other servants choose their masters many times, and change them when ill-treated; but "a woman to whom is denied any lot in life but that of being the body-servant of a despot," is refused (unless he add adultery to his cruelty) all release from him. this is in the strictest sense to be not a servant, but a slave.

Of course, when we think of the vast majority of kind and affectionate husbands there are in the world, of the number of households in which perfect equality prevails, and of the not inconsiderable proportion in which exists that highly undesirable state of things where the wife rules and the man is henpecked, all these strong statements of Mr. Mill seem misplaced and even preposterous. Not a few readers will feel indignant at them. But, as he goes on to say, we are not talking of what use men make of their power when they are good, but what use the law allows them to make when they are bad. "Because men in general do not inflict, nor women suffer, all the misery which could be inflicted and suffered if the full power of tyranny with which the man is legally invested were acted on," it only proves that human nature is better than the law. "Not a word can be said for despotism in the family which cannot be said for political despotism." Nobody doubts that slaves may love their masters, and that much happiness may be enjoyed under the absolute rule of a kindly-disposed tyrant. But marriage is meant not for good men only, but for bad; nor does the law take the slightest precaution to ascertain the character of the person to whom it delegates a power no longer to be found elsewhere in the civilized world.

But in the midst of these arguments, we are always pulled up by the question, put with the conviction of its unanswerable force, "How is the family to exist without a head? When the will of husband and wife differ, how is the case to be decided if there be not an acknowledged master?" May we for a moment quit the guidance of Mr. Mill, and treat this question from our own point of view?

Many matrimonial principles are very mysterious to the celibate mind, but none of them more puzzling than this: What is the force of this commonplace about the necessity of a ruler in a house where two people happen to live as man and wife? We are poor outsiders, but we have always fondly believed that "wedded love" was a sort of glorified friendship. We read in our Prayer Books with awe, if not with envy, of "Holy" Matrimony, and of all the pretty things which M. and N. promise to do and be to one another. Judging from the mere old-bachelor or old-maid point of view, we should at least have taken it for granted that the aforesaid M. and N. would find it at least as easy to "live in unity and godly love" as Mr. A. and his sister Miss B., or the two sisters C., or the two friends D.

and E., or the two heads of that flourishing firm, Messrs F. and
G. None of these good people, male or female, are in the habit
of calling on Jupiter to get their wheels out of the mud when
they happen to stick in it. The law settles none of their terms of
agreement; but somehow they manage to rub on, and their
houses do not tumble down in the apocalyptic manner
threatened to married couples in consequence of being divided
against themselves. Nothing is more common in such cases
than for the partnership to be complicated by the joint charge
of children. But even then, we do not hear of those fearful wars
and disasters always prophesied in similar cases for married
people unless the husband be invested with absolute authority.
Can the truth - we tremble to write it, but we must expose the
depth of our difficulty - can it be that, after all, marriage is not
so very - well, not such entirely and perfectly delightful a yoke
as we have been always informed? A most amiable dog of our
acquaintance, who never growls at anybody when at large, is
apt to grow savage and bite viciously all round when any one
holds him by the tail. We do not mean anything, of course, by
alluding to this fact of natural history; but still, if marriage
does make such very exceptionally dear friends, how is it that
married couples need, more than any other friends and
partners, to be kept from fighting, by always supplementing
Ponto's superior strength by the "legal intervention" of the
gamekeeper's whip over Fan's shoulders?

Mr. Mill suggests various plans of "limited liability partnership" for husbands and wives, the most obvious of course being
that the man should regulate the out-door concerns of the firm,
and the woman those of the house. Such arrangements might
easily be agreed on before marriage, and be only rescinded with
the consent of both parties afterwards. But now that a woman
has no independent "sphere," not even her larder or linen-
closet, into which her spouse may not poke his nose, what can
be expected of her but to retaliate by meddling in her husband's
departments? We are all sick of being told on every occasion
that "we must draw a line somewhere." But if people would
only draw a line leaving wives some small field for their
independent wills, we should see fewer specimens of that
distressing animal, the Grey Mare. Schiller warns wisely -

Vor dem Sclaven wenn er die kette bricht
Vor dem freien Menschen, erzittert nicht!

The rightful (and ample) share of work for a wife, as Mr. Mill earnestly sets forth, is the care of the children and the household. She ought not, save in most exceptional cases, to have further labour. But though this task is commonly enough left to her, she is in discharging it at every moment liable to authoritative interference. If the husband have a crotchet about baby's pinafores, the wife has no right to say, "Mind your own affairs!" A wiseacre we have heard of (a wealthy gentleman), ordained that his children till two years old should wear no clothes whatever, and should sleep at night, like so many chrysalises, in boxes filled with bran. The poor wife remonstrated in vain, as her infants pined and shivered out of the bran into their graves. The sublime law of England left the question of their little shirts to be decided beyond appeal by the sage to whom they exclusively belonged.

Our diminishing space warns us to pass more rapidly over the latest chapters of Mr. Mill's book. They are devoted to arguments touching the admission of women to the franchise, and to every profession in which their abilities may enable them to obtain entrance, and also to the consideration of the oft-repeated assertions of the intellectual inferiority and moral superiority of women. As to the latter point, Mr. Mill is somewhat indignant at the men who at the same time tell women that they are much better than themselves; and then, as if it were a proper *sequitur*, that they ought to be in subjection to them. "It is the only case," says Mr. Mill, "in which it is supposed fitting that the better should obey the worse." He does not think that women are morally superior to men, and considers the attribution to them of such goodness a compliment of a very doubtful character. For our own parts, we are inclined to think that in this matter Mr. Lecky's admirable sketch of women's character, at the close of his splendid History of European Morals, is very near the truth. Certainly in the peculiarly Christian virtues of self-sacrifice, purity, patience, mercy and piety, the majority of women are superior to the majority of men. Even where the servile vices engendered by their condition have eaten into their souls, when the woman whose feeble voice is constantly drowned by masculine bluster takes to deception instead of honest, above-board argument, and when the woman who cannot give her child the things she knows it needs, has recourse to mean arts of wheedling or concealment to obtain them, – even then the sin is rather one of circumstance than of nature. The spontaneous cruelty of the school-boy, the wholly selfish passion and sensuality of the man, are things most rare in a girl or woman. Even in courage of the moral sort, in trying with all her little power to "deliver him that is oppressed from the hand of the adversary," a woman is commonly much more willing to act the Quixote, and put herself out of her way and into trouble, than the supposed more chivalrous sex. Such principles of religion and morality as she has found, she generally makes an effort to act up to, in some sort of way; and does not (as a great divine once complained to us of his masculine scholars) let them all run off like water from a duck's back.

But however all this may be, the question of women's comparative moral excellence, and also, we think, their intellectual capacity, has nothing to do with the argument in question. If they are better than men, then it is monstrous that the better should obey the worse. If they are worse than men – more cruel, more selfish, more drunken – even then, so long as they are admitted to be morally responsible beings and are subject to the same criminal laws, there is no ethical reason why every woman should have a despotic master. The laws punish crime sufficiently without selling all the individuals of the criminal classes into perpetual slavery.

Again, for the intellectual equality of women with men, we are sorry not to be able to follow Mr. Mill without misgivings. Admitting that no woman has ever created a masterpiece of literature or art, he argues that the conditions in which women have hitherto lived have made such success all but impossible to them. We fear that, though of course the negative cannot be proved, the presumption is terribly strong in its favour. One single really *great* work of ancient or modern times achieved by a woman, in poetry, in history, in sculpture, in painting or in music, only *one* in which creative power had beyond all doubt or question built an enduring trophy, and we should cease to hesitate. But till that work is done, women cannot "speak with their enemies in the gate" with any confidence. It is all a matter of conjecture. Yet if the utmost scepticism on this point by justified, it is still absolutely irrelevant to the argument concerning the political and domestic independence of women. It is not as sculptors, painters and musicians that men are permitted or wanted to exercise civil rights. The Anglo-Saxon and Roman nations

have been supposed always to be inferior in artistic genius to
the Celts and the Greeks, but they have not on that account
been ruled by Celt or Greek. Suppose that, beside our English
lack of first-rate sculptors or musicians or painters a century
or two ago, it had happened that both Shakespeare and
Milton had died in infancy. Then an Italian statesman of the
period might have written of us that we were a race which
had never produced a masterpiece of Art. Would he have
proceeded further, and argued on that slender foundation
that Italians had a right to rule over England? Of course, if it
could be equally proved, or even a presumption shewn, that
women had not those powers which civil order demands
should be possessed by all who have a share in it; if they had
no moral sense, or no comprehension of matters of public or
private economy, then, indeed, there would be reason in
bringing up for discussion their intellectual status whenever
their claims are being examined. But nobody pretends that
there exist such disabilities in the sex, or even that the
average female capacity is beneath that of the lowest stratum
of male voters to whom the franchise has now been accorded.
Nay, the curious fact is, that the deficiency of women in art
and literature is curiously compensated for in the field of
politics among the very few who have had a chance of
shewing their power. The proportion of great female
sovereigns and regents in the ancient and modern world,
among the score or so of women who have ever reigned, is
nothing less than a marvellous phenomenon. From the half-
fabulous Semiramis, the brave Artemisia, and the noble
Zenobia, down to Maria Theresa and Isabella and Elizabeth,
it seems almost the rule that Queens should be great and wise
sovereigns, and the exception when they are merely, like
Queen Anne, on the average of male royalty. Mr. Mill
indignantly scouts the *dictum* concerning these sagacious
rulers by which masculine vanity has generally soothed itself,
namely, that when a man is on the throne women rule, and
vice versa. In the first place, women do not generally rule
under a king; and, in the second place, it is not the
relinquishment, but the practice and highest achievement, of
good government to select and maintain able and upright
ministers. In nothing is kingcraft so thoroughly manifested.
Mr. Mill adds:

"If a Hindoo principality is strongly, vigilantly and economically governed, if order is preserved without oppression, if cultivation is extending and the people prosperous, in three cases out of four that principality is under a woman's rule. This fact, to me an entirely unexpected one, I have collected from a long official knowledge of Hindoo governments."[4]

We cannot leave this part of the subject without expressing the most emphatic agreement with Mr. Mill's passing observations on one of the hitherto unnoticed causes which, perhaps more than all others, has kept women's capacities from due expansion. He says, that one reason "why women remain behind men even in the pursuits which are common to them and men, is, that very few women have time for them. This may seem a paradox, but it is an undoubted fact. The time and thoughts of almost every woman have to satisfy great previous demands on them before she can turn her attention to any chosen pursuit. The superintendence of a household, even when not laborious, is extremely onerous to the thoughts," and causes constant interruptions of study; and just as a woman rises in wealth and social importance above household cares, so she enters a sphere of labours connected with party-giving and party-going, visiting and note-writing, even more distracting. Many a man who despises women's intellect, would go mad if subjected for a week to the swarm of small cares for ever buzzing about his wife's ears. How many masculine works, we marvel, would be suppressed, if all the quite Temple chambers, all the silent libraries and unapproachable studies, were shut up and the authors had to scribble in a drawing-room, with children, nurses, notes and visitors pouring in and out all the day long? Only a woman knows how impossible it is to train even the most submissive of servants to refrain from breaking in on the hours of abstrusest study, to ask how the lace is to be sewn on an evening dress, and whether the cook is to order soles, since the mackarel are not fresh. It is an evidence of the real intelligent sympathy Mr. Mill has given to female affairs that he has "spotted" this evil under the sun, and observed, "If it were possible that all this number of little practical interests (which are made great to them) should leave women

4 P. 100.

much energy or leisure to devote to art or speculation, they must have a greater original active faculty than the vast majority of men. A woman is expected to have her time at the disposal of everybody. Hardly can she give her own business precedence over other people's amusement. Everything a woman does is done at odd times." This is the reason why a resident College for young women, such as that projected by Miss Davies and founded by the munificence of Madame Bodichon and the devotion of Mrs. Manning (the first Lady-Warden), is indispensable, if there is every to be real study for ladies. Not one daughter or sister in five thousand can command three hours – two hours – one hour – of unbroken study under her father's roof.

But, as we have said from the first, the moral or intellectual capacity or defects of women are matters irrelevant to the questions at issue. It is as sensible to classify sex politically as it would be to classify politically men under the height for military service. The inferiority of women to men, to make the most of it, is the most indefinite and variable of all forms of inferiority. Nobody is agreed on what it is, save in the general inferiority of physical height, strength and size of brain. But many women are taller and stronger than thousands of men, and Mr. Mill tells us that the largest brain yet weighed belonged to a woman. The moral inferiority of women is more often denied than asserted, and the average intellectual inferiority under equal conditions seems less certain after each of the Cambridge Local Examinations. Yet this (real or supposed) indefinite and indescribable inferiority is hard to constitute, what no other kind or sort of inferiority now constitutes in any civilized state, namely, a permanent bar to political rights and domestic equality, and to open competition in every department of honourable employment. There is mockery in calling such inference from such a fact an argument. Let us imagine some class of male individuals, say coal-heavers or iron-puddlers, proved to have never produced a first-rate work of art among them – of being more often drunk than other men, and of general ignorance of classics and mathematics. What would be said of the Member who should rise in Parliament and gravely propose to exclude them from the benefit of the Reform Bill on the above grounds? And what should we think further, if another Senator maintained that such inferior beings ought each of them to be "subject" for life to some individual belonging to the classes who create works of art, and do not often drink and swear, and obtain degrees at the University? Not till "inferiority" is made equivalent to "serfdom" somewhere else than in the case of woman, is there any meaning in harping upon it whenever the subjection of women is under discussion.

He who thinks that Mr. Mill's proposals would lead, if adopted, to the ruin of conjugal happiness, ought not to close his book without at least noting his observations as to what, in accordance therewith, he thinks marriage ought to be. We are, as we confessed long ago, poor outsiders, somewhat staggered between ideal matrimonial felicity as found in novels (only occasionally in them in these days), and certain revelations which come to us through the Divorce Court and other channels as to what may be the domestic happiness really enjoyed in England under the present order of things. A wise and loving woman, wife of a very worthy man, but a thorough disciple of the despotic school, bestowed on us two apophthegms as a general guide to the life we were then about to enter: "Remember this, my dear: Woman proposes, but Man opposes." "Married women appear happy; single ones are so."

In sober seriousness, we can testify that among the multifarious acquaintances of a life-time, the happiest and most united marriages we have known have been those where, according to the religious opinions of the parties, no "obedience" was vowed or expected. And the most miserable, were those wherein the husband considered it a portion of his duty as well as his pleasure to keep his household in subjection.

Let us end this discussion, which, however we may try to lighten it by jests, has ever a painful jar in it, by rising to the noble "note" Mr. Mill has struck in conclusion:

"What marriage may be in the case of two persons between whom there exists that best kind of equality, similarity of powers and capacities with reciprocal superiority in them, so that each can enjoy the luxury of looking up to the other, I will not attempt to describe. To those who can conceive it, there is no need. To those who cannot, it would appear the dream of an enthusiast. But I maintain with the profoundest conviction, that this, and this only, is the ideal of marriage, and that all opinions, customs and institutions which favour any other notion of it, by whatever pretences they may be coloured, are relics of primitive barbarism. The moral reformation of mankind will only really commence when the most fundamental of the social relations is placed under the rule of equal justice, and when human beings learn to cultivate their strongest sympathy with an equal in rights and in cultivation."

MILL ON THE CONDITION OF WOMEN

The Subjection of Women. By John Stuart Mill. Second Edition. London: Longmans. 1869.

Among the features which characterize the present age, none is more remarkable than the widespread tendency to look with suspicion on the customs and opinions of former generations, and to call in question principles and institutions which were once fondly imagined to be settled on a firm and abiding basis. The same spirit is rife amongst us which was long ago noted by the poet:-

> "Qui fit, Mæcenas, ut nemo, quam sibi sortem
> Seu ratio dederit seu fors objecerit, illa
> Contentus vivat, laudet diversa sequentes?"

but while in the days of Horace it was their individual condition, it is now their political and social state which men regard with discontent. This disease – for such it may fairly be called – may, and no doubt does, by its presence, effect for us a riddance of other long-standing maladies; but at the same time it ought to be narrowly watched and kept in check, as being itself fraught with danger to mankind. "Meddle not," says the wise man, "with them that are given to change"; and while we readily admit that an unreasonable adherence to an old institution, and a mistaken adoption of a new one, are alike evils, we have no hesitation in saying, that of the two the former is in general the less pernicious; involving, as it for the most part does, a merely negative, instead of a positive, injury.

We therefore wholly dissent from Mr. Mill when, in the Essay before us, he asserts that, in reference to the condition of women, the burthen of proof lies on those who uphold the existing state of things, as against those who, like himself, would impugn it. Of course, as Mr. Mill admits, the state of public opinion upon the subject does, in point of fact, force him to support the views which he advances by positive arguments; but we hold that it does so rightly, and that the advocate of a theory which, as we think, so far from being a natural development, is a total subversion of the relations hitherto established between the sexes of the human race, is bound to adduce conclusive proofs of its truth before he can claim or expect its adoption.

At the outset of the Essay the proposition which is sought to be established is thus stated:–

> "That the principle which regulates the existing social relations between the two sexes – the legal subordination of one sex to the other – is wrong in itself, and now one of the chief hindrances to human improvement; and that it ought to be replaced by a principle of perfect equality, admitting no power or privilege on the one side, nor disability on the other."

Mr. Mill looks upon what he is pleased to call the subjection of women as the one remaining vestige in civilized countries of the sovereignty of physical force, and as a solitary remnant of the institution of slavery – an institution which is the distinctive creature of that sovereignty. While the slavery of the male sex has been abandoned by the nations of civilized Europe, divers reasons have conspired to cause the retention of that of the female sex. But it is a state of things wholly at variance with the principles of personal freedom and individual action which now prevail.

> "At present, in the more improved countries, the disabilities of women are the only case, save one, in which laws and institutions take persons at their birth, and ordain that they shall never in all their lives be allowed to compete for certain things. The one exception is that of royalty. . . . The social subordination of women thus stands out an isolated fact in modern social institutions: a solitary breach of what has become their fundamental law: a single relic of an old world of thought and practice, exploded in everything else, but retained in the one thing of most universal interest. It is as if a gigantic dolmen, or a vast temple of Jupiter Olympius, occupied the site of St. Paul's, and received daily worship, while the surrounding Christian churches were only resorted to on fasts and festivals. This entire discrepancy between one social fact and all those which accompany it, and the radical opposition between its nature and the progressive movement

which is the boast of the modern world, and which has successively swept away everything else of an analogous character, surely affords to a conscientious observer of human tendencies serious matter for reflection."

Surely it does; and we wonder that it has not suggested to Mr. Mill's mind the obvious reflection, that possibly, after all, the 'entire discrepancy' and 'radical opposition' may be found to exist more in imagination than in reality.

But to proceed. After pointing out that the condition of women through all the progressive period of human history has been approaching nearer to equality with men, Mr. Mill proceeds to combat the argument, that the *nature* of the two sexes adapts them to their present functions and position, and render these appropriate to them.

"Standing," he says, "on the ground of common sense and the constitution of the human mind, I deny that any one knows or can know the nature of the two sexes, as long as they have only been seen in their present relation to one another. If men had ever been found in society without women, or women without men, or if there had been a society of men and women in which the women were not under the control of the men, something might have been positively known about the mental and moral differences which may be inherent in the nature of each. What is now called the nature of women is an eminently artificial thing."

Hence Mr. Mill concludes that no argument can fairly be based upon the existence of alleged natural differences·between the sexes against their social and legal equality.

Having thus cleared the ground by dismissing the teaching and experience of past ages as of no value in the discussion of the question, Mr. Mill proceeds to consider more in detail the condition of women as it is, and to state what, in his opinion, it ought to be, in reference to the marriage state, and to the admissibility of both sexes alike to all functions and occupations. With respect to the former subject he says:-

"We are continually told that civilization and Christianity have restored to the woman her just rights. Meanwhile, the wife is the actual bond-servant of her husband: no less so, as far as legal obligation goes, than slaves commonly so-called. She vows a life-long obedience to him at the altar, and is held to it all through her life by law. Casuists may say that the obligation of obedience stops short of participation in crime, but it certainly extends to everything else. She can do no act whatever but by his permission, at least tacit. She can acquire no property but for him; the instant it becomes hers, even by inheritance, it becomes *ipso facto* his."

The whole of this statement is highly coloured, and the last clause of it is positively incorrect. Real estate, the only property which, in the strict sense of the term, comes to the wife *by inheritance*, does not become the property of the husband by devolving upon her. We are not, however, called upon to maintain that the relations between husbands and wives, or generally between men and women, are, in this country and at the present time, absolutely perfect. Even while we write, a Bill is in progress through Parliament, and has been entertained with marked favour by the Lower House, which, if passed into law, would materially affect the rights of married women over property acquired by them. But nothing less than a fundamental alteration of the whole relation between husband and wife will, in Mr. Mill's eyes, satisfy the requirements of justice and expediency. There must be real, unequivocal, unqualified equality – as much as between two partners in a business firm – and the only preponderance to be allowed to either party, except so far as it may be regulated by law or by ante-nuptial contract, must depend upon the comparative qualifications of the two. The influence of greater age is generally on the side of the husband, but that which is derived from bringing the means of support to the family will, under the new régime, be as likely to be found on the side of the wife as on that of the husband. For Mr. Mill desires the free and unrestricted admission of women to all the functions and occupations hitherto retained as the monopoly of the stronger sex. "On this point," he says,

" . . . I should anticipate no difficulty in convincing any one who has gone with me on the subject of the equality of women in the family. I believe that their disabilities elsewhere are only clung to in order to maintain their subordination in domestic life, because the generality of the male sex cannot yet tolerate the idea of living with an equal."

Mr. Mill would remove all legal disabilities which at present stand in the way of a woman entering any path of life whatever, trusting to individual choice or sense of fitness, and the natural laws of success and failure to regulate the due allotment of members of both sexes to the discharge of the several employments and duties of society. It cannot be doubted, he urges, that there are some women capable of discharging functions which are at present in the exclusive grasp of the male sex; and if the majority of them are not so, we shall find that majority instinctively, and without the necessity of legal intervention, avoiding the function for which it is unsuited.

In the last chapter of his Essay, Mr. Mill sums up the benefits which are, in his opinion, to be expected from the social revolution which he advocates. First and foremost he places "the advantage of having the most universal and pervading of all human relations regulated by justice instead of injustice."

> Marriage is the only actual bondage known to our law. . . . So long as the right of the strong to power over the weak rules in the very heart of society, the attempt to make the equal right of the weak the principle of its outward actions will always be an uphill struggle; for the law of justice, which is also that of Christianity, will never get possession of men's inmost sentiments; they will be working against it even when bending to it."

In the next place, Mr. Mill expects by his scheme to double the mass of mental faculties available for the higher service of humanity.

> "Where there is now one person qualified to benefit mankind and promote the general improvement as a public teacher or an administrator of some branch of public or social affairs, there would then be a chance of two. . . . This great accession to the intellectual power of the species, and to the amount of intellect available for the good management of its affairs would be obtained partly through the better and more complete intellectual education of women, which would then improve *pari passu* with that of men."

Again, the opinion of women, which has always possessed a great influence, would then possess a more beneficial influence upon the general mass of human belief and sentiment. And lastly, the most direct benefit of all would be "the unspeakable gain in private happiness to the liberated half of the species; the difference to them between a life of subjection to the will of others, and a life of rational freedom."

Now we do not deny that, like everything that bears the "*liberté, egalité, et fraternité*" stamp, there is something at first sight somewhat fascinating in the picture which Mr. Mill has unfolded to our view. But the subject is far too momentous for determination upon first impressions. Let us accept Mr. Mill's invitation, and enter into the discussion "as a real discussion, descending to foundations, and not resting satisfied with vague and general assertions."

There can be no doubt, that in the history of the human race the progress of civilisation has been attended by a gradual triumph of intellectual over physical strength, and a gradual amelioration in the condition of the female sex. Mr. Mill apparently regards the alteration which he advocates in the relations between the sexes as the natural and logical issue of these two processes of development. We think, however, that he has formed a mistaken estimate of the possible limits of the one, and of the tendencies and direction of the other.

When Mr. Mill, in dealing with the problem before him, ignores altogether the physical side of human nature, and confines the natural differences between the two sexes to their mental and moral characteristics, treating men and women as if they were disembodied spirits, we are constrained to ask whether the element of physical strength can be thus reduced to a nullity, and become a matter of absolute indifference. Surely there can be but one answer to the question. Intellectual power may assert an undisputed superiority over physical force, but can never effect its annihilation. A man in possession of intellectual faculties of the highest order, if health and strength of body fail, will be seriously impeded in employing those faculties for the advantage of himself and other, and may even be absolutely debarred from doing so. And, given two individuals of equal mental ability, but endowed with different degrees of bodily power, we can predict with certainty which of them will obtain the superiority. We cannot, therefore, in considering the natural differences between the sexes, treat the word *natural* as synonymous with *metaphysical*, and disregard, as beside the question, the inferiority of women to men in bodily strength and power of endurance, and the physical distinctions of sex, with all that these involve. On the supposition, then, that the mental and moral capabilities of men and women are equal – a supposition with respect to which Mr. Mill affirms that neither he nor anyone else can possible know whether it is correct or not, but of which we are willing, for the sake of argument, to concede the truth – we are, when we take into account the material side of the question, forced to the conclusion, that the female sex has been placed by nature in a position of inferiority as compared with the male. Now, where there are two things, between certain component parts of which there exists an inequality, any attempt to create equality between the remaining portions must necessarily tend to produce disparity between the wholes. This, however, is precisely what Mr. Mill proposes to do. The mental and moral characteristics of the two sexes are, according to our assumption, equal, but their physical capabilities are unequal, and Mr. Mill proposes to equalize in every respect their legal and social condition. What will be the effect of this, but to leave the physical disparity unbalanced by any counteracting elements, and to create a state of things in which the sum total of the terms involved will be unfavourable to the female sex? The fact is, that the abolition of all legal and social distinctions between men and women cannot result in placing the latter upon an equality with the former, unless there is some difference between the metaphysical power of men and women which will compensate for the inferior physical strength of the female sex. That there is no ground for supposing the existence of such a difference as this, Mr. Mill has taken great pains to prove, being well aware that, if its reality could be demonstrated, it would go far to shake the plausibility of his proposition for equalizing the legal and social condition of men and women. Hence, if Mr. Mill really desires the equality of the two sexes, he appears to us to be confronted with the following dilemma. Upon the supposition of an equality in the metaphysical powers of men and women, some distinctions in their artificial condition, which may counterbalance the discrepancy between their physical capabilities, are essential to the preservation of equality between them; but if such distinctions are rendered unnecessary, owing to the physical discrepancy being counteracted by some existing difference between the sexes in mental or moral power, this very difference is a strong argument in favour of maintaining artificial distinctions between them.

But, says Mr. Mill, I am merely carrying out to its inevitable conclusion another process of development which has ever advanced with the civilization and improvement of mankind. "Through all the progressive period of human history, the condition of women has been approaching nearer to equality with men." Yes, to *equality*, but not to *identity*. The two are not convertible terms. You cannot have identity without equality, but there may well be the latter apart from the former. We desire *equality* between the sexes, and it is precisely because we do so that we oppose the scheme which Mr. Mill sets forth for our adoption. Create an absolute identity, legally, socially, and politically, between men and women, and their physical differences will be an insuperable bar to their equality. Supplement the physical differences by suitable artificial distinctions, and an equipoise of the balance may be obtained. We do not say that, in the present state of society among civilized nations, this result has been absolutely and accurately attained; to allege this, would be to ascribe to one branch of human institutions a perfection at which we do not believe that any of them can ever, in the present order of things, arrive; but we do affirm that a nearer approach to that equality may be expected from the maintenance, as respects the female sex, of certain legal and social disabilities on the one hand, and on the other of the privileges which chivalry and courtesy have, in consequence of those disabilities, accorded to women; rather than from a ruthless demolition of the former, which would at the same time involve an abrogation of the latter, and would launch women in a career of universal competition with men, in which, however complete might be their intellectual equality, their physical inferiority, no longer relieved by the customs and sentiments which now exist as a counterpoise to it, would make itself felt at every step, and would tend to reduce them to a state of irretrievable subjection and degradation.

But while such would be the result, as regards women themselves, of their identification with the stronger sex, its effect on society at large would be no less disastrous.

Mr. Mill anticipates from his scheme "a doubling of the mass of mental faculties available for the higher service of humanity." Granted that some such advantage would be secured; yet we very much question whether, on Mr. Mill's own showing, the gain would not be attended by a loss for which it would afford no adequate compensation. For what does he tell us of the intellectual benefit which women in their present condition confer on the human race?

> "Looking at women as they are known in experience, it may be said of them, with more truth than belongs to most other generalizations on the subject, that the general bent of their talents is towards the practical. . . .
> "This gravitation of women's minds to the present, to the real, to actual fact, while in its exclusiveness it is a source of errors, is also a most useful counteractive of the contrary error. . . . *Hardly anything can be of greater value* to a man of theory and speculation, who employs himself, not in collecting materials of knowledge by observation, but in working them up by processes of thought into comprehensive truths of science and laws of conduct, than to carry on his speculations in the companionship and under the criticism a really superior woman. *There is nothing comparable to it* for keeping his thoughts within the limits of real things and the actual facts of nature. A woman seldom runs wild after an abstraction. . . . Women's thoughts are thus as useful in giving reality to those of thinking men, as men's thoughts in giving width and largeness to those of women. In depth, as distinguished from breadth, I greatly doubt if, even now, women compared with men are at any disadvantage."

Now, to what do we owe these peculiar characteristics of the female mind, which are of such incomparable utility in the evolution of intellectual processes? Mr. Mill does not speak positively on this point; but he evidently leans to the opinion, that they are due, not so much to natural differences, as to the artificial distinctions between the condition of the sexes.

> "No one,' he says, "can safely pronounce that if women's nature were left to choose its direction as freely as men's, and if no artificial bent were attempted to be given to it except that required by the conditions of human society and given to both sexes alike, there would be any material difference, or perhaps any difference at all, in the character and capacities which would unfold themselves."

If no one can pronounce decidedly upon this point, how can Mr. Mill think it safe to venture on an experiment which may result in depriving mankind of advantages than which "*hardly anything can be of greater value"* – to which *"there is nothing comparable"*?

In point of fact, as Mr. Mill partially recognizes when he admits that the amount of mental power resident in the female sex is even now not totally lost, woman in her present condition is, in a more or less perfect degree, fulfilling her part in the destiny of the race, as a "help meet" for man. Her function is not inferior to his, but is its indispensable and worthy complement; and it is, we think, scarcely more reasonable to imagine that the mental power of the human race would be increased by converting this complement into that of which it was intended to supply the deficiencies, than to conceive that an electric battery could be doubled in force by removing the copper and substituting an equivalent amount of zinc, or the virtue of the atmosphere increased by changing all the hydrogen into oxygen.

And while we should anticipate from the adoption of Mr. Mill's views an irreparable intellectual loss to the human race, on the practical side the damage would, as it seems to us, be no less grievous. The relative amount of the duties which are now looked upon as peculiar to either sex would of course, under the new state of things, remain the same, and would equally as before demand attention. But the admission of the female sex to the functions and occupations of men, on becoming to any extent a practical reality, would necessarily entail the diversion of a portion of that sex from the pursuits which have hitherto been considered as its peculiar province; and the deficiency thereby created, as well as the fact that there would otherwise be a surplus amount of agency for the performance of what we will call the masculine duties, would require that a corresponding number of men should devote themselves to feminine duties. The result would, in our opinion, be a great deterioration in the manner in which both sets of duties would be performed. At present the two sets are kept distinct, and one part of the human race is from early childhood destined and education for a public, and the other for a private and domestic life. But what shall the education of our children be under Mr. Mill's system? Shall boys and girls alike be brought up with a view to the contingency of their filling either position? Then their education and training must needs be either lamentably colourless or flagrantly inconsistent; and when it is completed, they will prove, it may be, in a condition to fill either station of life tolerably, but assuredly neither well. Or shall this boy and that girl be brought up for public life, while another boy and another girl are educated for domestic duties? But how, in that case, shall the particular fitness of the children for the life to which they are thus arbitrarily destined be, in their tender years, ascertained; and if mistake in that respect could be avoided, how shall we so regulate the course of the affections, that a domestic man shall be wedded to a woman whose vocation is of the public and active character, and a man destined for public life select a wife who is capable of discharging the duties of home?

These considerations remind us that we have as yet made no comment upon the views put forth by Mr. Mill on that most important of all social institutions – marriage.

"Marriage," he tells us, "is not an institution designed for the select few." He admits that in the present state of things, "the natural motives which lead to a voluntary adjustment of the united life of two persons, in a manner acceptable to both, do, on the whole, except in unfavourable cases, prevail." He readily admits "that numbers of married people, even under the present law (in the higher classes of England probably a great majority), live in the spirit of a just law of equality." And yet because, forsooth, the power of the husband over the wife is sometimes abused, Mr. Mill would upset the whole of the relations between married persons, and introduce the element of anarchy into every family. Marriage is to become a mere partnership on equal terms; and, for the sake of avoiding disputes, Mr. Mill suggests that the peculiar departments in which husband and wife should reign supreme might be settled before the marriage. Of course, the partnership must be carried on under the joint name of the two partners; for that the family should be known by the surname of the husband alone, would be a lingering badge of a condition of slavery wholly incompatible with the spirit of freedom which would then pervade society. We wonder that Mr. Mill has not carried his argument further, and denied the propriety of allowing parents to have authority over their children on the ground of its not unfrequent abuse. But this he distinctly disclaims; this is a point to which even the school of modern thought has not yet arrived. Meanwhile, equality in marriage is defended on account of its abstract justice. The change proposed by Mr. Mill would secure the advantage of having "the most universal and pervading of all human relations regulated by justice instead of injustice." Now, it is easy to talk of justice in the abstract, but not always so easy to ascertain its limits in particular cases. Upon the question before us, however, Mr. Mill has pointed out where he would have us ascertain the requirements of justice. It is from a source to which we may resort with implicit confidence. He speaks of "the law of justice" as "also the law of Christianity."

In appealing to the teaching of Christianity, Mr. Mill is aware that he must meet some preconceived notions with respect to the drift of that teaching, which are the very reverse of favourable to the views which he advocates. Referring to the duty, as it is commonly considered, of submission on the part of the wife to the husband, Mr. Mill says:-

"The Church, it is very true, enjoins it in her formularies, but it would be difficult to derive any such injunction from Christianity. We are told that St. Paul said, 'Wives, obey your husbands;' but he also said, 'Slaves, obey your masters.' It was not St. Paul's business, nor was it consistent with his object, the propagation of Christianity, to incite any one to rebellion against existing laws. The apostle's acceptance of all social institutions as he found them, is no more to be construed as a disapproval of attempts to improve them at the proper time, than his declaration, 'The powers that be are ordained of God,' gives his sanction to military despotism, and to that alone, as the Christian form of political government, or commands passive obedience to it. To pretend that Christianity was intended to stereotype existing forms of government and society, and protect them against change, is to reduce it to the level of Islamism or of Brahminism."

Having thus, as he thinks, refuted the notion, that the positive teaching of Christianity contains anything opposed to the equality which he would establish between husband and wife, Mr. Mill appeals, in support of that equality, to the general principle of the equality of human beings, which, according to him, "is the theory of Christianity, but which Christianity will never practically teach while it sanctions institutions grounded on an arbitrary preference of one human being over another." We fear that if the predominance of the husband over the wife in the married state is such an arbitrary preference as Mr. Mill alludes to, he must make up his mind to Christianity never teaching the equality of human beings. Mr. Mill, when he wrote this part of his Essay, can hardly have had before him the writings of the Apostle to whose teaching he refers, or he would not, we think, have ventured to dismiss the subject without offering some explanation of that remarkable passage in the Epistle to the Ephesians, which, while it points to a mystery which far transcends the limits of our present finite knowledge, grounds upon that mystery very plain and intelligible teaching on the subject of the relations between husband and wife.

> "Wives, submit yourselves unto your husbands as unto the Lord. For the husband is the head of the wife, even as Christ is the head of the Church; and he is the saviour of the body. Therefore, *as* the Church is subject unto Christ, *so* let the wives be to their own husbands in everything."

If Mr. Mill's views are really,a she would make them out to be, in accordance with the teaching of Christianity, then our religion teaches us either that the relations between the Church and her Divine Lord and Master are to change as the ages roll on, and are, with the progress of human development, to approach more and more nearly to terms of equality - a proposition to be rejected as blasphemous by every Christian - or that, whereas in the earlier period of man's history marriage has been, to use the words of Mr. Birks, "a figure of the highest mystery of the Gospel, and a type and earnest of the coming glory of the Church, the bridge of Christ, in the day of the resurrection,"[1] this is not its ultimate or perfect form, and it can never rise to its true dignity until it has sunk to something merely earthly and secular!

Inasmuch as we entirely dissent from these views on the institution of marriage - inasmuch as we are unwilling to come to the conclusion, that, except for the purpose of perpetuating the race, all distinction of sex in human beings is meaningless, and ought to be disregarded, and that in all the affairs of life men and women should be mixed together without distinction or discrimination - to question, in short, the wisdom of the

---

[1] "Church and State," p. 283. We commend to our readers some excellent remarks in this recent work of Mr. Birks (pp. 282-285), on the sacred character of the ordnance of marriage, and the danger of degrading it into a mere secular institution.

Almighty in having created difference of sex at all, when He might have ordained a means of propagating mankind independently of such a useless institution – inasmuch, lastly, as we look upon an identification of the two sexes as no less practically dangerous than it is theoretically false, we feel constrained to give an emphatic and uncompromising negative to the proposition which Mr. Mill has in his Essay submitted for our acceptance.

MR MILL ON THE SUBJECTION OF WOMEN
[Anne Mozley]

Blackwood's Magazine Vol. 106, Sept. 1869.

After a careful perusal of Mr Mill's essay *On the Subjection of Women*, we find some few paints to stand out from the rest in such distinct prominence that it may be well to state them at starting, as the readiest way of conveying a general impression. The foremost of these is the scarcely-veiled assertion of himself as the sole advocate among men with fairness and perception enough to plead woman's cause, to discern what she is capable of, and to indicate her real work in the world. Strong in the conviction that no man can at once honestly and rationally differ from himself, we see Mr Mill fearlessly meeting the whole human race single-handed. He exactly corresponds to the lunatic who proved logically that all the rest of the world was insane. It is nothing to him that mankind from the beginning has seen the matter in another light. Custom, he calmly tells us, however universal, affords no presumption, and ought not to create any prejudice, in favour of woman's subjection to man. Neither men nor women have hitherto had an idea of woman's true vocation. Nor are the arguments by which he seeks to prove his points less bold than the attitude assumed of seer and discoverer. He pooh-poohs all opposition at starting, and in one sweeping statement drives all his countrymen out of the field of controversy. There is less human nature, he tells us, in England than anywhere else; consequently we have had less opportunity than other men of studying its manifestations, and have no right even to a view. And if Englishmen know nothing of human nature generally, because in England rule has substituted itself for nature, still less do they know anything of woman's nature, which is, in fact, a sealed book, not only to him but to herself. All that Mr Mill allows is, that certain tendencies and aptitudes are characteristics of women, as woman has hitherto been. "I do not say," he cautiously adds, "as they will continue to be, for I consider it presumptuous in any one to decide what women are and are not, can and can not be, by natural constitution."

It is among the notable points that Mr Mill is especially dissatisfied with his countrywomen in what they can and do do at present; from which we may infer that they have disappointed him by coldness to the efforts he has made for their emancipation. He is evidently ashamed of them for consenting to marry while the laws are in their present infamous league with man's brutal despotism. Their efforts to please their masters disgust him as sycophancy, while their dull acquiescence in a bondage under which they ought to writhe is the worst sign of all. In fact, we gather that Mr Mill finds his countrywomen the great hindrance to progress, and he is angry and jealous accordingly. He hopes to subvert society as it now stands, and the conservativeness of women is an impediment which would make anybody despair but a philosopher of Mr Mill's school. But he clearly aspires to eradicate the feminine element out of woman's nature. Woman, as she is, is his enemy. "White women are so unlike men as they are now" – for so he puts it – Mr Mill expects no social amendment; but this difference does not discourage him, because it is one apparently not of nature's, but of despotic man's and the laws' making, and he is taking both in hand. Alter the marriage laws, and the thing is done. The moral regeneration of mankind will only really commence (p. 177), he tells us, when marriage is placed on the footing he recommends, and all ideas of authority on the one hand and obedience on the other give place to an exact equality – a mercantile firm where neither partner leads being the model proposed. At present no slave ever was a slave to the same lengths and in so full a sense of the word as a wife is, and she is a slave for life. The analogy of the *firm* suggests the idea of dissolution at will; but Mr Mill tells his readers that the question of divorce is beside his present inquiry, which we should not have thought if he had not said so. Lastly, however little in favour woman as we know her is with Mr Mill, he has a bright future in store for her if she will take his advice. He believes that old women have it in them to manage our finance – the finance not of the family but of the nation; – old women, not of the class the world has often trusted with its chiefest affairs, but veritable grandmothers and old maids, and widows who, having brought up their families, will be at leisure to devote the decline of life to their country. Mr Mill, in conclusion is pre-eminent in his indifference to ridicule; he is impervious to the absurd side of a view; – a peculiarity which is magnanimous or otherwise as he can see a joke or not. There is not much evidence that he *can* so far sympathise with his kind in the present volume. He evidently piques himself on being able to waive aside the coarse frivolities of brutal power; but take it as we may, we must feel that a patronage of old women is among the most respectable eccentricities of an abnormal self-esteem.

The tone of this work is so surpassingly insolent towards the whole human race, – it involves such an insult not only to men, but to women as we love and admire and desire to keep them – to the ideal woman as man's helpmate, – that we might wonder at the civility and seriousness with which it has been received by the world of readers as represented by the press, but that the subject of the relation of the sexes, however treated, meets a question of the day. And wherever people criticise an existing state of things, they are pretty sure to hit some palpable blots which demand consideration, and create sufficient sympathy between reader and author for reasonable discussion.

We must believe that Mr Mill has acquired his ideas of the aspirations and claims of women, possibly, too, of their capabilities for work not yet given them to do, from a limited and not average experience. He allows us to suppose him the recognised confidant of the class who by no means take their idea of woman's place and office in the world from St Paul. The fair members of the American convention for changing everything are evidently in communication with him; this correspondence, and an implied more intimate personal acquaintance with a few gifted women, roused by circumstances, – and possibly by his arguments and teaching, – into discontent, suggest to him a state of feeling among women at large which has no foundation in fact. Outside of these grateful sympathisers, his knowledge of the condition of women, their treatment by their masters, and their place in the world, might seem to be derived solely from police reports and other law columns in the *Times*.

If never has been denied in any age of the world that there are women of genius and of extraordinary administrative power, nor has mankind ever been unwilling to recognise this power and genius when it has declared itself. Only men and women of the old traditional way of thinking see – believe they see, at least – that these are exceptional cases which must not alter the existing relation between the sexes, or the apportionment on a large scale of the work of the world. It is this common-sense view which irritates Mr Mill against his countrywomen. They have no idea of sacrificing the ground they already hold by grasping for a new territory. Taking experience and observation as against his theory, they are disposed to laugh at his cry for liberty on their behalf. When he tells them that society makes the whole life of a woman in the easy classes a continual self-sacrifice, and exacts from her an unremitting restraint of her natural inclinations, they will not see it. Even the bribe of allowing women to take the initiative, and make the offer, which Mr Mill's theory of a "firm" clearly involves, loosening the present cruel restriction to "yes" or "no," will not tempt them to wear his colours. The idea of dependence upon men does not weigh unpleasantly upon women in the abstract; rather they have their own notion of liberty only to be attained through men, which is precisely his notion of bitter bondage. Take, for instance, his glowing praise of liberty as a sensation. Word for word, we believe it to represent the sensation of a woman of spirit in entering that married life which, according to Mr Mill, makes her the "body-servant of a despot" for the remainder of her life. "Let any man," he exclaims, "call to mind what he himself felt on emerging from boyhood – from the tutelage and control of even beloved elders – and entering upon the responsibilities of manhood. Was it not like the physical effect of taking off a heavy weight, or releasing him from obstructive, even if not otherwise painful, bonds? Did he not feel twice as much alive, twice as much a human being, as before? And does he imagine that women have no such feeling?" Now, of course, many a bride finds herself mistaken in her notion that married life brings freedom of action – though perhaps not so much oftener than man in his first dream of independence – still the fact that such an impression possesses the female mind should qualify some of Mr Mill's hard hits at his fellow-men. But not only do his countrywomen disappoint Mr Mill by insensibility to their slavery in the everyday routine of life – he complains of them still more when they assume an attitude of self-assertion, and yet do not assert his views. Because they will not treat the sexes as enemies, and marshal their sisters to the battle, he says that women who write dare not say anything that men don't like to hear; and that the greater part of what women write about women is mere sycophancy to men. Nay, he is so unhandsome as to hint further, that in unmarried authoresses much of what they write is intended to "increase their chance of a husband," and that with this aim they overstep the mark, and disgust the men they seek to attract by a servility beyond what is desired or relished in any man but the vulgarest. But if English authoresses, either through despair of attaining an object Mr Mill holds not worth all this pains, or because it is attained already, write without the fear or hope of men before their eyes, yet they are "such artificial products" that he does not attach the value of a grain to anything they can say on this subject where it differs from his own opinions. As we have said, a certain asperity of tone shows that in claiming from woman rights she does not now possess, Mr Mill is as much influenced by resentment for the use she makes of the power now in her hands, as by any real desire to see her sphere enlarged, unless in the change she loses more influence than she gains. It is because women stand in his way, are a drag upon what he considers progress, that he wants to change their status, and make them more like men. He has some chance with a young man, he seems to say, till he marries, and then it is all over with him – the interests of the family hold him down, and all through the wife's narrow views of life. Of course, till we know what Mr Mill considers the good held in check and abeyance by woman's narrowing influence, we cannot argue the question. It is certain that women now – and we believe the same is natural to them in every normal condition of society – have an especial eye to the private and particular. The family carries it often over public claims, always over vague theories of public good. We say vague, because where, as in religious questions, the advantage is realised, they do not yield to men in sacrificing not only personal but family interests to higher considerations. But this shyness of theory is not necessarily an evil; checks and drags are essential in all complex machinery. Families are as much institutions as states, and the people who have the care of them must hold loyally to their charge. Nor ought Mr Mill to lay the blame of desertion from the ranks of innovation and change upon women mainly: it is the fashion of his school to do so, and to denounce the frivolity of women accordingly; but time exercises the same feminine sway upon most minds – time and work. When men begin to act as well as talk and speculate, they sober down in the fashion so offensive to Mr Mill; for action brings the real sense of weight and place in the world. It is very well to be a master speculator; but always to speculate as a disciple, which must be the fate of most, is unsatisfactory – to be always fighting another person's quarrel with society, and whatever is established and received for truth. Above all must the faith of youth in a universal upset – the hope in mere change and subversion – fade along with youth itself: and it is not unfair, after reading this book, to assume that it is this particular faith of which Mr Mill laments the decay. Of such are "the young men of promise, who generally cease to improve as soon as they marry."

When we view Mr Mill as the head of a movement, it is important to enforce that he aims at changing the very nature of woman. His object is to make her something radically different from what we know her. He sneers at the natural fear of change in this vital social question, and assures his readers that of one thing they may be certain – that what is contrary to woman's nature to do, they never will be made to do by simply giving their nature free play. But a country's institutions are not only moulded by the national character – they also mould it; and no one can pretend to say that the reticence and contented domesticity which Mr Mill complains of in his countrywomen, and which men in general respect as an especial feminine virtue, will undergo no change under the call to publicity and rivalry with men which he would force upon them. Not that all women would respond to his appeal; there would be under his *régime* public women and private women – a recognised division from which we can imagine many inconveniences. The private section would be a class by themselves, subject to the temptation of recommending themselves to men through the strong contrast of their pretensions with those of their more ambitious sisterhood. They would have a character for frivolity and subservience to keep up. Poor creatures, simpletons, pretty dolls, and the like, would be at premiums such as they have not yet attained.

Nor can we imagine the stronger division of the sex such intellectual gainers as he supposes, by being urged into a new arena. Mr Mill, in his gallantry, or in his serious conviction, will not grant as *proved* any intellectual inferiority, scarcely a difference; but no woman with any claim to be attended to has ever asserted this equality: on the contrary, it has always been the reproach of clever women that they despised the common-alty of their sex. "If any one were to write down the conversation of women among themselves," said Mademoiselle Scudery, "it would make the worst book in the world." She spoke thus to stimulate her friends to a higher tone; but this and similar disparaging comments on the weakness of their sex from many vigorous female intellects, is in fact an admission on their own part of a need of masculine support in their higher efforts. While conscious of some exceptional powers in which they stand comparison with the men they compete with, yet they own a need of sustentation from without. They know themselves to be brighter, stronger, more far-seeing in intercourse with men of superior intelligence. Even where this tone towards their own sex is offensive, an admission of some needs lies at the bottom. We do not say that Mr Mill will meet with no woman to agree with him; but, from admissions constantly implied, we do feel confident that no woman of clear reason and wide experience fully acquiesces in his line of argument, or adopts his tone in her own person. We will go so far as to suspect that the most masculine-minded woman is conscious of a strain in continuous intercourse with men of vigorous thought, from which it is pleasant to relax into the amiable trivialities at present allowed to her sex, but which under a transcendental reign would be a giving in, a falling away, a desertion of the cause. In the contemplated rivalry in the same field of work, women aiming at posts and professions now filled by men would have a credit to keep up, a constant sex assertion to maintain, which might issue in eccentricities of tone, manner, habit, and costume not pleasant to think of. Now we are men and women. A modern school of philosophy threatens us with a third estate, which, in so far as it got a footing, would scarcely affect for good the other two. The argument that woman will never do what it is not her nature to do, therefore that there is no harm in opening every door to her energies, will never go for much with people who are persuaded in their own minds. It is the nature of many people to do things badly, and the nature of a great many other people not to know when a thing is bad or good, well or ill done. To open certain callings to women, which, because unsuited to their powers, they would fill with inferior average success, would be doubling the incompetence, instead of, as Mr Mill says, doubling the world's stock of intellectual power; and while every profession is, as with us, over-stocked with men, there is surely some plea from nature against doubling the candidates. Of course when we say, in answer to the plea for the education of women, that women are not constituted by nature for the same strict, systematic, long-sustained course of study by which men are prepared for the intellectual professions, we are met by the reply, that the physical training of women amongst ourselves is at fault for this. Let girls, we are told, have the same exercise and liberty of limb that boys have, and they will show themselves as little subject to nervous and other weakening influences. This is said, not because it tallies with any experience, but because it is the only thing to say, because it is *some* answer, because in certain cases of distinguished female intellect the girlhood has been passed a good deal in boy fashion. But if we inquire into these cases, the boyish sports – nay, even the boy's dress – were not a training, but an educational experiment, but an early stirring of conscious power, an eccentricity of genius in embryo. All women who have distinguished themselves hitherto, Mr Mill says, have been self-taught; and he argues that if they were taught like men, the proportion of highly-trained literary power with what is self-taught would be the same among women as it is among men. This can only be true under Mr Mill's hypothesis of the world's ignorance:–

"Hence, in regard to that most difficult question, What are the natural differences between the two sexes? – a subject on which it is impossible in the present state of society to obtain complete and correct knowledge – while almost everybody dogmatises upon it, almost all neglect and make light of the only means by which any partial insight can be obtained into it. This is an analytic study of the most important department of psychology, the laws of the influence of circumstances on character. For however great and apparently ineradicable the moral and intellectual differences between men and women might be, the evidence of there being natural differences could only be negative. Those only could be inferred to be natural which could not possibly be artificial – the residuum, after deducting every characteristic of either sex which can admit of being explained from education or external circumstances. The profoundest knowledge of the laws of the formation of character is

indispensable to entitle any one to affirm even that there is
any difference, much more what the difference is between the
two sexes considered as moral and rational beings; and since
no one, as yet, has that knowledge (for there is hardly any
subject which, in proportion, has been so little studied), no
one is thus far entitled to any positive opinion on the subject"
– (P. 41.)

As a comment on this profound passage, we quote Lord
Penzance in a recent debate:–

"I understand that there has been a recent discovery by
profound thinkers that there is no moral or intellectual
difference between the sexes such as to lead to the
subordination of the one to the other. Truth, however, in the
common affairs of life, lies very near the surface, and those
who dig and delve into the lower strata of thought sometimes
bring up ingenious theories, but rarely practical truth."

As *we* think we know women, we see in them a greater capacity
for self-teaching, a greater power of imbibing knowledge from
collateral sources, a greater aptitude to catch the tone of
thought about them without direct instruction, than in men,
together with less power of sustained attention and concent-
ration of the mind on a given subject. And all this fits, or seems
to fit, in with what has hitherto been regarded as nature's plan.
Up to a certain age girls and boys can learn together. A
divergence is observable just at the time when life opens to
both. Girls, it is said, cease to study because they see no
practical end in it. There comes a reaction into idleness with
the girl at a time when her brothers are urged to their utmost by
the sense of working for a career. Nature has something to say
for this reaction. It would not, we believe, suit the average
female constitution to go through a university course of study
from eighteen to two-and-twenty; but also, we will allow,
comes the question to her, Where is the practical use? what will
this labour do for me? and we can foresee no period in the
world's history where the answer can be the same as to men.
Therefore, because the majority of mankind cannot work their
minds for learning's sake, but only for some intelligible end, we
do not believe the education of women can ever be conducted
with the same system and severity as for men, because the
question of marriage acts with diametrically opposite influence

on the two. Mr Mill sneers at man's notion that the natural
vocation of a women is that of a wife and mother, and at his
educating her accordingly. "They might," he continues, "be
supposed to think that the alleged natural vocation of women
was of all things most repugnant to their nature, insomuch that
if they were free to do anything else – if any other means of
living or occupation of their time and faculties is open which
has any chance of appearing desirable to them – there will not
be enough of them who will be willing to accept the condition
said to be natural to them." Mr Mill is certainly hard upon man
in this matter of female education, and lays much to deliberate
intention which is inevitable in the nature of things. Few men
are educated for remote contingencies, as he would have all
women to be. It is true that one woman in a million may have
the organisation, physical and mental, which would qualify her
for a Chancellor of the Exchequer, or to shine in debate in the
British Parliament, or to perform a difficult operation, or to
construct a railway, or to build a cathedral, or to conduct an
intricate lawsuit, or to sway a fierce democracy; but the
chances are too infinitesimal to found a system upon. People
must be educated for probabilities, and make their way to
possibilities by themselves. If women are to compete with men,
their education for the task must begin from the cradle. It does
not occur to Mr Mill to consider, not what philosophers in the
abstract, but what the father with a family to provide for, must
do in any given circumstances. Education for a profession is
expensive. It may be taken for granted that young people
expect to marry. Now marriage, in the case of a man, is a
stimulus to exertion in the ordinary course of things; he is a
better, more sedulous doctor or lawyer for being married. The
father has not to put the question to his sons as to whether they
will or will not marry; but with his daughter of eighteen it is a
different matter. He spends his money on a mere chance of its
helping her on in life. No one can say that a woman is more
eligible as a wife or mother for pursuing a profession; and if she
does not pursue it, the cost of her education is wasted. Hence it
seems to us that women, whatever their liberty of choice in the
higher lines of employment, must always struggle into it on a
different footing from their brothers, and always be at a
disadvantage, unless, that is, fathers are relieved from the
charge of their children by the State, too enlightened to
consider sex at all.

Mr Mill is extremely severe on men assuming superiority by virtue of mere physical strength; but how is it possible to ignore or suppress in himself the natural effects of a fact on his moral consciousness? He quotes with recoil and disgust the title of lord as having been actually applied by the wife to her husband, and tolerated by him; but we do not see how this physical superiority can help carrying with it some sense of lordship over every condition of life wanting in his power to enforce his will. The boy of three who proves by rude experiment that he is stronger than his sister of four, receives an impression that can never be erased. If he uses his new-found power to bully, he must be snubbed; but all the teaching of his anxious mother only confirms in him the fact of his strength as a gift not to be ignored, but used. It belongs to the yearning in a good man to protect and defend the weak where they are weak. It does not interfere with a frank recognition of superiority in the nobler functions where he sees it in woman, but it does involve a claim to supremacy where he sees fit to exert it. The groom who sits behind his mistress, and takes the reins from her hands when he sees the horses need a stronger hand, feels this as an inevitable consequence of being the strongest. In fact, the whole question must turn upon this. Mr Mill's argument does not go upon women being more than the intellectual equals of man – if they were, they would have been his master long ago; if, therefore, they are physically weaker, the theory of equality falls to the ground, even without the argument from analogy, which leads most men to expect a mind softer, more open to control, less fitted for intense labour in a less robust frame. Equality that rests on sufferance ceases to be equality; it cannot affect the mind as such. The notion is a mere inflation that ends in bluster. Mr Mill's whole line is really that women are not equal to men, but we are to act as if they were. He calls upon the law to defend the weak, which, in truth, is the law's one business; but the fact that they are dependent on law is subversive of the theory of equality. Was there ever, Mr Mill asks, a domination which did not appear natural to those who possessed it? – a plausible ground for mistrust of our innate conviction, which, however, will not stand his tests. Aristotle, he says, held the opinion that the Greeks were of a free nature, the Thracians and Asiatics of a slave nature, and time has proved him mistaken. But this view was always open to the appeal of physical strength. Nobody could say in Aristotle's day that it was physically impossible for these slaves to throw off the yoke. The theory was perhaps acceptable, as quenching uneasy fears to the contrary. In all the cases he adduces, this last appeal has determined matters. Mr Mill cannot pretend that women will ever be able to secure their own independence by force of arms; and even if men were to do it for them, it would be mere favour, a make-believe, a pretence. The physical strength of slaves must always have been an element of insecurity. This insecure tenure can never be felt by men in regard to women. What men decide by law they are sensible of being able to abrogate when they please. Mr Mill has a Utopia in prospect, in which human nature will not only be weak, as in England, but absolutely done away with altogether as we know it. He writes as if nature was in his future to present no hindrances to a perfect uniformity of pursuit. With this we have nothing to do. In the world, as we and all mankind that has preceded us have known it, women under no conceivable circumstances can have the law on their side but by the permission of men; therefore they seem to us to act wisely by owning a natural law of subordination, and submitting to "subjection" as a Bible word – a justification for its use we need not say of little weight with Mr Mill. The discussion must, in fact, always want the last touch of reality. Nothing that we have said militates against the right of women, though physically weak, to justice; but it has much to do with what constitutes just claims. There may be certain privileges which men may think justly theirs – privileges founded on their different and stronger organisation.

The fact – for which we see nothing but that it must always remain a fact – that woman's influence over men will always be most potent before she has attained to her fullest mental development, must limit her influence, or rather determine its nature. There is this difference between the sexes' view of each other's time of most perfect charm and fascination, – woman early arrives at a perfection of grace and manner – the body ante-dates the mind. She is most persuasive, most irresistibly attractive, while still a girl. The term girl is clung to; the period of girlhood is that of sway. With women, boyhood is a term almost of reproach. With a girl in her teens, "a mere boy" means something raw and irresponsible – the mind still unformed. The man grows in her regard and interest as he matures – a very natural variety of standard if the one sex acknowledges a protector and superior in man, the other a being to shield and guide in woman, but altogether irrational under Mr Mill's view. However, with his notions of the perfectibility of the race, this is nothing – a mere temporary infatuation in men. Hitherto such and such ideas have influenced mankind; it is no reason whatever that they should continue to do so. At any rate, while the infatuation lasts, we regard it as a natural barrier potent on both sides against that severe application, that emulation between the sexes, which is to issue, according to this philosopher, in the regeneration of the world.

However much we have shown ourselves to disagree with Mr Mill's treatment of this subject, we cannot but consider his book opportune at the present juncture. It is well that people generally should realise that meddling with the marriage laws is dealing with the edge-tools, and that no alteration on the existing state of law and opinion can be thought of without serious consequences for good or evil. Mr Mill shows a perfect indifference to the enormous risk of his proposed changes. Probably there would be some difference between him and ourselves as to what constituted them. Christian morals, we are given to understand, elsewhere are going to be put on their trial. This essay may be a contribution to the argument. He begins by complaining of the power the present state of the law puts into the hands of a brutal husband; but his whole argument leaves such considerations far behind. To place women on the standing he claims for them, the relation of marriage must cease to bind as it does now. He exacts the right on both sides of separation at will on grounds which would now be regarded as frivolous, and therefore, will not allow marriage to be a tie; for that is no tie that holds neither party against the will of the hour. He makes no allowance for the reconciling effects of the indissoluble; he seems to eschew altogether the view of taking "for better for worse." Husband and wife with him are to join in raising funds, are to be equal as partners, are to dissolve the contract at will. He abstains from the question of absolute divorce – his faith in the revolution he would effect blinds him, we believe, to consequences; but few people can contemplate the natural results of boundless legal separations without foreseeing consequences to morals hideous in the eyes of the humdrum respectability in which English society, by these transcendentalists, is supposed to wallow, to the smothering of all finer perceptions. No one can be other than ashamed of the leniency too often shown to brutality by the administrators of the law, or by the law itself, where the wife is the victim. The story told by Professor Newman is likely to be true enough, of the fellow who grumbled at his sentence of six months' imprisonment for ill-using his donkey, on the ground that he had only had two for beating his wife nearly to death. It is quite of a piece with the line of defence taken by a Yorkshireman before the coroner: "This I can say, I never felled my wife in my life – and that's a great thing to say;" a plea drawing from one of the jury the hearty response, "Ay, Tummas, it is." But it must not be supposed that an alteration of the marriage laws will have any prompt effect in restraining these excesses. Any inquiry into such atrocities shows that they are quite as common where the contract between the man and woman is not marriage. Indeed it is noticed by the curious in human nature that a woman will put up with more from the man who is not her husband than from one that is; and we have known it inferred that a man and woman who lived as man and wife were not married, or she never would have put up with what she did from him. What, we would ask, would be the consequence to women of the lowest classes if the right of separation was established on the ground of incompatibility of temper? We hear much in these days of the superfluity of single women. Might there not, then, be another class on the world's hands infinitely more helpless and *de trop*? As has been well remarked, if the wife is a slave, at any rate a man, as the law now stands, can have but one slave. So long as physical strength remains on the man's side, he must have the advantage in change. A husband and wife separating at fifty, which of the two, we would ask Mr Mill, will have the best of it, or the most chance of an eligible new alliance? The truth is, his whole line is for exceptional women, either in power of mind, or in circumstances, or in temper, aims, and ambition. The vast body of women, we cannot doubt, know themselves to be better off now than they would be if thrown upon their own hands for support. As the American fine lady said to Mr Hepworth Dixon, to account for her not joining the "woman's rights movement," "You see I like to be taken care of." It will be a bad time, we believe, for women whenever it is announced to her as her privilege through the length and breadth of her ranks that hence forth she must take care of herself. Margaret

Fuller, the great American exponent of the new claim, required that woman should enter into competition with man on every field now exclusively his own, and also that he should yield to her every gallant and chivalrous observance. She exacted to be allowed to speak in the Senate, to preach in the pulpit, "to be a sea-captain, if she will;" and also expected to have his arm as her support when she crossed a room that he should pick up her handkerchief to save her the trouble of stooping, and give up his seat to her whenever she chose, – that woman should, in fact, be at once his idol and his rival. The experiment can never in the nature of things be fairly tried; and we believe it is fortunate for woman that it cannot, and that she should betray, after all, more real appreciation for the tenderness of a voluntary courtesy than the "rights" which she is persuaded to clamour for. The one class of women who owe least to the chivalry of men are those least aggrieved by the laws as they now stand. In fact, a single woman of spirit has not much to complain of from the law beyond political disabilities. As things now stand, she can do most things she wants to do. If she chooses, she may regret that her education did not fit her for a profession; but if she has any candour, she must own the grievance an after thought – she can scarcely admit to herself that any such destination would have found favour in her youth. It is the fashion with theorists to enlarge upon the growing army of single women, as though the State should education every woman to form one of its ranks. Mr Mill even aspires so to present the ignominy of married subjection to women, that she shall refuse the yoke; and speaks sneeringly of an irresistible *entrainement* as her one cause for submitting to it; but opinion and nature are powers scarcely to be subverted by such taunts.

If is often easy to go along with Mr Mill half way, a companionship no doubt worse than valueless in his eyes. Thus some rights married women certainly have bearing upon his tribute to their powers of government and domestic management. They belong, however, to custom rather than law. Every woman has a right to know the state of her husband's affairs. She has a right to know what she may afford to spend. If he has secrets from her on this point, one of two things is certain – he either has not chosen prudently, or believes himself not to have done so; or his secrets are anxious, painful, or discreditable ones. Openness on these points has often more to do with the right relation between husband and wife, is a greater check upon the frivolity and expense which are so frequent a charge against the sex, than any other consideration. Prudence and economy must have some basis to act upon. Men constantly treat their wives as if they were fools, and then are angry because they are foolish. Such unjust want of confidence causes a waste of that administrative power attributed to woman as her peculiar gift. We agree also in much that Mr Mill says on the self-abnegation men conspire to expect from women as such, and to treat as an especial feminine virtue. "All the moralities tell them that it is the duty of women, and all the unreal sentimentalities that it is their nature, to live for others, to make complete abnegation of themselves." In so far as this view, enforced as a characteristic of sex, encourages the selfishness of men, it must be a false one. It is too true that men are still trained in the idea that the women connected with them do only what is natural and right when they sacrifice their property, and often their only means of living, to the exigencies of *their* selfish extravagance. But this is scarcely an occasion for entering upon such questions, Mr Mill carries his readers so far beyond reforms of mere detail either in law or practice.

In treating with indignant contempt the sum and collective wisdom of mankind on these vital points, Mr Mill bases his right on intimate experience: he says to his readers, "I know what I say." He has been happy enough, he leads his readers to infer, to know in the closest relation a woman who has taught him to respect her whole sex as by right of nature the intellectual equals of man. "Who can tell," he asks, "how many of the most original thoughts put forth by male writers belong to a woman by suggestion, to themselves only by verifying and working out? If I may judge by my own case, a very large proportion indeed." While, in justification of his view of marriage in the only condition which he considers worthy of respect, we read in the conclusion:–

> "What marriage may be in the case of two persons of cultivated faculties, identical in opinions and purposes, between whom there exists that best kind of equality, similarity of powers and capacities, with reciprocal superiority in them – so that each can enjoy the luxury of looking up to the other, and can have alternatively the pleasure of leading and of being led in the path of development – I will

not attempt to describe. To those who can conceive it, there is no need; to those who cannot, it would appear the dream of an enthusiast. But I maintain, with the profoundest conviction, that this, and this only, is the ideal of marriage; and that all opinions, customs, and institutions which favour any other notion of it, or turn the conceptions and aspirations connected with it into any other direction, by whatever pretences they may be coloured, are relics of primitive barbarism." – (P. 177.)

These indications of the source and inspiration of the present essay impart interest and sentiment, while they detract from its value as an argument. Where the affections are deeply engaged, we maintain it is impossible to pronounce authoritatively on such points as these passages decide. We, who write in absolute ignorance of Mr Mill's data, perceive only that his personal individual experience has determined his line of thought on a question which has occupied the mind of mankind ever since there were men to think, in defiant opposition to their conclusions. It is a great privilege to have known one eminently intellectual and noble woman; but as an argument for the abstract equality of the masculine and feminine intellect, a man's self cannot be the judge from personal experience. Whatever shortcoming there may be in woman's capacity, the power of seizing upon another's thought almost in the act and moment of conception, and making it her own, has never been denied her. It is this that makes the clever woman's conversation so brilliant. She not only produces her own store, but she is the mirror of all the minds about her. Neither she nor they may detect it, but this is the reason why many a woman surprises us where there is quick interchange of thought, who collapses into a very ordinary thinker, with her pen for her only inspiration. This is mere generalising in face of a particular experience; but we believe our readers' own observation will prove on our side. We own we should have accepted Mr Mill's instance of intellectual independence as more conclusive if there had been less unanimity of thought. But we cordially enter into the charm of the union he pictures. How many happy, mutually beneficial marriages there are without any approach to intellectual equality is beside the present question. We believe them to be beyond count. The ordinance of Providence's own appointment is not dependent for its success on mere intellectual balance or exact harmony. The principle of due subordination, the sense of a larger and a lesser sphere of action, tell with soothing power even where there may be wide divergences of opinion; and, above all the deep religious acquiescence in the law, human and divine, that the marriage union is indissoluble, is one of magical force to smooth and reconcile, though this is a force wholly alien to Mr Mill's sense of right.

Where an author writes *in memoriam*, a sympathy is aroused in his readers which must mingle some tenderness with the strongest opposition to his views. He is advocating not only a cause but a person; his arguments have a power to himself borrowed from a stronger influence than reason. He represents a lost pleader of the cause he advocates; he has to do justice to something dearer than abstract truth; hence much of the harshness and unfairness we have to complain of; hence, perhaps, some share of the arrogance, as though he were the solitary possessor, the monopolist, of the truth and fact on which the whole question turns. People are never so arrogant as when they speak in their own person what they have derived from a source they have implicit trust in. Hence too, perhaps, that deadness to ridicule we have remarked on as so prominent in this onslaught on universal opinion, a sensitiveness which people are seldom quite self-reliant enough to overcome if they have only self to back them; though, no doubt, a positivist philosopher has advantages on this point beyond other men.

It is observable that all men who take women for their theme argue upon an extremely limited knowledge. We may generally form a safe conjecture on the view a man will take of the whole sex if we know what his particular experience has been. Mr Mill says the same, though without personal application: "The most favourable case which a man can have for studying the character of a woman is that of his own wife; and in fact this is the source from which any knowledge worth having on the subject has, I believe, generally come. But most men have not had the opportunity of studying in this way more than a single case; accordingly one can, to an almost laughable degree, infer what a man's wife is like from his opinions about women in general."

There are persons so keenly sympathetic in their own natures that the want of sympathy in Mr Mill excites a strong antagonism. His intense arrogance, his incapacity to do justice to the feelings or motives of all from whom he differs, his intolerance of all but his own disciples, and lastly, in natural consequence of these qualities, his want of playfulness in himself and repugnance to it in others, all combine to create something like antipathy. There are not points enough in common for argument. With the exception of these emphatic protesters, it is curious to observe – in the discussion and comment of which, – either in seriousness or banter, – the present essay is a fruitful source, how readily it is granted to be clever, well written, logical, and so on. Nobody is afraid to praise Mr Mill, whatever side they take in the argument; for this reason, we believe, that everybody, man and woman, feels to be outside the region of severe fact. Turn from his page to society and experience, and his whole edifice crumbles to dust. In their inmost heart all are equally convinced of the unreality of the thing – we do not say of the details, but of the conclusions they are to prove. It is understood there is a fallacy somewhere, which Mr Mill shows his cleverness in hiding out of sight. Where the logic gets most commended, the innate difficulties are regarded as so many puzzles for which Mr Mill finds plausible solutions. He has found out the only answer, such as it is. Thus it is ingenious to call woman an artificial product, in reply to those who argue for the natural dependence of woman upon man. It is ingenious to call the subordination of women the single relic of an old world of thought and practice exploded in everything else; it is ingenious to give as a reason why women remain behind men in the pursuits open to both, that they have not time for them because society assigns to them other duties – that, especially, of being charming. It is *the* answer, of course, to attribute the contentment of woman with her present lot to ignorance of the value of self-dependence. The case of a mercantile partnership adduced in refutation of the time-honoured argument, that where two ride together one must ride behind, is of the same nature. The reference to Mrs Grundy, where our present ideas of propriety are threatened, is commonplace, but still *the* retort where sarcasm is the only answer. Everybody agrees that there is an immense amount of truth in what Mr Mill says, as there generally is in men's quarrel with an existing state of things; but the conclusions he derives from his truths all demand just a little fresh adjustment of nature. If only Mr Mill were a good Catholic, says the *Tablet*, in return for his defence of the priest as a check upon the tyranny of the husband – if only women were men in petticoats, says another – if only his plans for removing present evils would not admit a hundred worse, says a third, – then we might do something more than admire Mr Mill's ingenuity; then we might not only defer to his assumption of especial enlightenment – of a philosophic vantage ground from which he is justified in despising the wisdom of mankind from the very beginning of things, – but we might also accept him for our guide.

MILL ON THE SUBJECTION OF WOMEN
[Margaret Oliphant]

Edinburgh Review, Volume 130, October 1869.

ART. XI. - 1. *The Subjection of Women.* BY JOHN
STUART MILL. London: 1869.
2. *Woman's Work and Woman's Culture: a Series of Essays.*
Edited by JOSEPHINE G. BUTLER. London: 1869.

Of all writers on the claims of women, Mr. Mill alone has
treated the question on its fundamental principles. The
apologists of woman have eluded the first dilemma in many
ingenious ways. They have not ventured to go to the
fountainhead and begin with the beginning. We have heard
much talk about moral superiority and mental equality, but
more in the shape of guesses than of argument; and we have
had an amount of wild statement on both sides which it is
amazing should have been tolerated in any reasonable discussion. Men have gravely informed us that women were
incapable of self-government, or of any share in the serious
work of the world, notwithstanding the patent facts which we
have only to open our eyes and see; and women, with equal
gravity and more heat, have endeavoured to impress upon us
the belief that they were competent to undertake the work of
men, not instead of, but in addition to, their own. We have
been told that the one sex is better and that it is worse than the
other; that it is full of intuitive wisdom and intuitive folly; that
it is stronger, that it is weaker, that it is purer, that it is
wickeder. We have been told that most of the harm done in the
world has originated with women; and we have been told that
all the good comes from their influence and soft example. In
the face of such assertions what is the puzzled spectator to do?
If we could imagine an intelligent being looking on, who was
neither man nor woman, and had no prejudices one way or
another, listening to all this babble, yet casting his eyes around
him in the world in the exercise of an independent judgment,
what should we imagine his real impressions to be?

Looking down from some angelic height he would see a mass of creatures moving about on the face of the earth on that general level of humanity which is the first standing ground of the children of Adam. The chances are that his first look would convey to him an impression of intense similarity, almost uniformity. He would see the two halves of humanity not divided into two armies, but mingled and mixed up together with the most curious absence of primary identity. He would find on the whole that motive of a very similar character actuated the mass; that some were lofty and some petty, some wise and some foolish, some able and some stupid, with wonderfully little distinction of sex. The first glance would reveal this to him in a curious confusing way, and would probably make the conditions of human life a very bewildering problem. And when those distinctions which do really mark out sex from sex became apparent to him, he would be more puzzled still. He would find many things expedient that are not altogether just. He would find necessities which nature imposed, but which abstract equity turned against. He would find indeed a great troubled confused uncertain world, ruled by anything but logic, not even ruled by justice, in which century after century had over again demonstrated the impossibility not only of perfection in action or agreement in thought, but even of any universal infallible code of right and wrong as applied to the most intimate relations of life.

One can imagine a young and romantic angel putting his inexperienced hand to the work with the idea of bringing light out of darkness, and absolute order from the midst of this confusion. But we fear the chances are that he would soon withdraw in consternation from the difficult task. He would find conflicting claims too fine to be ever discriminated; interests which even the balance of the sanctuary would be unable to weigh and divide; rights and wrongs so involved and complicated that no trenchant steel of keen justice coming down upon them could do other than cut and sever many heartstrings in its descent. We who are not angels but men and women of the nineteenth century, very reluctant to allow that any hardship can exist for which a remedy is impossible, must inevitably find the matter a still more difficult one. And no doubt it is the inherent human consciousness of its supreme difficulties which has so long placed it out of the sphere of discussion. Now, however, when even this barrier is insufficient to restrain the audacity of argument, the question has become one which must be looked in the face; and the more seriously we can do it, and the less trust we put in those picturesque and sentimental pleas which tempt the advocates on both sides, the more likely we shall be to come to some real and satisfactory conclusion.

It is, however, humbling and painful to the serious inquirer to find that a subject so important should be introduced, even by a great writer and thinker from whom we might at least hope for facts and reason, by a fancy picture. Even Mr. Mill, whose genius is not dramatic or pictorial, cannot sufficiently wean himself from natural prejudices as to refrain in this matter from an attempt at the picturesque. Before he tells us what reforms he hopes for, or even explains to us his conception of the proper position and relations of men and women, he sketches for us their actual state. And as the sketch is one we can all verify or disprove the moment we turn our eyes from his pages upon the world around, the preface is of the most daring description. The subject woman is his heroine. He sets her before us, laden not only with personal chains, but with the shadow of those fetters in which her mother and all her female ancestors have been bound. As he writes there rises up before us the enormous shade of a despotism vaster and more monstrous than any other ever conceived by man – a tyranny which enslaves its victims before their birth, which freezes the fountain of their life, which never relaxes, never varies, which skilfully seizes upon God's gifts to make them instruments of devilish oppression, which turns one half of the race into minute and scientific tyrants, and the other into blind and servile slaves. Selfishness has been often declared to be the moving principle of the world, but Mr. Mill has given a new aspect to selfishness. In those primeval days when Adam delved and Eve span, as soon as there were two creatures to have mutual relations with each other, the grand sentiment of Sex, according to his description, came into being – not that sentiment which inclines one soul towards the other and knits between them the closest and most subtle of all bonds, but a brutal sense of superior strength and determination to subjugate and oppress. The first Husband, whoever he may have been, saw in a moment, with an instinctive clearsighted-ness which does him infinite credit, the advantage of having a bondwoman. And from that moment to this the primitive

conception has grown and intensified with every new generation. Thus the world itself is founded upon the basis of a vast
injustice, a code of oppression more wide-spreading and deeply
penetrating than any other which has cursed humanity. Other
tyrannies have confined themselves to one race, or nation, or
period. Some countries have still been free when others were
enslaved; but this slavery has regarded no geographical
bounds, and has extended over the entire face of the earth. In
every community despotism has had its day, but there have
been times when the empire has been a republic, when the
tyrant has been set aside by the patriot, and the slave has tasted
the delights of freedom. But between man and woman there
have been no lapses into liberty. The hardest, most minute, and
most galling of all despotisms has reigned with unbroken force
in all times and all nations. It has paralysed the very root and
origin of the human race. It has entered into every house and
pervaded the most private, the most sacred moments of
existence. There are times when the veriest slave who breathes,
in his hovel, or even his dungeon, may retire within himself and
feel that there at least beyond the reach of his tyrant, he is free
before God and a sympathetic heaven. But even this refuge has
been denied to a woman. In her very thoughts she must bear
the yoke – the hours which bring privacy and the relief of
solitude to other slaves are her hardest moments of bondage.
She cannot put her chains off her for a moment. The world
which has come to reject and abhor the idea of slavery as
respects a man, has no pity, no thought of her in her blacker
captivity. And the marks of a servitude more bitter, and long,
and universal than any other bondage which this earth has ever
known have eaten into her very soul. She is debased without
knowing her debasement. She has sunk to that lowest depth of
degradation at which the captive hugs his chains. She is an
object of contempt, more or less openly displayed, to her
husband who rules over her, to her sons whose birthright it is
to rule over other women, to her brothers who have grown up
beside her, to her father who has trained her for this long
course of servitude. They are her nearest and her dearest, and
yet one and all they put their feet upon her neck. This is the
terrible picture which Mr. Mill places before us. So deeply has
her bondage entered into her nature, he says, that after all these
thousand years we are in no position to say what a woman can
or cannot do. She has never had the ghost of fair play. She has

been so held down, silenced, and oppressed, that we can
scarcely even form a right idea of what she wishes, nor does she
herself know what she wishes, her faculties being benumbed by
the damps and chills of the prison-house in which she was
born. The spectator is struck dumb by the appalling tableau on
which he is thus invited to gaze. If it is so, what can this world
be but a worse pandemonium, a darker hell? Even in hell, the
miserable beings give each other what ease they can in their
everlasting sufferings – but here, of each two one is the
oppressor, the other the slave – one exults in his mastery, the
other obeys with trembling – one is everything, the other
nothing. Weak in body, crushed in mind, all hope and courage
and natural delight gone out of her, the feeble creature drags
her lengthening chain, the stronger mocks her with taunts, with
jeers, with new impositions. Dante might have found a new
torture for the wretched had he but dreamt of this theory of
wedlock. Talk of binding a dead man to a living one as a
supreme act of cruelty! It is a bagatelle in comparison with the
burning chains, the insulting barbarous fetters, which eat into
the soul of every woman who is a wife.

This is no exaggerated picture of Mr. Mill's statement of the
past and present history of woman. And it would be little
wonder if the mere thought of such a subjection should rouse
and excite any generous mind. It is like the story with which an
ancient minstrel might have roused the knights in Gloriana's
court. Where is this dismal country? one can fancy Sir Artegal
crying. One can imagine a jar of the armour, a clank of spur
and scabbard, as one indignant warrior after another, flushed
with rage and pity, sprang to his feet at the spirit-stirring tale.
And even when it is told by ourselves in days which are no
longer those of chivalry, it is not to be denied that the breath
quickens and the breast heaves. But as the fumes of the tale
disperse and float away into the common daylight, a certain
chill comes upon our enthusiasm. We ask ourselves with
astonished voice, where is the home of such cruelty? What! can
it be here in this smiling, weeping, loving, struggling, ordinary
world that these things be? here, where though there are storms
and troubles by times, the dew falls nightly and the sun rises
every day, and millions of unconscious people take hands and
smile upon each other without knowing that they are masters
and slaves? Is this that country of despair? It is hard to
recognise it when we turn from the gloomy image conjured up

in the philosopher's study to the fresh daylight outside, and all that is being enacted before our eyes, between the green sod and the blue sky. There are subjects upon which such a writer speaks with authority what is all but supreme. We do not yield our judgment to him, yet his word has a weight which attaches to the utterance of few of his contemporaries. But this is not one of those special subjects. This is a matter on which we are all qualified to form an opinion. What we see and know has inevitably a greater influence with us than what we are told, and common experience, common eyesight, contradict Mr Mill's picture at every turn. Was it not unwise at the very outset of a philosophical inquiry to put himself in sharp collision with the evident and visible? It is not a proof, perhaps, that his theory is wrong, but it is a proof that his judgment is sometimes warped by theory, and that he does not approach this subject at least with the candour and impartiality which become a great thinker. Should not we all have been more impressed by his arguments, more disposed to listen to his reasoning, had he allowed that, after all, the system he condemns had not worked badly in the majority of cases? He admits as much grudgingly, in half a dozen lines after he has given three times as many pages to the strangely fictitious picture we have just described. This is not to strengthen but to weaken the force of the real case which we are ready to suppose he has in reserve all the time. When Mr. Mill asserts that slavery is the basis of the law of marriage, he forgets that it is a contract by which the master is bound to labour for the slave, not the slave for the master.

And even after this preface which has somewhat shaken our confidence in him, it is disappointing to find that such an authority as Mr. Mill takes us to no higher ground in his attempt to clear up the old question between men and women than that limited arena of equality upon which so many futile duels have been fought. Of all doubtful questions, this is one which must be the most doubtful to any thoughtful mind. Is there such a thing as equality, not only between men and women, but between any two creatures in the whole round of existence? Mr. Mill's very argument settles the question between the sexes without a moment's difficulty; for the fundamental and undeniable difference of bodily strength, which alone would make the subjection be describes possible, throws the balance so overwhelmingly in favour of one of the claimants, that the superiority of the other in point of intellect and character would need to be immense in order to neutralise that first advantage. Intellect is a great power; and no doubt in the long run it is that which solves all the difficulties, and finally settles the movements of humanity; but it does not reign at first hand, nor is it the undisputed monarch of the universe; and even did woman possess a monopoly of it, which is so far from being the case, it is doubtful whether that would have sufficed in the rude conflicts of the ages to enable her to hold her ground as an antagonist and athlete against the greater strength, the bolder temper, and the uninterrupted robustness of man. But, strangely enough, it is in this aspect alone that Mr. Mill apparently cares to consider it. It is to him no complicated matter which a hundred subtleties of nature combine to render difficult, but a simple question to be settled by that sleight of hand which is called legislation. It is strange to find so profound a mind taking so superficial a view. Even were his theory of equality a perfectly right and just one, did men and women stand upon precisely the same ground, adapted for the same work, framed on the same model, qualified to perform the same functions in the world, yet the very fact that for so many centuries they have not realised this, and in the meantime have been weaving themselves up in confused and intricate webs of prejudice and tradition, should move the philosopher to a keener sense of the infinite difficulties of the subject. These difficulties, which to us seem well nigh insurmountable, are in his opinion overcome by a simple change of conditions. He mixes up the fundamental question – which we may call that of the official superiority of man in the economy of the world – with local laws of marriage and individual hardships resulting from the same; strangely conceiving the greater to be produced by the less, and not the less by the greater. And looking on the matter in this light, the remedy becomes easy enough. It is but to repeal the laws which subject women to the legal authority of their husbands, and to place the sexes on a footing of external equality. These words no doubt describe an outward revolution which would change, though not so much as appears on the face, many circumstances of our lives. It would not, however, change in one iota the laws or conditions of nature. The alteration would be simply external. The disabilities of woman removed, the superstition of her different standing in the world abolished, her equality recognised, her rights guaranteed, a perfect legal level of position established between men and women – this is Mr. Mill's remedy for all her evils. He does not flatter us, indeed, that the immediate result will be perfect blessedness, for she is, he thinks, too profoundly debased by her subjection to recover all in a moment. But the acknowledgment of her equality is all that is wanted in the long run; and as soon as she has become accustomed to her enfranchisement her griefs will disappear by degrees, and Woman for the first time will be happy, being free.

This is a summary way of settling the difficulty, and, if it were possible, would be a very easy one; but Mr. Mill does not seem to perceive that any law on such a subject must be but an expression of some deep primitive sentiment, and that while the former can be dealt with, the latter is beyond the reach of legislation. For our own part, we agree with Mr. Mill to a great extent as to the injustice of some existing laws which press very hardly upon women; and are perfectly disposed to accept the alterations he suggests, believing that they would furnish a real remedy for a distinct grievance. We believe that a great and universal injury – the injury of an insult – is done to all women by the present state of the marriage law in England. Were it universally – as it is in the vast majority of cases – a dead letter, it would still outrage the sensibilities of one half of the race; and no end that is worth serving can be served by that. To say that a woman loses all rights, all property, all identity, as soon as she is married – although it is the merest legal fiction and idle breath – is in its actual words an insult to every woman. Nobody believes that the bride, when her husband leads her from the church door over the scattered flowers, herself the very flower and blossom of humanity, the perfection and the origin of life, is the chattel of the man by her side – a thing transformed, lost to the world and the race, absorbed in him, and with no further claim to personal existence. But yet the law says as much in the plainest language, and Mr. Mill builds upon this his dismal survey of the condition of women. It is not true, and all the enactments in the world could not make it so; and – not to speak of marriage settlements and the precautions of anxious parents – that mutual dependence which is the law of nature, and love which is the origin of wedlock, and the most ordinary good sense and good feeling suffice, except in individual instances, to nullify the law. The grievance chiefly complained of is, let us say, a sentimental grievance, and practically makes very little difference to the happiness of married women generally; but there are not perhaps a hundred married women in England to whom at one time or other the phraseology of the law has not conveyed a stinging sense of humiliation and insult. This has little to do with the abstract question of equality – it does not affect the subordination of the wife to the husband or the virtual authority of the bread-winner. It is a gratuitous offence and an actual falsehood. And at the same time it sets a door of opportunity open to the exceptional monsters of the race. 'Absolute fiends are as rare as angels, perhaps 'rarer,' says Mr. Mill; but when the fiend appears, as happens at intervals, the law hands his victim over to him with cheerful readiness. It provides the knife and the cord, and places every instrument of torture within the reach of the operator. It will not let him kill her, unless he is exceptionally gifted; but it lets him rob her, starve her, ruin her, beat away her hands from every help she clings to, neutralise all her efforts, take the bread out of her mouth and the children out of her arms, and make her life a continued torture. All this can be done in the name of the law which insults the happiest wife, while it thus crushes the unfortunate. This is a question altogether apart from the general question between the sexes. It is a special practical matter, susceptible of amendment. The Married Woman's Property Bill, without offering any facilities for separation, or interfering in any way with the husband's position as a husband, offers a remedy which will cancel the sentimental grievance, and do as much for the real evil as can be done in this life. For at the best it is doubtful, when there is really a bad man or a bad woman in the case, if law can do anything that will be really effectual. It cannot enter into the privacy which secludes husband and wife from all the world. It can endow a woman with the control of her own property, but it cannot prevent her from being wheedled or bullied out of it at any of the many moments in which a married pair are alone together. Even in this point, the only one in which it can do anything, it is astonishing how little the law can do. But we have no room to enter into this part of the question. We repeat, the Married Woman's Property Bill would remove to a great degree the actual injustice Mr. Mill complains of, would bind bad men from the exercise of exceptional tyrannies, and relieve some suffering women; and it would free all from a statute which is an injury and an offence. But it would not affect, except nominally and in the most limited way, those arrangements which to him seem its artificial produce and to us appear the laws of nature. The bond of marriage is too intimate, and the parties are left too completely at each other's mercy, to make any external code absolutely supreme between them. We must search farther and go deeper before we can see where the foundation of the matter actually lies.

And strangely enough in this unjust and cruel and insulting law of marriage there is a germ of natural truth, which recognises something deeper in the question than Mr. Mill is disposed to recognise. 'The two,' he says with indignation, 'are called one person in the law for the purpose of inferring that whatever is hers is his; but the parallel inference is never drawn, that whatever is his is hers; the maxim is not applied against the man, except to make him responsible to third parties for her acts, as a master is for the acts of his servants or his cattle.' Here then is the hypothesis which Mr. Mill will not take into consideration, but which we are compelled to take into consideration, and which in reality affects the whole question. They are 'one person in law.' This Mr. Mill asserts to be a cruel fiction. It is utterly contrary to the idea of two equally endowed, similarly able persons entering into a contract of mutual profit and assistance. It is here that we completely join issue with the so-called champion of women. It is here also that the real principle comes in, which he has treated, externally, as a matter of legislation alone – and far though we should be from placing ourselves on any other question on the same level with Mr. Mill, we have a conviction that in this point we speak with a fuller knowledge of the feeling of women, who are the parties most concerned. And we assert that this faulty law has yet amid all its offensive and tyrannical enactments caught sight of the principle in which lies all the difficulties of the question, and which Mr. Mill ignores. It is, that the man and the woman united in the first of all primitive bonds, the union upon which the world and the race depend, *are* one person. We say it not sentimentally or poetically, but with the profoundest sense of reality and seriousness. If they were two the matter would be easy. It would but be to establish the balance by law as Mr. Mill suggests and to keep it even; a business requiring the watchfulness of Argus, yet probably manageable by dint of pains and trouble. The secret of all that is hard and dangerous and bewildering in the matter, is simply the fact that in very truth the two *are* one.

We cannot, indeed, believe that any candid reader can fairly look the question in the face, and accept an explanation of it which so resolutely skims the surface. If the highest claim of woman was, as Mr. Mill declares, that of being a perfectly equal and similar creature, occupying exactly the same ground and possessing the same powers as man, in respect to intellect, character, and endowments, then there could remain no doubt of woman's fundamental inferiority on any reasonable mind. We repeat: if they are precisely the same kind of being with no differences except those which are physical, then we allow without a moment's hesitation that women are the natural inferiors of men. Equality must embrace the whole being; it cannot be taken as belonging only to a part of it. And woman is confessedly and unmistakeably man's inferior in one part of her being; therefore, unless she is as unmistakeably his superior in another, she can have no claim to consider herself his equal. Now it cannot be asserted for an instant that she is notably his superior in intellect; all that the boldest theoriser ever dreams of asserting is that she is equal with him in that particular, while she is manifestly not equal to him in bodily strength and personal courage. Thus in every way in which we can put the comparison, so long as we examine the two as competitors for one prize, her inferiority is marked and undeniable. If we could say, the woman is weaker, less courageous, incapable of the violent exertion which comes natural to her companion, and which is necessary for the maintenance of life; but at the same time she has a greater power of thought, a much higher grasp of the necessities of the position, a mind which can guide him in his ruder work – we should then be at ease in the contrast and feel that the point of equality had been reached. But this it is altogether out of our power to say. That her intellect is as good as his, is all that we can assert, and even this with hesitation and uncertainty; but then intellect is but one part, and her other powers are not so good as his. Must we therefore conclude that the woman is inferior? Taking Mr. Mill's ground that she is exactly the same kind of creature as the man, we are certainly driven to that conclusion. We cannot get out of it by any expedient of logic. We have no superfluity on one side to put against the want in the other. Equal in one point she is deficient in another, and deficiency means inferiority. With all our desire to make out a flaw, we are obliged to yield before the facts which will allow no comparison. Not being a man's superior anyhow, in natural constitution, she cannot be man's equal, let us twist the matter how we will.

But let us turn for one moment to the other view of the question. It is that a woman is a woman, and not a lesser edition of man. The competition in which we are for ever labouring to involve them, has no existence in nature. They are not rivals, nor antagonists. They are two halves of a complete being. The offices they hold in the world are essentially different. There is scarcely any natural standing ground which we can realise on which these two creatures appear as rivals. The very thought is preposterous. Shall the woman challenge the man to a trial of strength? Shall the man pit himself against the woman for delicacy of eye and taste? Shall she plough the heavy fields with him, wading through the new-turned mould, or shall he watch the children with her, patient through the weary vigil? An exchange of place and toil, the man taking the indoor work and the woman the outdoor, in order to prove the futility of their mutual discontent, was a favourite subject with the old ballad-makers; and the witty minstrel is generally very great on the domestic confusion that follows, and gives the wife the best of it. But the fact is that such a rivalry can by nothing but a jest. The two are not rivals, they are not alike. They are different creatures. They are one.

To illustrate this theory we have but to look at the life which they lead together. Civilisation has a wonderful faculty for altering and confounding the natural conditions of existence. But in primitive circumstances it is always the man who is the bestower of material advantages; it is his to give, to provide for, to labour, to protect. He is the bread-winner – the strength is his. It is he alone who without intermission can face the outside world, and force a subsistence out of the reluctant soil or the barren seas. When the typical pair set out together who are to found all human economies, all domestic relations, and from whom the new life is to proceed – and every new pair is but a repetition of the first – nature places them at once with a certainty beyond theory in their traditional places. The woman has an office to perform which renders unremitting labour impossible to her. She is the fountain of life, bound by all the laws of her nature to guard the sacred seed and bring it forth to crush the serpent's head, and fill the world with increase and gladness. The man may shirk his work, but hers she cannot shirk. And in the pride and joy of her special office there mingles a sacred shame which compels her to intervals of seclusion and avoidance of the world's gaze. Her life is interrupted, broken up into morsels; now she can go forth, can work if it be needful, can use in any way that may be necessary the faculties that God has given her: and anon there comes a time in which all such labours must be suspended in consideration of something else which God has given her to do. But the man has no interruptions to his life; his strength is steady without breach or variation. What partnership is there that can have any analogy with this? Let us suppose that they laboured together in their Eden a little while, scarcely knowing which was which in the first sweet unity of being. And then the time came when he went out alone to labour, and she in her sanctity of weakness stayed at home. When he returned how could it be otherwise than that one for whom he had been toiling all day should meet him with offices of service, with domestic ministrations, with grateful lessening of herself and magnifying of him? From that moment must not equality have fled to the winds like all other foolish pretences? The man was out all day toiling, struggling, meeting the winds and the storm, the sun beating on his head, the powers of nature resisting him; what could he be but king when he returned to that first hut or hovel and stretched out his weary limbs by the new-lighted fire? Service was his due. The food he had earned, must it not be offered to him, with observances copied afar off from those with which the gifts of His giving were offered back again to God? The imagination refuses to believe in, refuses to frame, any other conception. His inferior – that might or might not be – but his servant, yes – his minister, the natural Second, the born solace and consolation. When we cast our eyes back to the primeval husband and wife – when we turn to any subsequent pair who have ever set out upon the world like Adam and Eve, we find the same course of events recurring in infallible sequence. This is fact and nature let theory say what it will. The woman in such a union is in no way called upon to be the man's inferior. She may be intellectually his superior even, and it will not change the course of nature. She will serve him should all the world interfere to prevent her. She will spread his table, and watch his wishes, and give him of his own, with rites of gratitude, with flowers and incense, and a whole liturgy of ministration. Eve would have done it had Mr. Mill been there ever so distinctly, shaking his head at her, and bidding her remember the rules of equality. Equality! what does it mean? Has it any existence as between any two people in intimate relations on the face of the earth? And were it established over and over, were it measureable by line and weight like any tangible material, what place is there for its consideration between the two thus linked and bound together, the one the supplement of the other? Man goes out to his work and labour till the evening. Woman prepares for him, waits for him, serves him at home. So natural is this, that when, as the case may be, it is a woman who is the bread-winner for a household of women, the worker is turned into an impromptu superior on the spot, and served and waited on as the man in other circumstances is waited on and served. It is the hire of the labourer, the reward of the provider; an instinctive law which antedates all legislation, and lies at the very root and beginning of all human affairs.

Thus, though we have declared without hesitation our belief that the law which takes all property and all right from married women is an insult and injustice, equally cruel and unwise, we are ready to grant as frankly that the economical position of man is that of the superior, the first in the natural hierarchy. He it is whose office is to maintain, support, and protect. He may not always be equal to the duties of this office. He may by nature be no more powerful, no more stedfast, no more trustworthy, in fact, than the wife who is recognised as dependent on him. But in his official position he stands first, and has in his favour all the instincts and prejudices of nature. It is vain to assert of a rule which is so universal that it originates in the arbitrary will of the stronger half of the species. We might say on the contrary, with much greater appearance of justice, that it is women who have framed this infallible law. Every observer, whose eyes are open to the common facts about him, will see it re-enacted every day by every bride who crosses the threshold of a new household. Mr. Mill will tell us that this is the result of defective education, and of the long habit of slavery; but let him take the most high-spirited young woman he can find, trained in his own school, and roused to full defence of the theoretical rights of her sex by the enthusiasm of youth and vehement sectarian education, and let her but marry a man she loves, and the philosopher will find the code re-established, it may be secretly, it may be with a sense of guilt and confusion, and even treachery to her own cause, ere she has well taken her place in her new kingdom. She may rule her husband even, yet she will serve him; she may lead him blindfold by right of love, or wit, or superior character, and yet she will minister to him, wait upon him, offer him sacrifices as if she were the commonest daughter of Eve. For were the confusing conditions of our civilisation abolished, along with dowers and laws of property and marriage settlements, would it not be his office to work for her? His it must be to protect her, whatever external dangers come their way; his to toil when Providence forbids her from toiling; his to stand between her and the world, and screen off from her at those moments when nature demands seclusion, the offensive gaze of the crowd. Far be it from us to dwell with prurient sentiment upon the details of that grand function which is the distinguishing work of woman in the world. But any theory of her being which ignores it, or gives it a secondary place, or in any way whatever leaves it out of the calculation, is inevitably a futile theory. Let us imagine even that at other times she may be capable of maintaining her own independence and securing her livelihood apart from the help of man – yet at these times she is not so capable. It is then that his strength who is liable to no interruption asserts its superiority. He has nothing to do which calls him off his day's work, prompts him to seek the covert, puts him aside from ordinary employments. Such a fact makes rivalry utterly impossible. It would be as reasonable to expect that a soldier engaged in a dangerous campaign, and with the necessity upon him of periodically confronting death, and running all the risks of a battle, should at the same time compete with a civilian in some art or handicraft. The comparison is weak, for there is no reason why the soldier should not be in robust health up to the moment of marching, and it is his own life only which is concerned. But the women who are men's wives are bound in most cases to undergo periodically a risk which is as great as that which any individual soldier encounters in a battle. And they have not only to brace their nerves to encounter this danger for themselves, but it is their grand moment of responsibility, when they must vindicate the trust reposed in them by God and the world. Can there be any doubt that this essential element of her life at once and for ever disables a woman from all trial of strength and rude equality with man? Nobody but a fool, we believe, will assert that the burden of this great trust stamps her as inferior. It would be just as reasonable to say that it gave her a superior place in the economy of nature as the possessor of a faculty more utterly essential to the continuance of the race. But there can be no doubt about the fact that it separates her and her work and her office from the office and work of man. The two are not made to contend and compete and run races for the same prize. There is no natural opposition, but on the contrary harmony unbounded in their differences of nature – harmony which can never be attained by two creatures framed on the self-same plan.

And thus, we repeat, the old harsh contemptuous law which Mr. Mill condemns, and which we no less condemn, melts into a certain sense of the necessities of nature which he refuses to acknowledge. With an economic provision for this most important of woman's disabilities, it qualifies her husband to act for her at all times, and binds him to provide for her. Marriage has its conditions which are hard upon him as well as upon her. He cannot be free any more than she is. By the laws of equality, might not he too demand to leave off his work by times, and let her shift for herself? The hardships are not all on her side. He must go on whether he likes it or no, while she may pause and rest; there can be no break in his labours, for everything depends upon him; not only the moral but a legal obligation binds him hand and foot. He is as subject as his wife is. The claims made upon him by her needs and the needs of her children impede his natural liberty as completely as the yoke of conjugal submission does hers. An unmarried man moves lightly about the world, consulting his own pleasure or advantage, following the suggestions of his own fancy, taking the path that pleases him best, or changing his course as inclination and circumstances suggest. But all this freedom of action is lost for a man when he marries. He has given, as we say, hostages to society. He has to do henceforward not what he likes, but what he must; he has to earn bread not lightly for one, but painfully for two, or three, or any indefinite ever-increasing number. He has to sustain and shield and bear with the weaknesses of a companion, whose private share of the troubles of life must prevent her from being always the delight to him which she is supposed to be at the outset. Thus he buys his economic post of superiority dearly enough; and he cannot

abandon it. He, too, may find it oppressive by times, and if
he is not insulted by any assault upon his identity on the part
of the law, he is subject to the onslaught of Mr. Mill, for
example, no contemptible assailant, and has to submit to be
told that he is a tyrant and oppressor, the representative of a
long line of oppressors, the last slaveholder left in a reformed
world. While we write, a sense of pity for man comes over us.
And he behaves very well on the whole under the circumstances. He utters very few serious moans over his disabilities
and his bondage. Sometimes, it is true, the poor soul permits
himself a jeer, not so much at his wife as at her friends. But
when we think of it, it is seldom he who discloses the secrets
of the prison-house, or laments over his lost liberty. Is there
not here a certain self-renunciation as well as on the other
side? Another kind of equality not recognised by Mr. Mill –
the equality of common sacrifices, common self-denials,
mutual aids, interposition of the strength of one to succour
the weakness of another, of the service of one to recompense
the fatigues of another, of perpetual interchange, sympathy,
and help – reveals itself when we look at the world through
the daylight and not through any philosophical spectacles. As
a speculation, we might almost say that the theory of man's
position as the sustainer and protector of woman was man's
invention – and that the theory of woman's subjection was
woman's corollary to that first grand principle. Did Mr. Mill
succeed to-morrow to free the weaker sex from all disabilities, and proclaim their absolutely equal rights, he
would find the ancient circle recommence from the moment
that the two recommenced their life. Next day the new
bridegroom would go forth from his chamber rejoicing to toil
for the being he loved best, and next evening the bride would
fly to her door to greet the returning labourer, would spread
his board and serve his food, and recognise herself as the
Second, not the First. Amen! In such a union we recognise a
dignity and harmony which exists in no other partnership.
Men are bad and women are bad, and the whole matter
sometimes ends in misery, and chaos, and warfare, all the
most dreadful because the bond ought to produce the highest
peace and content. But that is not the fault of law or of
nature, or of anything but those evil tendencies to which the
race is undeniably liable, and from which we have no present
prospect of being ever completely set free.

As for the possession of political power by a married woman in independence of that possessed by her husband, we cannot but feel the idea to run counter to the whole theory of married life. This is not to say that the woman is to take no interest in politics, to form no opinions, to be politically dead. But there is no social justice in giving to two people so closely bound by all the complications of nature as to be, to all intents and purposes one, two voices in the commonwealth. This is as much as to abrogate altogether the family constitution, the first primitive constituency. We have pointed out, we trust with sufficient clearness, the impossibility of woman holding her own as against man in any race of individualities; but when she is united to man, perfecting and being perfected by the conjunction, it is unjust to the rest of the world that this composite being should have two voices in the sway of the world. It is one, not in imagination but in reality, and why should it speak as for two? Nobody who has ever come into collision (being but a solitary individual) with a pair of married persons will fail to see the weight of this. The double being is so strong in its double sense of one interest, so curiously wrapt in its compound adherence to its one opinion, that the single opponent is generally wound to a point of exasperation which no encounter with another solitary would produce. For there can be little doubt that the two will almost invariably agree, whether by better information on one side – and that without doubt the man's – or by stronger feeling on some special point, which may just as likely be the woman's – in which case the effect would be simply that one opinion would obtain two expressions. If, on the contrary, the two disagreed, it would not only introduce a jar into their union, but would be a simple stultification of the family voice and obliteration of its influence. In this, as in so many other things, it seems to us a positive impossibility to sever the two who are one. They have one home, one interest, one place in the world; the one, whenever absent, is represented in an expressible but perfectly real way by the other. We cannot explain how it is, but we know that it is. They agree together, whatever may be their differences between themselves, to maintain in almost all ordinary matters a policy of unanimity before the world, knowing well that their one voice thus united is worth far more than it would be divided. Nature thus demonstrates the wisest mode of procedure; for there is no law which forbids a woman in other matters from standing on her own opinion and saying her independent say; and we are not blind enough to believe that she is so intimidated as to be afraid of expressing herself on common subjects. Here, once more, it is not a matter of individual right, but of social necessity and policy, and what we may call the economics of humanity. The two have given up their separate privileges, which is the fundamental question – they have relinquished the right to live where they like, to do what they like, with little less abandonment on one side than the other. And to give one interest two voices, one thought two expressions, would be not to ease but to complicate the workings of government, whether in its higher or in its lower levels.

This part of the subject brings us suddenly to an entirely new class and new matter of discussion. Mr. Mill's book is in a great measure about wives and their miseries, but the atmosphere in it is not the atmosphere of wedlock. We seem to perceive as we read the presence around the philosopher of an audience totally different from that common mass of humanity which toils along the weary ways of the world two by two, with minds so much occupied by practical toils and difficulties as to have little time for fine discussions. A woman in the heat of her natural work, with her husband to care for, and her children to bring up, has seldom leisure to measure herself against him or any other man she meets and speculate which is the tallest. Neither has an ordinary man, with his daily work to do, much time to waste in such speculations. In ordinary life, notwithstanding what the newspapers say and the 'Saturday Review,' men do not generally despise their wives. They have got to know in most cases after a few years what each other's opinion is practically worth. And their consultations are not biassed by any theory about the abstract weight attaching to a man's or a woman's advice. The fact is it is Mary's opinion and not the abstract woman's which her husband cares for. And when she asks herself what John will say, it is not any immediate sense of subjection to the abstract man which mingles with her anxiety. But apart from these matter-of-fact ordinarily-occupied people, who fulfil the duties of their several sexes without carrying the distinction consciously about with them, there is a class of which we desire to speak with all respect, which is gradually becoming more and more influential, so far, at least, as speech goes, to which all Mr.

Mill's arguments more distinctly refer, and which, indeed, in some degree occupies the theoretical position he claims for womankind – we mean the class of highly cultivated, able, mature, unmarried women who have never undergone the natural experiences of their sex, and really feel themselves in the position to compete with men, without fear or favour. This class is rarely taken into account in any discussion of the claims of women, yet it has inspired all such discussions, and is the only portion of the sex which can really benefit by them. Their influence is apparent in everything Mr. Mill says – which may be supposed an injurious suggestion to make, but is not really so – for they are, without doubt, intellectually superior to the ordinary mass of women, and still more certainly are much more like men. We repeat that we desire to speak of them with all respect. Looking at them from a point of view totally different from their own, we can yet grant to these exceptional women the applause due to high motives, high spirit, great activity and independence of thought, perfect purity of intention, and the most generous desire to help and further all good works. At the height of life and health, superior to other women by their exemption from all the disabling consequences of marriage, superior to men by their more perfect temperance and self-restraint, it is but natural that they should resent with fiery indignation not unmingled with a certain bitter amusement, the vulgar theory of woman's inferiority. They know themselves full of power to work and act as men do, and can perceive no reason why they should be limited to those arts of domestic management and industry which are the natural accompaniments of a life interrupted by childbirth and absorbed in family cares. Their lives are subject to no interruption; they are as free as men, as able for fatigue, as ready to embark in any venture. Their education may not be so thorough – at least it is probably not classical – but in knowledge of the world and experience of it, in acquaintance with modern literature and the habits of the modern mind, they feel themselves no whit inferior. And if they ever dreamt of union with the other section of humanity, the dream has either passed away or changed in character. To them the plea of equality is natural – they have declined to accept any other standing-ground. Why should not all the professions of men be open to them? why should they lie under arbitrary disabilities which have not been laid on them by nature? Our old scruples and precautions are simply unmeaning to them, not because of any unwomanliness on their part, but because they have passed the age at which one set of scruples operate, and have kept themselves free from those engagements which promote another. And if Mr. Mill or any other social reformer asks us candidly why these women should not exercise the suffrage or any other right they happen to covet, we feel ourselves driven into a corner, and have no answer to make. They are as strong, as courageous, as clever as their masculine contemporaries. They have no occasion to hide themselves, no mystery going on within them which shrinks from the eye of day. Their lives stretch on clear before them like those of men, unhampered by any of the usual feminine burdens. In short, they are quite able to stand up and try their strength against the first-comer. And if we are to be asked why should not they? we can give no satisfactory reply. Why not if they like it, is all the faltering response we can make. We might jeer at their boldness, but that is a cheap and not very telling argument. We might thunder against their unwomanliness and beat them back to the level of their sex, but that would be futile, and it would be foolish. They are quite able to judge for themselves, and we have no right to beat them back. If they like it why should not they have votes? Their position is exceptional, and so it is quite possible may be their rights. There is no precedent on the subject. Such a class has no place in the primitive records, and frankly we have no reasoning to bring to bear upon them. They are very well able to manage their own lives and those of their dependents, and we can give no reason why they should not be able to manage a learned profession or some department of public life. We have our prejudices, but we have no right to guide our fellow-creatures by our prejudices; and no rational creature can assert, at least with any hope of being able to believe his own assertion, that a young fellow of four or five and twenty, just emancipated from the bondage of education, is by mere right of his manhood able to judge on any public or political question better than a highly educated woman ten or fifteen years his senior, who probably fills a much more important place than he does in the world. Any such assertion would be ridiculous. The woman has most likely fifty times more experience, more practical knowledge, possibly more common sense, almost certainly more education except as regards Latin and Greek; and to tell us that she is not equally able to choose her county member, or for that matter if she likes it, to propose him on the hustings, is simple nonsense. Why should not she do it, if she has a mind? The question is so utterly unanswerable that it awakens within us a certain comic bewilderment. Why should not she? For our own part we know of no reply.

If she likes it, the chances are that she would be of admirable use in many practical matters, and could work upon committees, and manage poor-laws, and education, and reformatory movements, and boards of works, and all the benevolent-political work of the country, as well as any set of men. She is as she declares herself to be, a force unemployed, a capacity going to waste, and if she chooses to enforce and insist upon her rights, we cannot see what reasonable argument can be brought against her: nor have we any doubt that she will obtain them in the long run, if she perseveres; and she is sure to persevere.

This is one curious fact, however, to be noted in passing, on this branch of the subject. When the class of independent, house-holding, and wealth-possessing women is referred to publicly, it is generally described as composed of the unmarried and widows. Many of the latter, we all know, have a man's work and responsibility thrust upon them, in respect to everything but politics; they have estates to manage, children to bring up, the well-being of many dependents in their hands. And they have gone through all the experiences of life, and have had a double share of its practical education. The curious fact to which we have referred is, that very few, if any, women of this class have publicly joined the agitation for political rights. Their claim would be even less answerable than that of the unmarried. Yet they do not seem to think the privilege worth asking for. How does this happen? Wives demand it, who have already a share in their husbands' voice; but the widow makes no demand. Is it that life is too busy with her to leave room for the franchise, or too serious to be lightened by it? The silence is as strange a fact as any in the story of this agitation.

But the able, stedfast, self-sustaining being above described is not a type of ordinary women; she is not even a type of the mass of the unmarried, whose numbers we have so perpetually dinned into our ears, but for whom Mr. Mill on the whole has but little to say. On the other hand, the authors of 'Woman's

Work' have a great deal to say for them, and enforce their rights to labour with reasonings sometimes sensible, but sometimes infinitely droll; as when Miss Jessie Boucherett appeals to the men and hairdressers of England with a highly-wrought and sometimes indignant eloquence to emigrate, and leave their places to the unemployed women! This question, too, is of an entirely practical character, a matter which cannot be settled on any general principle, but rather by the rules of possibility and expediency. We believe, for our own part, for instance, that educated medical women well qualified to treat female diseases would be a great boon to society. In one special branch of practice they would be simply invaluable, and such a consolation to suffering women as only women can fully understand. Even now in the existing state of affairs, the services of women imperfectly educated are eagerly taken advantage of, and the comfort it would be to many a painworn creature to see a person of her own sex at her bedside is simply incalculable. Doctors are very kind and sympathetic as a rule, and the whispered scandals which sometimes breathe about the corners of society as to the disadvantages in point of morality of their close attendance upon their female patients are, we believe, as diabolically unfounded as Miss Jex-Blake in her article on the subject of Medical Education for Women indignantly declares them to be. But still every medical man must know how women shrink from the statement of their own symptoms in serious and delicate cases; and how universally the patient's story has to be filtered through some female attendant, who may on her part boggle over the tale, and is certainly not bound to understand it. It is easy to laugh at Dr. Mary and Dr. Lucy; and, indeed, laughter has for long been the understood way, and a very cheap one, of begging the whole question. But this special advantage is one which we believe medical men themselves will not deny the truth of, and which women in general, who must be the best judges in the matter, would pray for with all their hearts. There would be of course, to start with, a certain terror of trusting themselves in untried hands; but this doubt has but to be removed to make women unanimous, we believe, on this point.

This is one thing, however, and the education which qualifies for it is another, and there are difficulties in respect to that, and all other professional training which are far from easy to deal with. Miss Jex-Blake in the essay already referred to, and which is beyond question the most valuable of the series, has given a very clear account of the difficulties attending medical education as respects admission to universities, studying along with the ordinary students. &c. From this it will be evident to the reader, that the steady energy and devotion to her object which a woman must possess in order to acquire the knowledge necessary to her entrance into this profession, are of so high an order as to raise her entirely above the level of those ordinary unenthusiastic neophytes who do their work because they are obliged to do it, and are doctors because their parents destine them to be so. It can only be a personal choice, and the strongest bias of mind and sense of duty, which could nerve a young woman to confront all these obstacles, and force her way in spite of them. We avow that we do not understand how it can be done at all – but it has been done, and we are not called upon to understand but only to acknowledge the fact. We ought to add to all we have already said, a hope that henceforward the barriers will be removed and the entrance into those fields of learning made easy for every woman who chooses it. But the hope fails somehow at the moment of utterance. Not that we dislike female doctors, or fail to appreciate the admirable places they might fill and the good they would do; but because, frankly, professional education for women is a thing in which our belief is very limited. Of all the numberless crusades of the day there has been none more warm and lively than that which takes up the question of female education generally. There have been so many words expended on the subject that we are reluctant to enter into it with further waste of breath; but yet it is a branch of the general subject, and cannot be dismissed without notice. The result of the present commotion of the public mind on this point seems to be a general feeling that to extend that monotonous classical training in respect to which, for our boys, we now and then take a cold shiver of apprehension, asking ourselves with doubts which it is difficult to silence, is this really the best we can do for them? – to our girls, is to do them the fullest justice, and to provide for all possible necessities. We are aware, all the same, that when the preparation for actual life commences in any but an academical career, we have to tear our sons away from the traditions of school and compel them to 'go in' for a totally distinct kind of training; but yet we are told that an entirely superior new generation of women will be produced when we succeed in tying our girls to the system of education thus proved futile for all but one special class of our boys. This is surely a very unreasonable conclusion. So far as the higher classes are concerned, who can choose their own education, it seems to us that there is a great deal to be said in favour of the present theory, which makes living languages the portion of the sister, while the brother is fighting his way through Ovid and Catullus: and if, as so often happens, it is she, and not he, who reads Dante and Goethe, is she really so much his inferior in point of intellectual training? It is far from our desire to say a word which should imply indifference to the spread of education; but if women are virgin soil, as people say, in this respect, why should we conclude indiscriminately that the thing best to do for them is to extend to them the monotonous supremacy of an education which many of us regard as unsuitable for half at least of the minds at present subjected to it? If ever there was a case for selection, surely this would be the opportunity; though the authorities generally seem to prefer imitation and uniformity. With the same curious repetition of past efforts, we find that the courses of lectures which were to make our working men into sages and heroes, are cropping up again for the benefit of women. Even in such a matter as this are we never to find anything new under the sun?

But when we turn to the consideration of professional education for girls, we feel that we have returned to the general fundamental conditions of women, and can only argue the one question by an appeal to the other. Professional education in man occupies all the season of youth. He has reached his majority at least before he is qualified to put his powers to the test, and exercise the knowledge he has gained. Unless he steps into an exceptional position, reaping the benefit of some one else's labours, the first ten or fifteen years of manhood are spend in a struggle for position more or less hard in proportion to his talents and his character, and his power of awaiting a slow result. Under favourable circumstances, of course, this struggle is not mortal, but it always requires the man's full force, his clearest judgement, and most careful labour. If he is prosperously established in the exercise of his profession at thirty-five, with a clear prospect of gain and social honour, he has done as well as he could possibly hope, and can look forward with tolerable confidence on the career before him.

During this early struggle he has to exert all his powers; if he pauses for a moment he knows that it is at the hazard not of losing that moment alone but of sacrificing ten times its value. The road is so uphill that he slides down one step for every three he makes, and is aware that to stop short or turn aside on the way is destruction. A temporary illness sometimes neutralises years of labour: he must be always at his post, pushing on with speed unbroken. Should he fall some one else is ready to jostle him out of the already too crowded way. Such is a very ordinary statement of the usual difficulties which beset the path, say, of a young physician; and the other professions are not less toilsome. Let us see what effect these obstacles would have on the career of the candidate were it a woman and not a man.

The first thing we have to imagine is that the girl's entire youth, its bloom, and softest years should be passed like that of the young man in the steady pursuit of knowledge. At one-and-twenty, by the devotion of all her youth, she is qualified to enter upon the practice of her profession; when lo! there appears at the threshold of life the most natural of all interruptions to a young woman's career, a young husband ready to take upon himself the charge of her fortunes. She is married let us suppose, her education being no bar to the exercise of the primitive duties of her sex; and let us also imagine that she is loth to sacrifice at a stroke the labours of so many years, and that she attempts to combine professional exertions with the duties of a wife. She works for a year, let us say with intermissions, finding it more and more difficult to maintain her place against the lively competition of men who have no divided duty. Then she is stopped short by the inevitable discharge of the primary function of woman. This business over, she resumes again with a heart and attention sorely divided between the claims of the infant she leaves at home and the duties she finds outside. During the interval of her seclusion, however restricted in point of time, every one of her male competitors has made a stride before her. Faltering and discouraged she resumes her laborious way; and if she has the energy of half a dozen men in her single person, if her courage is indomitable, and her determination sublime, she perhaps manages by a strain of mind and body which it would be impossible to continue long, to make up half of the ground she has lost; when lo another interruption comes, and she has to step aside again and bear her feminine burden, and see her competitors, light and unladen, stride past once more. This is the inevitable course, known only too well to every woman who has endeavoured to combine professional exertions with the ordinary duties of a man's wife. Other complications such as we shrink from mentioning, probably come in to to take all the elasticity out of a mind so burdened. Her children born amid these cares, and injured before their birth by the undue activity of brain which weakens their mother's physical powers, come into the world feeble or die in her arms, quenching out her courage in the bitterest waves of personal suffering. This is no fancy picture. At every step in her career it becomes less possible for her to maintain the unequal conflict. Her competitors have marched far before her, while she toils and strives midway on the steep ascent. They have gone on without intermission; she has had to stop short again and again in her course. With what sickness of heart, with what a weary hopeless sense of the unattainable, and desperate consciousness of the mistake, she maintains the struggle, only they can tell who have done it, and happily the number is not great. Such is all that a woman has to expect who attempts to combine the work of a man to which she has been trained with the common duties of female life.

On the other hand, let us suppose that she puts aside the profession she has acquired and gives herself up to domesticity and wifehood until the period of childbearing is over, and her special responsibilities so far accomplished. This period cannot be estimated at less than twenty years. It may be considerably shorter; it is sometimes longer; but we are not understating the possibilities if we grant that at forty she may consider herself emancipated from woman's natural disabilities, and may stretch out her hands towards the tools which she put from her all new and shining at one-and-twenty. Will these tools have improved or will they have deteriorated in the meantime? Will her training of twenty years ago come back all fresh to her memory as if it had been but twenty days? Will the world be so good as to stand still in the meantime and keep everything just as it was in the days of her apprenticeship that she may begin again with some chance of success? Alas, no! this is precisely what the world will not do. She will find her fellow-students a hundred miles ahead of her, and their sons ready to tread on her heels and gibe at her old-world principles. She will be of the old school, before she has even begun to put in practice her

rusty knowledge. She will feel in herself the painful consciousness of faculties blunted by want of use, and powers numbed
by long inaction. If she is a wonderful woman, with the energy
of half a dozen men, she will perhaps make a desperate effort
and force her way alongside of some plodding bungler whose
indolence or stupidity have left him out of the race. This is the
best that can befall her is she adopts this second course and
waits until she can give to her profession the matured and
steady powers of middle age.

There is, however, an alternative open to her. She can take a
vow of celibacy. She can throw off altogether the yoke of
nature, and fit herself to compete with man by consciously and
voluntarily rejecting the life of woman. This is a possibility
which is not to be rejected with disdain as out of the question.
If all is true that we continually read about the number of
women who cannot marry, it is no unfit question for the more
resolute souls among them, whether they should not make up
their minds that they will not marry, and thus qualify
themselves by one severe yet effectual effort for an existence
resembling that of man. By this means alone can they procure
for themselves fair play in the world, or a reasonable chance of
success in any profession. But this is a penalty which perhaps
not one of all their male fellow-students would undertake to
pay; and it is the most cruel renunciation which can be exacted
from a human creature. Thus success in a profession – nay, the
mere initiatory possibility of success – requires from a woman
not equality with man, but an amount of intellectual and moral
superiority over him, which can only be found in the rarest and
most isolated cases. To him the prospect of marriage is the
strongest incentive to industry and exertion. To her it is simple
ruin, so far as her work is concerned. If then she has the
magnanimity and self-devotion to cut herself off from all that is
popularly considered happiness in life – from all that youth
most dreams of, and the heart most cares for – she is free to
enter into and pursue, and very likely will succeed in a
profession, which men, with all solaces of love and help of
companionship, pursue by her side at not half the cost. Perhaps
even then, after she has made this sacrifice, she will find that
she is the pot of earth making her way among their pots of iron;
and that their superior physical powers and bolder temperament will carry them beyond her, notwithstanding the superior
devotion she has shown and the price she has paid. But this is

the best we can promise her when all is done – to (perhaps) succeed as well, at the cost of everything, as her competitors who go into it with the commonest of motives and at no cost at all.

This is a very serious, very weighty consideration at the outset of a career. Professional education too is very costly, and the parents of young women to whom self-support is necessary are not generally rolling in wealth; can we then wonder at their reluctance to purchase dearly such a training for their daughter knowing that the expense will most probably be all in vain, and indeed hoping that her first step in actual life will be to render herself incapable of her profession by a happy marriage? We do not for one moment deny that the picture we have just drawn, and the truth of which we are but too certainly aware of, is the very contrary of encouraging to those hapless women who are seeking work to do and know not where to find it. We acknowledge sadly that it is not encouraging, but it is better to face the truth than to ignore it. These things would remain true were all the colleges in Christendom thrown open to-morrow with all their means of instruction to the girl-graduates, who, we are told, thirst for improved education. By all means, we say, let them be thrown open. Let all contemptuous laws that teach fools to sneer at the mother who bore them be erased from our statute-book. Let the women who stand apart from woman's natural existence, be it by choice, be it by necessity, be permitted to assume men's privileges if they choose. And what then, oh daughters of Eve? The most of you will still be wives, will still be mothers all the same, will still lie under nature's own disabilities and be trusted with nature's high responsibilities, and have your work to do, which no man is capable of doing instead of you. Legislation may help the surplus, the exceptional women. If it does really aid them to find a practicable standing ground it will do well; but for the majority, legislation can do little and revolution nothing at all.

There are a great many more points in both the books before us which we should have been glad to notice had our space served. There are, for instance, a number of impertinences in some of the essays in 'Woman's Work,' especially those contributed by men, which we should imagine the ladies concerned must find it hard to swallow. Mr. Stuart, for instance, is so good as to tell us, as several gentlemen have done recently in the newspapers, that women are capable of understanding popular lectures about science, and can put very pertinent questions, and write very creditable papers, – information which we receive without astonishment, and we fear with scarcely so much gratification as it is intended to produce. And Miss Boucherett, as we have already said, appeals eloquently to every young hairdresser, and to most young men, whether it would not be better for them to emigrate without more ado, and leave their work to their sisters, who otherwise would find no occupation. But why should the poor fellows emigrate? This is carrying chivalry to a very fine point indeed, and the woman who calls upon men to make such a sacrifice has evidently a beautiful faith in them, such as rarely survives much encounter of reality. Then Miss Wedgewood, in her argument for the *Female Suffrage*, takes up the question which we have just been discussing from the opposite side, with a curious reversal of the argument. She complains of the fact that young women are hampered in their early education by the possibility which lies before them of an event which will influence the whole course of their lives. 'She may try to read history, to teach poor children, to cultivate a musical talent; but for a certain interval all is vague and difficult. The question, Is this to go on? takes the edge off any pursuit, and draws off interest to a possible future which has no continuity with the present. . . . She has to ignore the possibility which may change her whole framework of life as nothing changes a man's life, and to profess an entire absence of anticipation as to the one event which for a time fills her whole horizon.' This Miss Wedgewood considers an argument for the bestowal of the franchise, which will elevate the girl's mind, and turn her to thoughts of other matters more essential than the theory of domestic life, which she justly describes as the necessity of getting married. We should ourselves be much more disposed to say that it was an argument in favour of the French mode of managing matrimonial affairs, by which the young lady would be relieved from this vague interval of uncertainty; for after all, franchise or no franchise, women must marry or the world would soon come to an end. And the very fact that marriage 'changes the whole framework' of a woman's life as 'nothing changes a man,' is the proof of proofs that this possibility cannot be ignored, that it must influence education, and her maiden training, and her thoughts. But we have not room to enter at greater length into all the strange speculations which have grown around this subject. The singular way in which one writer after another accepts, without examination, a foregone conclusion, and builds upon a prejudice as if it were an unquestionable truth – the curious assumption by the very writers who set themselves forth as champions of women, of woman's profound ignorance, triviality, and want of harmony with the world around her, strikes the observer with the strangest sense of limitation and unreality. 'The mental gifts which would raise a man to the woolsack may make a cultivated woman,' says Miss Wedgewood; but why so? Women have money, and the best teachers in the world are to be obtained by money; they have leisure – too much of it they all tell us; printing was invented, how many hundred years ago? and all the books that are now printed are purchasable, and may be learned and read. To what then are we to attribute the extraordinary efforts necessary to make a cultivated woman? No doubt the writer herself is one. To our humble thinking there are a great many to be found about the world. And how bewildering, how unmeaning, how falsely sublime is this strange statement? On the other hand a curious list of learned women chiefly professors in Italian colleges in the Middle Ages seems to have been handed about from one essayist to another, and appears at full length three times at least, by way of proving that after all women are capable of something. Is there nothing in the world to show for that but the fact that Maria Gaetana Agnesi was a Professor of Mathematics in 1750, and that Betisia Gozzadini lectured in law in 1236? Good heavens, ladies! have you never an old nurse about your houses who has more good sense in her good grey head than half the men who moon about your salons? Do not we all know what our mothers were? and, whisper in your ears, have you not in your own persons a certain power of holding your own, were all Oxford brought against you? Such certainly is our belief. We are fully convinced that there are a great many highly cultivated women to be met with in these days. And Mr. Mill, who is probably a much better judge, thinks so too, with an oft-expressed devotion which cannot but soften towards him every feminine critic. Modern language and literature may not be equal to the antique; but yet they count for something, and women of the upper classes are at least free to attain perfection if they will in these branches of knowledge. And women of the lower classes possess in plenty, if not education, at least that gift of intelligence which, we confess to our own thinking, is the most attractive of all human gifts. We would not close a single classroom, nor shut up a single source of knowledge against those who thirst for it; we would gladly see all arbitrary restrictions upon individuals abolished; we would joyfully hail anything practical that anyone could suggest to touch the vast mass of misery which lies down in the depths, and which, as Mrs. Butler well and feelingly observes, attains an intensity of degradation which nothing can equal in man; though that no doubt partly arises from the fact that the standard of degradation in man and woman is different. But we cannot flatter Mr. Mill or his disciples, with any hope that the fundamental question between man and woman can be greatly altered; and we altogether reject his hypothesis that woman is man in petticoats. It is not so; it never was so; and devoutly we trust never will be.

THE SUBJECTION OF WOMEN
[Sheldon Amos]

1. *The Subjection of Women.* By John Stuart Mill. London: 1869.
2. *Woman's Work and Woman's Culture.* A Series of Essays edited by Josephine E. Butler. London: 1869.

As may be inferred from the difference in the sources whence they severally proceed, the contents of the two volumes before us are of very unequal degrees of merit. Although they are both directed to the examination of the same subject, or branches of the same subject, from an identical or nearly identical point of view, it is hardly practicable to institute a comparison between them. In scope, tone of thought, and method of treatment, they differ essentially the one from the other. In all these respects the first stands on a level so immeasurably removed above the second, that we seek in vain for any adequate means of determining, with an approach to accuracy, the extent of space which separates them. The work of Mr. Mill is by far the most thorough and complete discussion which has ever appeared of the fundamental principles lying at the base of the question to which it relates, as well as of the question itself in all its aspects and bearings. The series of essays by Mrs. Butler and her associates seems to us to be important principally because its publication affords further evidence, of no doubtful character that the just and rational conception of the normal *status* of one half of the human race, hitherto the exclusive possession of a few advanced and enlightened thinkers among us, is at last making itself felt throughout a wider circle, and gradually winning the universal acquiescence which we feel confident it is destined sooner or later to receive. It is an additional sign that the seed sown in times past by Godwin, Mary Wollstonecraft, Bentham, and James Mill, in our own time by Mr. Samuel Bailey, Mr. Herbert Spencer, Mr John Stuart Mill, and by the *Westminster Review* during nearly half a century, has taken root in the public mind, and promises in due season to bring forth an abundant harvest.

It would nevertheless be unfair were we not to notice that some of the essays are conspicuous for sound sense and correct expression; those, for example, entitled "Medicine as a Profession for Women," by Miss Jex Blake; "The Social Position of Women in the Present Age," by Mr. Boyd-Kinnear; and "Female Suffrage considered chiefly with regard to its indirect results," by Miss Wedgwood. The essays "On some Historical Aspects of Family Life," by Mr. Pearson; and "The Property Disabilities of a Married Woman," by Mr. Mozley, are mainly compilations, rather indifferently executed, from well-known text books, of which the necessary dulness is not much enlivened by such original observations as the authors have introduced. The essay on "The Final Cause of Woman," by Miss Cobbe, is written, as might be expected, with the point and fluency of a veteran scribe; that on "The Teaching of Science," by Mr. Stuart, is a treasury of platitudes and commonplaces; and that on "How to Provide for Superfluous Women," by Miss Boucherett, is a prolonged but unconvincing argument in favour of *male* emigration. The essays on "Education considered as a Profession for Women," by the Rev. G. Butler, and "The Education of Girls, its Present and its Future," by Miss Wolstenholme, are fair and judicious criticisms on the deficiencies of our existing system with regard to both female teachers and female pupils, demanding as a remedy what is no more than justice: the admission of both sexes, on equal terms, to the privileges and advantages of our national and endowed educational institutions. The "Introduction," by Mrs. Butler, commencing the volume, is a fervid, almost eloquent appeal to public sympathy on behalf of what we have ventured to designate "the suppressed sex," in general. The authoress does not scruple, like many "who really are so good, so pious, and so holy," to touch, although lightly and delicately, upon that great social evil, at once the foulest blot on our civilization, the cruellest consequence of our conventional notions of female propriety, and the *ne plus ultra* of female degradation. There is much in Mrs. Butler's essay with which we do not wholly agree, and a little which we do not altogether understand; but her evident sincerity and single-heartedness in the cause she has in hand, are deserving of every recognition and of all praise. As the essayists, to the extent to which they go, traverse the ground Mr. Mill has now made his

own, we will here take leave of them, and follow him for the
rest of our journey.

The main propositions which it is the purpose of Mr. Mill to
establish in "The Subjection of Women," are summed up in the
following passage from its opening page, namely –

> "That the principle which regulates the existing social
> relations between the two sexes – the legal subordination of
> one sex to the other – is wrong in itself, and now one of the
> chief hindrances to human improvement, and that it ought to
> be replaced by a principle of perfect equality, admitting no
> power or privilege on the one side, nor disability on the
> other."

This sentence may be regarded as the text on which the
remainder of the book is a continuous and elaborate commentary. Mr. Mill commences by attacking the prepossessions
aggregated in the popular mind around the subject he proposes
to illustrate; then he explains what are the present social
arrangements he holds to be objectionable; next, he shows the
capacity of women to benefit by the particular changes he
recommends; and lastly, he dwells upon the advantages which
may be expected to accrue to mankind generally should those
changes be effected.

The persistence of an opinion originating in sentiment rather
than in reason, instead of being diminished is usually increased
when it is proved to be logically untenable. If it were founded
on reasoning, its stability would be shaken should the
reasoning on which it is based be refuted. But when it "rests
solely on feeling, the worse it fares in argumentative contest,
the more persuaded its adherents are that their feeling must
have some deeper ground which the arguments do not reach,"
and there are so many causes tending to make the feelings
connected with the *status* of woman –

> "the most intense and most deeply rooted of all those which
> gather round and protect old institutions and customs, that
> we need not wonder to find them less undermined and
> loosened than any of the rest by the progress of the great
> modern spiritual and social transition."

And not only is the opinion against which Mr. Mill protests
a sentimental, but it is also an almost universal prejudice. The
obstacles in the way of dispelling it are consequently propor-

tionately augmented and multiplied. The established rules of
evidence and canons of logical discussion are either suspended
for its convenience, or reversed in its defence. In all other cases
the burden of proof is cast upon those who maintain the
affirmative; in this case it is thrown upon those who maintain
the negative side of the controversy.

> "Again, in practical matters the burden of proof is supposed
> to be with those who are against liberty; who contend for
> any restriction or prohibition, either any limitation of the
> general freedom of human action, or any disqualification or
> disparity of privilege affecting one person, or kind of
> persons, as compared with others. The à priori presumption
> is in favour of freedom and impartiality. It is held that there
> should be no restraint not required by the general good, and
> that the law should be no respecter of persons, but should
> treat all alike, save where dissimilarity of treatment is
> required by positive reasons, either of justice or policy."

But, where women are concerned, a departure is invariably
made from this salutary principle, and the à priori presumption
is at once assumed to be against all that it implies. It is then the
advocate, not the assailant of equality, who is called upon to
show cause why he should not, without further inquiry, submit
to a nonsuit.

It is frequently asserted that the subjection of women is
justified by the experience, and sanctioned by the practice of
mankind in every age and in every portion of the earth. But
although the generality of a custom may afford strong ground
for believing that it either is or once was conducive to laudable
ends, this is so only when it has been deliberately adopted as a
means to those ends, and carefully selected from among others
as the most appropriate for reaching them.

> "If the authority of men over women had been the result of a
> conscientious comparison between different modes of con-
> stituting society, if after trying various other modes of social
> organization, the government of women over men, equality
> between the two, and such mixed and divided modes as
> might be invented, it had been decided, on the testimony of
> experience, that the mode in which women are wholly under
> the rule of men, having no share at all in public concerns,
> and each in private being under the legal obligation of

obedience to the man with whom she has associated her destiny, was the arrangement most conducive to the happiness and well-being of both, its general adoption might then be fairly thought to be some evidence that at the time when it was adopted it was the best, though even then the considerations which recommended it may, like so many other primeval social facts, have subsequently, in the course of ages, ceased to exist. But the state of the case is in every respect the reverse of this. In the first place, the opinion in favour of the present system, which entirely subordinates the weaker sex to the stronger, rests upon theory only, for there never has been trial made of any other, so that experience, in the sense in which it is vulgarly opposed to theory, cannot be pretended to have pronounced any verdict. And in the second place, the adoption of this system of inequality never was the result of deliberation or forethought, or any social ideas, or any notion whatever of that conduced to the benefit of humanity or the good of society. It arose simply from the fact that from the very earliest twilight of human society, every woman (owing to the value attached to her by men, combined with her inferiority in muscular strength) was in a state of bondage to some man."

Nor is the dependence of women on men, as established at present in this and other civilized countries, –

"an original institution, taking a fresh start from considerations of justice and expediency – it is the primitive state of slavery, lasting on through successive mitigations and modifications occasioned by the same causes which have softened the general manners, and brought all human relations under the control of justice and the influence of humanity. It has not lost the taint of its brutal origin. No presumption in its favour, therefore, can be drawn from the fact of its existence."

On the contrary, the whole analogy of past and contemporary history tends to rebut it, and substitute an opposite presumption in its place. It is not easy for us to understand how completely the law of superior strength constitutes the rule of life in some phases of human evolution. In barbarism, might and right are always regarded as convertible terms, and even Plato's typical sophist, Thrasymachus, defines justice to be "the advantage of the stronger." It was only within comparatively recent times that the immorality of this doctrine was perceived and condemned by any one but philosophers and saints. The transition from compulsory to voluntary social arrangements was very gradually carried out, and then in the most advanced communities alone. But that transition is at present, among ourselves at any rate, almost perfectly accomplished. The difference of sex is now the sole natural distinction which we permit to operate as an absolutely irremovable disqualification for the discharge of certain of the functions of citizenship, and the pursuit of particular occupations. None but women are treated by us as political *pariahs*, and condemned to perpetual tutelage after they are of full age, while they are of sound mind, and before they are convicted of felony.

> "Their condition thus stands out an isolated fact in modern social institutions, a solitary breach of what has become their fundamental law, a single relic of an old world of thought and practice, exploded in everything else, but retained in the one thing of most universal interest, as if a gigantic dolman or a vast temple of Jupiter Olympus occupied the site of St. Paul's, and received daily worship, while the surrounding Christian churches were only resorted to on fasts and festivals."

Moreover, experience tells us –

> "That every step in improvement has been so invariably accompanied by a step made in raising the social position of women, that historians and philosophers have been led to adopt their elevation or debasement as, on the whole, the surest test and most correct measure of the civilization of a people or an age. Through all the progressive period of human history, the condition of women has been approaching nearer to equality with men. This does not of itself prove that the assimilation must go on to complete equality; but it assuredly affords some presumption that such is the case."

The argument that the *nature* of the two sexes adapts them exclusively to the respective parts they now occupy in social economy is manifestly irrelevant, because what is at present "called the nature of woman is an eminently artificial thing – the result of forced repression in some directions, unnatural stimulation in others." In the existing state of society it is impossible to obtain complete knowledge of the really natural differences between the characters of men and women.

"The profoundest knowledge of the laws of the formation of character is indispensable to entitle any one to affirm even that there is any difference, much more what the difference is, between the two sexes, considered as moral and rational beings, and since no one as yet has that knowledge (for there is hardly any subject which, in proportion to its importance, has been so little studied), no one is thus far entitled to any positive opinion on the subject."

As a matter of fact, we know next to nothing of the unsophisticated *nature* of woman, and the knowledge of most men does not go beyond one narrow, "although no doubt important," department of it – the amatory. Of this, however, we may be certain, "that what is contrary to woman's nature to do they never will be made to do by simply giving their nature free play." If they have a greater aptitude for some pursuits than for others, there is no necessity for laws or social inculcation to make them follow the former instead of the latter. What they can do, but not so well as men, they would be excluded from by competition in the ordinary way.

"Nobody asks for protective duties and bounties in favour of women;; it is only asked that the present bounties and protective duties in favour of men should be recalled."

We do not hold it requisite to make it illegal for all but strong-armed men to be blacksmiths. We simply leave weak-armed men to discover by experience that they may labour to more advantage elsewhere than at the forge. If women suffered under an insurmountable disability, or if even they were less able than men to be physicians or lawyers, clerks or chemists, carvers and gilders, or to pursue any other profession or calling, they would not be long in ascertaining the fact, and these employments would in practice be as effectually closed against them as they could be by Act of Parliament.

But it seems that marriage is the destination which society specially appoints for women. It is the prospect to which they are all of them brought up to look forward, and the single object which they are all of them taught to attempt to attain. Their training is directed to the same end precisely as the plot of fashionable three-volumed novels, and is intended to terminate "in the curate and St. George's," or some more or less exalted officiator and edifice. If other means of gaining their accustomed livelihood were thrown open to them, it is feared that they might perhaps prefer them to matrimony. And seeing how much the law has done to make the position of a married woman unattractive, it is not surprising that this apprehension should be entertained. In this country, indeed, it is more unenviable than it is, we believe, in any other part of Europe or America, except among the Indian tribes. In ninety-five out of every hundred marriages in England the operation of the Common Law makes the act of marriage on the part of the woman equivalent to high treason as far as the consequence of her rights of property is concerned, and little less than equivalent to it in its effect upon her right of personal liberty. In the other five per cent of marriages, taking place among the wealthier orders, some mitigation of the severity of the Common Law is effected through the medium of the Court of Chancery. But ordinarily –

> "The wife is the actual bond servant of her husband, no less so, as far as legal obligation goes, than slaves commonly so called. She vows a lifelong obedience to him at the altar, and is held to it all through life by law. Casuists may say that the obligation of obedience stops short of participation in crime, but it certainly extends to everything else. She can do no act whatever but by his permission – at least, tacit. She can acquire no property but for him the instant it becomes hers; even if by inheritance, it becomes *ipso facto* his. In this respect the wife's position under the Common Law of England is worse than that of slaves in many countries. By the Roman law, for example, a slave might have his *peculium*, which to a certain extent the law guaranteed to him for his exclusive use. The higher classes in this country have given an analogous advantage to their women through special contracts setting aside the law, by conditions of pin-money, &c., since parental feeling, being stronger than the class feelings of their own sex, a father generally prefers his own daughter to a son-in-law, who is a stranger to him. By means of settlements the rich usually contrive to withdraw the whole or part of the inherited property of the wife from the absolute control of the husband, but they do not succeed

in keeping it under her own control; the utmost they can do only prevents the husband from squandering it, at the same time debarring the rightful owner from its use. The property itself is out of the reach of both, and as to the income derived from it, the form of settlement most favourable to the wife (that called 'to her separate use') only precludes the husband from receiving it instead of her. It must pass through her hands; but if he takes it from her by personal violence as soon as she receives it, he can neither be punished nor compelled to restitution."

This is the wife's *status* with respect to her individual interest, and her *status* in regard to her children is of a piece with it. They are called in law the husband's children, and he alone has legal right over them. The wife can do nothing in relation to them except by delegation from him, and, even after his death, she does not become their guardian unless she has been appointed so by him.

The natural sequence and corollary from the state of things here described would be, that since a woman's whole comfort and happiness in life "depend on her finding a good master, she should be allowed to change, again and again, until she finds one." To those to whom nothing but servitude is permitted –

> "the free choice of servitude is the only, though a most insufficient alleviation. Its refusal completes the assimilation of the wife to the slave – and the slave under not the mildest form of slavery, for in some slave codes, the slave could, under certain circumstances of ill usage, legally compel the master to sell him. But no amount of ill usage, without adultery superadded, will in England free a wife from her tormentor."

When it is not superadded she has no means whatever of withdrawing herself from bondage. If she leaves her husband, she can take with her neither her property nor her children; and, as her services legally belong to him, the earnings of her ability or industry are his, and not hers, whether she lives apart or with him. If he chooses he can compel her, by judicial process, or by physical force, to return to him. It is only in the event of his actually deserting her, or being guilty of gross cruelty towards her, that the courts of justice are empowered to interfere for her protection when separated from her husband.

It is quite true that husbands in general, especially in the upper and middle ranks, seldom push their legal authority to tyrannize over their wives to its extreme limits. But laws are made for the purpose, not of confiding to what people will do, but of guarding against what they may do.

> "Marriage is not an institution designed for a select few. Men are not required, as a preliminary to the marriage ceremony, to prove by testimonials that they are fitted to be trusted with the exercise of absolute power:" and 'when we consider how vast is the number of men in any great country who are little higher than brutes, and that this never prevents them from being able, through the law of marriage, to obtain a victim, the breadth and depth of human misery caused in this shape alone, by the abuse of the institution, swells to something appalling."

And even independently of any abuse of it, the institution itself is at present calculated rather to depress than raise the standard of domestic virtue as far, at all events, as the husband is concerned.

> "If the family in its best form is, as it is often said to be, a school of sympathy, tenderness, and loving forgetfulness of self, it is still oftener, as respects its chief, a school of wilfulness, overbearingness, unbounded self-indulgence, and a double dyed and idealized selfishness, of which sacrifice itself is only a particular form; the care for the wife and children being only care for them as part of the man's own interests and belongings, and their individual happiness being immolated in every shape to his smallest preferences."

The wife, however, if she cannot resist, can at least retaliate. Hers is the "power of the scold or the shrewish sanction." But to this the amiable, or high-minded will not resort, and thus, when it is resorted to, it is usually against the gentler and more inoffensive variety of husband, so that the wife's capacity for "being disagreeable only establishes a counter-tyranny, and makes victims in their turn chiefly of those husbands who are least inclined to be tyrants."

Nor can it be maintained that the continuance of this order of things is necessary, because in voluntary associations some one member must be master, and it is requisite that the law should decide which of them it should be. In business partnerships, next to marriage, the commonest form of voluntary association among us, this is not the case. The law does not –

"ordain that one partner should administer the common business as his private concern, that the others should have only delegated powers, and that this one should be designated by some general presumption of law, for example, as being the eldest. The law never does this, nor does experience show it to be necessary, that any theoretical inequality of power should exist between the partners, or that the partnership should have any other conditions than what they may themselves appoint by their articles of agreement."

In practice, one member of a firm often does take the lead in its management, and oftener each member of it superintends a distinct department of business. But these arrangements are always the results of the assent of the partners themselves, and not the consequences of legislation. Were it not that settlements and compromises of a similar kind are effected by married couples, even now, in spite of our law of marriage, every household in the realm would be the scene of constant discord and disorder. There is in all decently well-regulated families a distribution of some sort or other of their respective functions, rights, and obligations between husband and wife. But –

"the division neither can nor should be pre-established by law, since it must depend on individual capacities and suitabilities. If the two persons chose, they might pre-appoint it by the marriage contract, as pecuniary arrangements are now often pre-appointed. There would seldom be any difficulty in deciding such things by mutual consent, unless the marriage was one of those unhappy ones in which all things, as well as this, become subjects of bickering and dispute."

The various circumstances of age and means, of mental or moral qualities, would naturally determine whether the husband or the wife should have the more potential voice in the practical conduct of affairs. They do so at present in nine cases out of ten –

"and this fact shows how little foundation there is for the apprehension that the powers and responsibilities of partners in life, as of partners in business, cannot be satisfactorily apportioned by agreement between themselves."

It may be suggested that an amicable apportionment of them between husband and wife is now common, because the resource of legal compulsion is known to be in reserve –

"as people submit to arbitration because there is a court of law in the background. But to make the cases parallel, we must suppose that the rule of the court of law was, not to try the case, but to give judgment always for the same side, suppose the defendant. If so, the amenability to it would be a motive with the plaintiff to agree to almost any arbitration, but it would be just the reverse with the defendant."

The equality of married persons before the law, with respect to both their personal and their proprietary rights –

"is not only the sole mode in which that particular relation can be made consistent with justice to both sides, and conducive to the happiness of both; but it is the only means of rendering the daily life of mankind in any high sense a school of moral cultivation. Though the truth may not be felt or generally acknowledged for generations to come, the only school of genuine moral sentiment is society between equals."

The effect of obliterating the legal ascendancy of the husband over the wife would be to place wives on the same footing towards the laws and institutions of the country as that now occupied by single women. At present, single women are endowed with all the rights, and subject to all the obligations appertaining to men, except that, unless as sovereign, they are allowed to take no part either in the legislative or executive privileges and duties of government. They are liable to be punished for their crimes and misdemeanours, and are enabled to procure the punishment of those who have been guilty of crimes or misdemeanours against them. They can acquire, possess, and dispose of property, both real and personal. They may sue and be sued in the Common Law Courts, file bills, and have bills filed against them in Chancery, and petition the Court of Bankruptcy either as debtors or as creditors. They are empowered to appoint agents, trustees, guardians and executors, and to act as agents, trustees, guardians, executrices and administratrices. On what ground, either of justice or expediency, then, are they debarred from taking a part in the making and administration of the laws in the nature and execution of which they are as fully and variously interested as men?

"In the last two centuries, when (which was seldom the case) any reason beyond the mere existence of the fact was thought to be required to justify the disabilities of women, people seldom assigned as a reason their inferior mental capacity, which in times when there was a real trial of personal faculties (from which all women were not excluded) in the struggles of public life, no one really believed in. The reason given in those days was not woman's unfitness, but the interest of society, by which was meant the interest of men, just as the *raison d'être*, meaning the convenience of government and the support of existing authority was deemed a sufficient explanation and excuse for the most flagitious crimes. In the present day power holds a smoother language, and whomsoever it oppresses, always pretends to do so for their own good: accordingly, when anything is forbidden to women, it is thought necessary to say, and desirable to believe, that they are incapable of doing it, and that they depart from their real path of success and happiness when they aspire to it. But it make this reason plausible (not valid), those by whom it is urged must be prepared to carry it a much greater length than any one ventures to do in the face of present experience. It is not sufficient to maintain that women on the average are less gifted than men on the average with certain of the higher mental faculties, or that a smaller number of women are fit for occupations and functions of the highest intellectual character. It is necessary to maintain that no women at all are fit for them, and that the most eminent women are inferior in mental faculties to the most mediocre of the men on whom these functions at present devolve. For if the performance of the function is decided either by competition or by any mode of choice which secures regard to the public interest, there needs to be no apprehension that any important employments will fall into hands of women inferior to average men, or to the average of their male competitors."

This argument applies to state offices as well as to private avocations. There is, however, one of the privileges of citizenship to the enjoyment of which the claim of women is entirely independent of any question that can be raised concerning their faculties. This is the suffrage, both parliamentary and municipal.

"The right to share in the choice of those who are to exercise a public trust is altogether a distinct thing from that of competing for the trust itself. If no one could vote for a member of parliament who was not fit to be a candidate, the government would be a narrow oligarchy indeed. To have a voice in choosing those by whom one is to be governed, is a means of self-protection due to every one, though he were to remain for ever excluded from the function of governing; and that women are considered fit to have such a choice may be presumed from the fact that the law already gives it to women in the most important of all cases to themselves; for the choice of the man who is to govern a woman to the end of life is always supposed to be voluntarily made by herself. In the case of election to public trusts, it is the business of constitutional law to surround the right of suffrage with all needful securities and limitations; but whatever securities are sufficient in the case of the male sex, no others need be required in the case of women. Under whatever conditions, and within whatever limits men are admitted to the suffrage, there is not a shadow of justification for not admitting women under the same."

If women are entitled to life, liberty, and property, they are equally entitled to be consulted as to the manner in which their lives, liberties, and properties shall be controlled and disposed of; and any control or disposition of them in which they do not participate is simply an usurpation and a wrong. If they are amenable to the laws, and called upon to pay taxes, they are merely slaves so long as they are prevented from authoritatively expressing their views as to what those laws and taxes ought to be. The title of men and women to the suffrage is based on exactly the same considerations, and its denial to the latter is iniquitous for exactly the same reasons that its denial to the former would be.[1]

1   Mr Herbert Spencer, speaking of the rights of women, says:- "Three positions only are open to us. It may be said that women have no rights at all: that their rights are not so great as those of men: or that they are equal to those of men.

In this connexion it is also curious to contemplate that the only things which women are ordinarily excluded from doing are just those things which they have proved themselves best able to do. There is no law or custom in force to prevent a woman from writing plays like Shakespeare or operas like Mozart, but there are laws and customs to prevent them from embracing a military or political career, and Joan of Arc and Queen Elizabeth are historical characters.

"If anything conclusive could be inferred from experience, without psychological analysis, it would be that the things which women are not allowed to do are the very ones for which they are peculiarly qualified, since their vocation for government has made its way and become conspicuous through the very few opportunities which have been given, while in the lines of distinction, which apparently were freely open to them, they have by no means so eminently

"Whoever maintains the first of these dogmas, that women have no rights at all, must show that the Creator intended women to be wholly at the mercy of men – their happiness, their liberties, their lives, at men's disposal; or, in other words, that they were meant to be treated as creatures of an inferior order. Few will have the hardihood to assert this.

"From the second proposition, that the rights of women are not so great as those of men, there immediately arise such queries as: If they are not so great, by how much are they less? What is the exact ratio between the legitimate claims of the two sexes? How shall we tell which rights are common to both, and where those of the male exceed those of the female? Who can show us a scale that will serve for the apportionment? Or, putting the question practically, it is required to determine, by some logical method, whether the Turk is justified in plunging an offending Circassian into the Bosphorus? Whether the rights of women were violated by the Athenian law, which allowed a citizen, under certain circumstances, to sell his daughter or sister? Whether our own statute, which permits a man to beat his wife in moderation, and to imprison her in any room in his house, is morally defensible? Whether it is equitable that a married woman should be incapable of holding property? Whether a husband may justly take possession of his wife's earnings against her will, as our law allows him to do? – and so forth. These, and a multitude of similar problems, present themselves for solution. Some principle rooted in the nature of things has to be found, by which they may be scientifically decided – decided, not on grounds of expediency, but in some definite philosophical way. Does any one holding the doctrine that women's rights are not so great as men's, think he can find such a principle?

"If not, there remains no alternative but to take up the third position – that the rights of women are equal with those of men." – *Social Statics*, page 156.

If we substitute, for "the intention of the Creator," either "the dictates of a moral sense,' or "conceptions of general utility," precisely the same conclusions may be drawn.

distinguished themselves. We know how small a number of reigning queens history presents in comparison with that of kings. Of this smaller number a far larger proportion have shown talents for rule, and many of them have occupied the throne in difficult periods. It is remarkable, too, that they have, in a great number of instances, been distinguished by merits the most opposite to the imaginary and conventional character of women – they have been as much remarked for the vigour and firmness of their rule as for its intelligence. When to queens and empresses we add regents and viceroys of provinces, the list of women who have been eminent as rulers swells to a great length."

The bad joke that queens are better than kings, because under kings women govern, but under queens men, is hardly worth serious examination. But it may be observed that it is not true, in the first place, that under kings women govern; and, in the second place, it is not true that under queens men govern, except in the same sense in which they govern under kings. With reference to kings, the cases are entirely exceptional; and weak ones have as frequently governed ill through the influence of male as of female favourites.

"When a king is governed by a woman merely through his amatory propensities, good government is not probable, though even then there are exceptions. But French history counts two kings who have voluntarily given the direction of affairs during many years: the one to his mother; the other to his sister. One of them, Charles VIII., was a mere boy; but in doing so he followed the intentions of Louis XI., the ablest monarch of his age. The other, St. Louis, was the best and most vigorous ruler since the time of Charlemagne. Both these princesses ruled in a manner hardly equalled by any prince among their contemporaries. The emperor Charles V., the most politic prince of his time, who had as great a number of able men in his service as any ruler ever had, and was one of the least likely of all sovereigns to sacrifice his interest to personal feelings, made two princesses of his family successively governors of the Netherlands, and kept one or other of them in that post during his whole life. They were afterwards succeeded by a third. Both ruled very successfully; and one of them, Margaret of Austria, was one of the ablest politicians of the age. So much for one side of the question: now as to the other. When it is said that under queens men govern, is the same meaning to be understood as when kings are said to be governed by women? Is it meant that queens choose as their instruments of government the associates of their personal pleasures? The case is rare even with those who are as unscrupulous on the latter point as Catherine II., and it is not in these cases that the good government alleged to arise from male influence is to be found. If it be true, then, that the administration is in the hands of better men under a queen than under an average king, it must be that queens have a superior capacity for choosing them, and women must be better qualified than men, both for the position of sovereign and for that of chief minister; for the principal business of a prime minister is not to govern in person, but to find the fittest persons to conduct every department of public affairs. The more rapid insight into character, which is one of the admitted points of superiority in women over men, must certainly make them, with anything like parity of qualifications in other respects, more apt than men in the choice of instruments, which is nearly the most important business of every one who has to do with governing mankind. Even the unprincipled Catherine de Medici could feel the value of a Chancellor de l'Hôpital. But it is also true that most great queens have been great by their own talents for government, and have been well served precisely for that reason. They retained the supreme direction of affairs in their own hands, and if they listened to good advisers, they gave by that fact the strongest proof that their judgment fitted them for dealing with the great questions of government."

It may be reasonably asked if the female relatives of princes have thus always proved themselves to be at least as fit as princes themselves to discharge the duties of the princely station, what is there in the nature of things to prevent the female relatives of all sorts and conditions of men from discharging the duties appropriate to the several stations of their fathers, husbands, and brothers? There is really nothing, but there appears to be something, because, while the rank counterpoises the sex of princesses in vulgar apprehension, the latter accident is not compensated by the former in the case of less exalted personages.

"The ladies of reigning families are the only women who are allowed the same range of interests and freedom of development as men, and it is precisely in their case that there is not found to be any inferiority. Exactly where and in proportion as women's capacities for government have been tried, in that proportion have they been found adequate."

All other women have been kept, as far as regards spontaneous development, in so unnatural a state that their nature cannot but have been greatly distorted and disguised. It is not, therefore, safe to –

"pronounce that if women's nature were left to choose its direction as freely as men's, and if no artificial bent were attempted to be given to it, except that required by the conditions of society, and given to both sexes alike, there would be any material difference at all in the character and capacities which unfold themselves."

As it is, however, women seem to be inferior to men in their powers of generalization, but superior to them in their powers of observation. Their perceptive preponderate over their speculative faculties. The general bent of their talents is towards the practical.

"What is meant by a woman's capacity of intuitive perception? It means a rapid and correct insight into present fact. It has nothing to do with general principles. Nobody ever perceived a scientific law of nature by intuition, nor arrived at a general rule of duty or prudence by it. These are results of slow and careful collection and comparison of experience, and neither the men nor the women of 'intuition' usually shine in this department."

It is not, however, an uncommon thing for "too much learning" to render men insensible to present fact. "They do not see in the facts they are called up to deal with what is really there, but what they have been taught to expect." This rarely happens with women of any ability. "Their capacity for 'intuition' preserves them from it. With equality of experience and of general faculties, a woman usually sees much more than a man of what is immediately before her." The vivid appreciation of the actual is the main distinction between practical and theoretical minds, and its absence is "the most characteristic aberration" of the latter. Thus women's thoughts "are as useful in giving reality to those of thinking men, as men's thoughts in giving width and largeness to those of women. In depth, as distinguished from breadth, it may be greatly doubted if even now women, compared with men, are at any disadvantage.

Again, women may be said to have more excitability of nerve than men, and more of those qualities which excitability of nerve produces. "They are the material of great orators, great preachers, impressive diffusers of moral influences." But they are not, on this account, disqualified for the discharge of the calmer and more dispassionate social functions. In the matter of nervous temperament there is as much difference between races of men as there is between men and women.

"Like the French compared with the English, the Irish with the Swiss, the Greeks or Italians compared with the Germans, so women compared with men, may be found on an average to do the same things with some variety in the particular excellence. But that they would do them fully as well on the whole, if their education and cultivation were adapted to correcting instead of aggravating the infirmities incident to their temperament, there is not the smallest reason to doubt."

The only evidence afforded by observation of the supposed mental inferiority of women to men, is the circumstance that no production entitled to the highest rank in philosophy, science, or art, has been the work of a woman. It is hardly three generations since, with very rare exceptions, women commenced to try their powers in any of those directions, and in the present generation alone have their attempts been at all numerous. It may therefore be questioned –

"whether a mind possessing the requisites of first-rate eminence in speculation or creative art, could have been expected on the mere calculation of chances to turn up, during that lapse of time, among the women whose tastes and personal position admitted their devoting themselves to these pursuits. In all things in which there has yet been time for – in all but the very highest grades in the scale of excellence, especially in the department in which they have been longest engaged, literature (both prose and poetry) – women have done quite as much, and have obtained fully as

high prizes, and as many of them, as could be expected from
the length of time and the number of competitors."[2]

If we contrast the literary and artistic works of women with
those of men in modern days, we shall find that their inferiority
resolves itself into one, but still a most material, defect,
namely, "a deficiency of originality." They do not, indeed,
exhibit a total want of it, for no production of mind of
substantive value can do so; but they have not up to the present
been marked "by any of those great and luminous new ideas
which form an era in thought, nor those fundamentally new
conceptions in art which open a vista of possible effects not
before thought of, and found a new school." Their compo-
sitions are mostly based on the existing fund of thought, and
their creations do not deviate widely from existing types; but in
point of execution, in the treatment of details, and in perfection
of style, their works are quite on a par with those of their male
rivals. The fact is, however, that –

"nearly all the thoughts which can be reached by mere
strength of original faculties have long since been arrived at,

2 "Whoso urges the mental inferiority of women in bar to their claim to equal
rights with men, may be met in various ways. In the first place, the alleged
fact may be disputed. A defender of her sex might name many whose
achievements in government, in science, in literature, and in art have
obtained no small share of renown. Powerful and sagacious queens the
world has seen in plenty, from Zenobia down to the Empresses Catherine
and Maria Theresa. In the exact sciences, Mrs. Somerville, Miss Herschel,
and Miss Zornlin have gained applause; in political economy, Miss
Martineau; in general philosophy, Madame de Stael; in politics, Madame
Roland. Poetry has its Tighes, its Hemanses, its Landons, its Browning; the
drama, its Joanna Baillie; and fiction, its Austens, Bremers, Gores,
Dudevants, &c., without end. In sculpture, fame has been acquired by a
princess; a picture like 'The Momentous Question' is tolerable proof of
female capacity for painting; and on the stage it is certain that women are
on a level with men, if they do not even bear away the palm. Joining to such
facts the important consideration, that women have always been, and are
still, placed at a disadvantage in every department of learning, thought, or
skill – seeing that they are not admissible to the academies and universities
in which men get their training; that the kind of life they have to look
forward to does not present so great a range of ambitions; that they are
rarely exposed to that most powerful of all stimulants – necessity; that the
education custom dictates for them is one that leaves uncultivated many of the
higher faculties; and that the prejudice against blue-stockings, hitherto so
prevalent amongst men, has greatly tended to deter women from the pursuit
of literary honours:– adding these considerations to the above facts, we shall
see good reason for thinking that the alleged inferiority of the feminine mind
is by no means self-evident." – SPENCER: *Social Statics.* p. 157.

and originality, in any high sense of the word, is now scarcely ever attained but by minds which have undergone elaborate discipline, and are deeply versed in the results of previous thinking."

There are very few women who have gone through this training, and every sort of obstacle is placed in the way of their obtaining it. They are deprived of all the advantages, and most of the motives, which men possess for acquiring even a decent amount of systematic education; and if we turn from philosophy and science to literature, in the narrow sense of the term, there are other obvious reasons why women's productions are in general conception, and in their leading features, more or less imitations of those of men.

"Why is the Roman literature, as critics proclaim to satiety, not original, but an imitation of Greek? Simply because the Greek came first. If women lived in a different country from men, and had never read any of their writings, they would have had a literature of their own. As it is, they have not created one, because they found a highly advanced literature already created. If there had been no suspension of the knowledge of antiquity, or if the Renaissance had occurred before the Gothic cathedrals were built, they never would have been built. We see that in France and Italy imitation of the ancient literature stopped the original development, even after it had commenced. All women who write are the pupils of the great male writers. A painter's early pictures, even if he be a Raffaelle, are undistinguishable in style from those of his master. Even a Mozart does not display his powerful originality in his earliest pieces. What years are to a gifted individual, generations are to a mass. If women's literature is destined to have a different collective character from that of men, depending on any difference of natural tendencies, much longer time is necessary than has yet elapsed before it can emancipate itself from the influence of accepted models, and guide itself by its own impulses. But if there should not prove to be any natural tendencies common to women, and distinguishing their genius from that of men, yet every individual writer among them has her individual tendencies, which at present are still subdued by the influence of precedent and example, and it will require generations more before their individuality is sufficiently developed to make head against that influence."

With respect to the fine arts, properly so called, the inferior originality of female genius appears to be most strongly marked. Although women are encouraged to cultivate them, and the chief portion of their education consists in their cultivation, they have fallen short of men more considerably in them than in almost any other line of exertion.

"This shortcoming, however, needs no other explanation than the familiar fact, more universally true in the fine arts than in anything else, the vast superiority of professional persons over amateurs. Women in the educated classes are almost universally taught more or less of some branch or other of the fine arts, but not that they may gain their living or their social consequence by it. Women artists are all amateurs. The exceptions are only of the kind which confirm the general truth. Women are taught music, but not for the purpose of composing, only of executing it; and accordingly it is only as composers that men in music are superior to women. The only one of the fine arts which women do follow to any extent as a profession and an occupation for life is the histrionic, and in that they are confessedly equal, if not superior to men. To make the comparison fair, it should be made between the productions of women in any branch of art and those of men not following it as a profession."

In some degree music is less than the other fine arts dependent on general mental power, and more dependent on a special gift. But this gift, to be made available, requires study and professional devotion to the pursuit. It is only in Germany and Italy that great musical composers have as yet appeared, and in those countries the education of women has remained far behind what it is even now in France and England. In Germany and Italy men who are acquainted with the principles of musical composition may be counted by thousands, and women barely by scores, "so that here again, on the doctrine of averages, we cannot reasonably expect to see more than one eminent woman to fifty eminent men, and the last three centuries have not produced fifty eminent male composers in either."

Besides all this, the time and thoughts of women have to satisfy considerable demands on them before they can be

applied to higher purposes. They have always domestic duties
to occupy them, except where the families to which they belong
are sufficiently rich to delegate their superintendence to
servants. Moreover, the desire for distinction which impels so
many men, without, or over and above, the pressure of
necessity, to "scorn delights and live laborious days," is
suppressed, or at any rate discouraged, in women. Ambition,
"the last infirmity of noble minds," is regarded as "daring and
unfeminine."

If we pass from the intellectual to the moral differences
between the two sexes, we find the distinction is commonly
drawn in favour of women.

> "They are declared to be better than men – an empty
> compliment which must provoke a bitter smile from every
> woman of spirit, since there is no other situation in life in
> which it is the established order, and considered quite
> natural and suitable, that the better should obey the worse. If
> this piece of idle talk is good for anything, it is only as an
> admission by men of the corrupting influence of power, for
> that is certainly the only truth which the fact – if it be a fact –
> either proves or illustrates."

As some compensation to this dictum, it is also usually asserted
that women suffer from a greater liability to moral bias than
men. "Their judgment in grave affairs is warped by their
sympathies and antipathies;" but,

> "assuming that it is so, it is still to be proved that women are
> oftener misled by their personal feelings than men by their
> personal interests. The chief difference would seem in that
> case to be that men are led from the course of duty and the
> public interest by their regard for themselves, women (not
> being allowed to have private interests of their own) by their
> regard for somebody else."

We frequently hear, for instance, that women care for nothing in
politics but personalities, and form their opinions of measures
from the men identified with them, and not of the men from the
measures they propose or support. This is only what is to be
anticipated from the way in which they are brought up. They
have been and are invariably instructed to limit their horizon to
their family circle at most, and by no means to extend it so as to
embrace their country, much less mankind; and it is not

surprising if they have learnt a lesson faithfully which has been so long and so assiduously taught to them.

It may be inquired, What good are we to expect from the changes proposed in our customs and institutions? Would mankind be at all better off if women were free? If not, why disturb their minds and attempt to make a social revolution in the name of an abstract right? In respect to the alterations which it is urged ought to be made in the condition of married women, it is hardly requisite to reply to these queries. "The sufferings, immoralities, evils of all sorts, produced in innumerable cases by the subjection of individual women to individual men are far too terrible to be overlooked." The abuse of power cannot be very much checked while the power remains, and the marital power is one accorded not only to good or decently respectable men, but to all men who marry – the most brutal and the most criminal among them. "Marriage is the only actual bondage known to the law. There remain no legal slaves except the mistress of every house." In regard, however, to the larger question, –

> "the removal of women's disabilities – their recognition as the equals of men in all that belongs to citizenship; the opening to them of all honourable employments, and of the training and education which qualifies for those employments – there are many persons to whom it is not enough that the inequality has no just or legitimate defence; they require to be told what express advantage would be obtained by abolishing it."

To this it is to be answered, first, "the advantage of having the most universal and pervading of all human relations regulated by justice instead of injustice;" and secondly, the advantage secured by "giving to women the free use of their faculties, by leaving them the free choice of their employments, and opening to them the same field of occupation and the same prizes and encouragements as to other human beings," of "doubling the mass of mental faculties available for the higher service of humanity." The vast amount of gain to human nature which would arise from the former advantage it is scarcely possible to place in a stronger light than it is placed by merely stating it

> "to any one who attaches a moral meaning to words. All the selfish propensities, the self-worship, the unjust self-prefer-

ence which exist among mankind have their source and root in, and derive their principal nourishment from, the present constitution of the relation between men and women."

The fact that "where there is now one person qualified to benefit mankind and promote the general improvement, as a public teacher or an administrator of some branch of public or social affairs, there would then be a chance of two," is sufficient of itself to make the importance of the latter advantage manifest to all impartial persons.

"Mental superiority of any kind is at present everywhere so much below the demand, there is such a deficiency of persons competent to do excellently anything which it requires any considerable amount of ability to do, that the loss to the world by refusing to make use of one-half of the whole quantity of talent it possesses is extremely serious. It is true that this amount of mental power is not totally lost. Much of it is employed, and would in any case be employed, in domestic management and in the few other occupations open to women, and from the remainder individual benefit is in many individual cases obtained through the personal influence of individual women over individual men. But these benefits are partial: their range is extremely circumscribed."

And against them should be weighed the stimulus that would be given to the intelligence of men by the access of competition by women, "or, to use a more true expression, by the necessity that would be imposed on them of deserving precedency before they could expect to obtain it."

Added to these considerations are the effects to be anticipated from the proposed changes on the character and happiness of women themselves.

"The mere consciousness a woman would then have of being a human being like any other entitled to choose her pursuits, urged or invited by the same inducements as any one else to interest herself in whatever is interesting to human beings, entitled to exert the share of influence on all human concerns which belongs to individual opinion, whether she attempted actual participation in them or not; this alone would effect an immense expansion of the faculties of women as well as enlargement of the range of their moral sentiments."

They would become proportionately more fitted to develop what is commendable in their male associates, and to aid them in their nobler aspirations, instead of endeavouring, as they now too frequently do, to stifle everything in them which does not conduce to their immediate advancement, or that of their belongings, or which runs counter to, or out of, the current conventional opinion. "Whoever has a wife and children has given hostages to Mrs. Grundy;" and seeing how many have done so, it is no "wonder that people in general are kept down in that mediocrity of respectability which is becoming a marked characteristic of modern times."

At present the influence of women is probably not less real than it was in classical antiquity, or in the age of chivalry; but it is no longer of so obvious and definite a character.

> "Both through the contagion of sympathy, and through the desire of men to shine in the eyes of women, their feelings have great effect in keeping alive what remains of the chivalrous ideal – in fostering the sentiments and continuing the traditions of spirit and generosity. In these points of character their standard is higher than that of men, in the quality of justice somewhat lower. As regards the relations of private life, it may be said generally that their influence is on the whole encouraging to the softer virtues, discouraging to the sterner, though the statement must be taken with all the modifications dependent on individual character. In the chief of the greater trials to which virtue is subject in the concerns of life – the conflict between interest and principle – the tendency of women's influence is of a very mixed character. When the principle involved happens to be one of the very few which the course of their religious or moral education has strongly impressed upon themselves, they are potent auxiliaries to virtue, and their husbands and sons are often prompted by them to acts of abnegation which they never would have been capable of without that stimulus. But with the present education and position of women, the moral principles which have been impressed on them cover but a comparatively small part of the field of virtue, and are, moreover, principally negative, forbidding particular acts, but having little to do with the general direction of the thoughts and purposes. It is to be feared that disinterested-ness in the general conduct of life – the devotion of the

energies to purposes which hold out no promise of private advantages to the family – is very seldom encouraged or supported by women's influence. It is small blame to them that they discourage objects of which they have not learnt to see the advantage, and which withdraw their men from them, and from the interests of the family. But the consequence is that women's influence is often anything but favourable to public virtue."

There is nothing, except disease, indigence, and guilt, so fatal to the pleasurable enjoyment of life as the deprivation of a worthy outlet for the active faculties.

"Women who have the cares of a family, and while they have the cares of a family, have this outlet, and it generally suffices for them; but what of the greatly increasing number of women who have had no opportunity of increasing the vocation which they are mocked by telling them is their proper one? What of the women whose children have been lost to them by death or distance, or have grown up and married and formed homes of their own?"

They are, as a rule, driven to take refuge in philanthropy; the two provinces of it they chiefly cultivate being religious proselytism and charity.

"Religious proselytism at home is but another word for embittering of religious animosities: abroad it is usually a blind running at an object without either knowledge or heeding the fatal mischiefs – fatal to the religious object itself, as well as to all other desirable objects – which may be produced by the means employed. As for charity, it is a matter in which the immediate effect on the persons concerned, and the ultimate consequence to the general good, are apt to be at complete war with one another; while the education given to women – an education of the sentiments rather than of the understanding – and the habit inculcated by their whole life of looking to immediate effects on persons – make them both unable to see, and unwilling to admit the ultimate evil tendency of any form of charity which commends itself to their sympathetic feelings."

In marriage, again, the broad line of distinction there now is between the education and resulting characters of women and those of men, much more often than not, proves destructive to "that union of thoughts and inclinations which is the ideal of married life. Intimate society between people radically dissimilar to one another is an idle dream. Unlikeness may attract, but it is likeness which retains, and in proportion to the likeness is the suitability of the individuals to give each other a happy life. While women are so unlike men, it is not wonderful that selfish men should feel the need of arbitrary power in their own hands to arrest *in limine* the lifelong conflict of inclinations by deciding every question on the side of their own preference. When people are extremely unlike, there can be no real identity of interest. Very often there is a conscientious difference of opinion between married people on the highest points of duty. Is there any reality in the marriage when this takes place?"

It is, of course, not to be supposed that differences in taste and inclination exist between husbands and wives only because women and men are brought up differently. They would probably exist to a greater or less degree under every imaginary concatenation of circumstances. But it is not going beyond the mark to say that the difference in their bringing up aggravates those differences and renders them wholly inevitable.

"While women are brought up as they are, a man and woman will but rarely find in one another real agreement of tastes and wishes as to daily life. They will generally have to give up as hopeless and renounce the attempt to have in the intimate associate of their daily life that *idem velle, idem nolle*, which is the recognised bond of any society that is really such; or, if the man succeeds in obtaining it, he does so by choosing a woman who is so complete a nullity that she has no *velle* or *nolle* at all, and is as ready to comply with one thing as another if anybody tells her to do so. Even this calculation is apt to fail; dulness and want of spirit are not always a guarantee of the submission which is so confidently expected from them. But if they were, is this the ideal of marriage? What in this case does the main obtain by it, except an upper servant, a nurse, or a mistress? On the contrary, when each of two persons, instead of being a nothing is a something, when they are attached to one another, and are not too much unlike to begin with, the constant partaking of the same things, assisted by their sympathy, draws out the latent capacities of each for being interested in the things which were at first interesting only to the other, and works a gradual assimilation of the tastes and characters to one another, partly by the insensible modification of each, but more by a real enriching of the two natures, each acquiring the tastes and capacities of the other in addition to its own."

The following passage will appear, to those who have read a certain monumental inscription at Avignon, and still more to those who may have had the privilege of being personally acquainted with the gifts and virtues it records, to be characterized by peculiar pathos, the full depth and meaning of which it is impossible for others perhaps even partially to understand.

"What marriage may be in the case of two persons of cultivated faculties, identical in opinions and purposes, between whom there exists that best kind of equality, similarity of powers and capacities with reciprocal superiority in them – so that each can enjoy the luxury of looking up to the other, and can have alternately the pleasure of leading and of being led in the path of development – I will not attempt to describe. To those who can conceive it there is no need; to those who cannot it would appear the dream of an enthusiast. But I maintain, with the profoundest conviction, that this, and this only, is the ideal of marriage; and that all opinions, customs, and institutions which favour any other notion of it, or turn the conceptions and aspirations connected with it into any other direction, by whatever pretences it may be coloured, are relics of primitive barbarism. The moral regeneration of mankind will only really commence when the most fundamental of the social relations is placed under the rule of equal justice, and when human beings learn to cultivate their strongest sympathy with an equal in rights and in cultivation."

We have now presented our readers with an outline of Mr. Mill's argument, preferring on all occasions to give its leading points in his own powerful language rather than diluted in any paraphrase we could make of them. It is unnecessary for us to comment upon or criticise, his reasoning. To our minds it appears completely conclusive and utterly unanswerable. But we notice with regret that one branch of the subject of which

Mr. Mill treats, has been considered by him to be foreign to the
immediate purpose of his present work, and has been omitted
by him from examination. We refer to the question of Divorce
– the appropriate means of terminating the engagements
implied by marriage, and of enabling the parties to enter into
similar engagements with other persons. It was the opinion of
the illustrious William von Humboldt, that interference on the
part of the State with the arrangements, whether in respect to
their nature or continuance, which citizens of the opposite
sexes may think proper to make with one another for their
mutual association, is politically illegitimate and morally
censurable. He says:

"The manifest inference we would derive from these
considerations on the institution of matrimony is this:– That
the effects which it produces are as various as the characters
of the persons concerned; and that, as a union so closely
allied with the very nature of the respective individuals, it
must be attended with the most hurtful consequences when
the State attempts to regulate it by law, or through the force
of its institutions to make it repose on anything save simple
inclination. When we remember, moreover, that the State
can only contemplate the final results in such regulations –
as, for instance, population, early training, &c. – we shall be
still more ready to admit the justice of this conclusion. It may
reasonably be argued that a solicitude for such objects
conducts to the same results as the highest solicitude for the
most beautiful development of the inner man. For, after
careful observation, it has been found that the uninterrupted
union of one man with one woman is most conducive to
population; and it is likewise undeniable that no other union
springs from true, natural, harmonious love. And further, it
may be observed that such love leads to no other or different
results than those very relations which law and custom tend
to establish, such as the procreation of children, family
training, community of living, participation in the common
goods, the management of external affairs by the husband,
and the care of domestic arrangements by the wife. But the
radical error of such a policy appears to be, that the law
commands, whereas such a relation cannot mould itself
according to external arrangements, but depends wholly on
inclination: and wherever coercion or guidance comes into

collision with inclination, they divert it still further fi
proper path. Wherefore it appears to me that th
should not only loosen the bonds in this instance, an
ampler freedom to the citizen, but, if I may app , ...c
principles above stated (now that I am not speaking of
matrimony in general, but of one of the many injurious
consequences arising from restrictive State institutions,
which are in this one specially noticeable), that it should
entirely withdraw its active solicitude from the institution of
matrimony, and both generally, and in its particular
modifications, should rather leave it wholly to the free choice
of the individuals, and the various contracts they may enter
into with respect to it. I should not be deterred from the
adoption of this principle by the fear that all family relations
might be disturbed, or their manifestation in general
impeded: for although such an apprehension might be
justified by considerations of particular circumstances and
localities, it could not be fairly entertained in an inquiry into
the nature of men and States in general. For experience
frequently convinces us that just where law has imposed no
fetters, morality most surely binds: the idea of external
coercion is one entirely foreign to an institution which, like
matrimony, reposes only on inclination and inward sense of
duty: and the results of such coercive institutions do not at
all correspond to the designs in which they originate." – *The
Sphere and Duties of Government*: translated by Joseph
Coulthard, jun., pp. 33–5.

As society is at present constituted, however, the full measure
of personal liberty with respect to our sexual relations here
contended for, unspeakably desirable as we hold its attainment
to be, cannot perhaps be practically accorded, with due regard
to the interests of individuals or of the community at large. But
towards the attainment of it there is a growing movement,
particularly in the United States, and, to some extent, in this
country and on the continent. Among persons distinguished
rather for the strength than the weakness of their moral
convictions there is, on both sides of the Atlantic, an increasing
desire to emancipate their unions from conventional trammels,
and to avoid in their initiation the interchange of pledges which
it may be impossible in spirit, and, in that event, which would
be immoral, for them to observe. For we do not hesitate to

affirm that the prolonged cohabitation of a man and a woman, after it has ceased to be sanctified my mutual affection, is as essentially immoral when it arises from so-called religious feeling, as the pious prostitution of the ancient Babylonians in their temples, and when from considerations of worldly convenience or advantage, as essentially immoral as the mercenary prostitution of the streets of modern London and Paris.

Nevertheless, marriage in the existing order of things, and as they are likely to exist for a long time to come, entails civil and legal consequences so important, and frequently so intricate, that to us it seems the Legislature of any country in which this is the case, is not only justified but bound to direct the observance of certain public and ascertained formalities by those subject to it who intend to participate in, or to retire from participation, in the rights and obligations marriage confers and attaches. The effects of marriage do not terminate with the man and woman between whom it subsists. By it they assume a special relation towards the rest of the community of which they are members, and when they procreate children, other interests are with them brought into being, of which it is the duty of society to take charge. But the primary objects of marriage are the happiness and comfort of the parties to it, and it is susceptible of every variety of form which their consent can establish, if it be not contrary to these objects. The stipulations which the parties might see good to make with each other should be, like those of any other contract, capable of being legally enforced. Their terms, however, whether as to the incidents or the duration of the connexion, should be left to the choice and discretion of the parties themselves. We have not space at our command to do justice to these matters now, and we have referred to them simply because when we opened "The Subjection of women," we hoped that in it we should have found an expression of opinion on them from the acknowledged leader of British thought – an expression of opinion which we are convinced would have done more than anything else to dispel prejudice and diffuse sound views with regard to them. But as it is, Mr. Mill's book is emphatically a great work:– the writing of it is not the least among his many claims to our admiration and respect, nor will it, we venture to prophesy, prove among the earliest forgotten of his numerous titles to the esteem and gratitude of posterity.

MR. MILL ON THE SUBJECTION
OF WOMEN[1]
By Sir Henry Taylor, K.C.M.G. D.C.L.

Taking Mr. Mill's essay as the work of a philosopher applying himself on this occasion, not to an act of investigation, but to an act of advocacy, I cordially share the admiration generally bestowed upon it. Mr. Mill is of course intellectually incapable of overlooking, were he willing to perceive, much that lies beneath his argumentation and much that stands over against it; and his language of confidence and conclusiveness must be understood as belonging to the art of advocacy, dictating, for the moment and for the purpose, its own limitations to the reach and scope of his philosophic mind. He knew that to produce the effect he desired upon popular sentiments there must be no word, or but one word here and there, of doubt or hesitation, and that the most arduous and complex questions which human history and human life can present, must be dealt with by a bold, rapid, and decisive handling: and he knows also that this forensic suppression of half the question, and bogtrotting evasion of the difficulties, is perfectly justifiable in a philosopher when treating of a subject on which counter-advocacy is certain to be provoked; being indeed nothing else than the subdivision of labour in the cause of truth.[2]

But there is a third method of treatment which, though less popular, may not be without its use; and a sceptic who neither affirms nor denies many of Mr. Mill's conclusions may be

[1] *The Subjection of Women*, by John Stuart Mill. Longmans. A Bill entitled 'An Act to Amend the Law with respect to the Property of Married Women,' brought from the House of Commons 22nd of July 1869, and ordered by the House of Lords to be printed.

[2] It is observed by Miss Julia Wedgwood in her very admirable essay on female suffrage, that, 'It is not the act of a partisan, but of an earnest seeker after truth, to contemplate any large subject for a time steadily from one side.' – *Woman's Work and Woman's Culture*, p. 247. Perhaps, however, it should rather be said that, whether it be or not the act of a partisan (for it is only in rare and exceptional cases anything else), it may be, and often is, conducive to the establishment of the truth.

allowed to cast his weak and wavering glances here and there
upon two or three of them:

> Some will object that a comparison cannot fairly be made
> between the government of [by?] the male sex and the forms
> of unjust political power [political forms] which I have
> adduced in illustration of it; since these are arbitrary and the
> effect of mere usurpation, while it, on the contrary, is
> natural. But was there any domination which did not appear
> natural to those who possessed it?

And according to Mr. Mill what *is* natural is, that man should
not arrogate, nor woman undergo, any rule of the one over the
other.

If Mr. Mills' antagonists shall play upon the surface of the
subject in the way he thus supposes, it may suit his advocacy to
play with them, and I can understand how it comes that such a
shuttlecock of a word as the word 'natural' should be thus tost
backwards and forwards. Had it suited Mr. Mill's purpose and
his plea, he would have denounced the word as, in this
application of it, either unmeaning or demanding divers
developments in one direction and limitations in another to
give it significance. He knows that whatever is (miracles
excepted), is natural, and that that which is natural may just as
well be evil as be good. Of course, if the word is to indicate
anything that is relevant to the issue, it must have reference to
something in nature so elemental, stable, and durable, that
whether it be good or evil, time and circumstance will find it
indestructible, – something which, if evil, cannot be helped,
and not only cannot be helped in time present, but never can be
helped in this world's hereafter: it must mean that woman's
subjection, – as it was in the beginning, is now and ever shall
be, – arose not merely out of variable operations of nature,
which would make it natural in one sense, but out of an
universal and perdurable law of nature, which would make it
natural in quite another.

Taking the word in this latter sense, his arguments from
assumed political analogies, – the conditions of slavery, of
military subjugation, of civil despotism, – all mutable and
perishable, – are misdirected. Russia subjugates Poland, and
the subjugation and consequent subjection is natural, but
natural only in the sense of being a result of nature variably
operant through variable circumstances. It is according to

nature that, in the main, governments should be the results of peoples. But peoples are subject to time and change. The people of Poland were, at the time of their subjugation, a people to whom anarchy and faction were natural. In this their condition, subjugation by a foreign power, and the consequent subjection, was natural; – natural, not by an immutable law of nature, but by a terminable operation of nature. The question is in which of these senses the subjection of woman to man is natural. Mr. Mill assumes that it had its origin in mere inferiority of physical strength; and could I concur with him in his assumption, I should so far concur with him in his inferences as to perceive that, if there is no other reason for it than that, the intention of nature might very possibly be that it should come to an end. Nature does not often mean what she begins with; and nothing is more natural than that physical strength, except in so far as it ministers to intellectual energies and mental health, should play a continually diminishing part in civil and social relations. It is, or seems to be, a permanent law of nature that woman should be inferior to man in physical strength; but the physical strength of man operates powerfully or faintly according to circumstance. In savage tribes, and in the lower classes of civilised communities, it operates power-fully; and if the subjection of women were found in these alone, the inference might be that it was natural only as belonging to nature's fugitive operations; for savages may cease from the earth, and the lower classes may be raised to the level of the higher. But the subjection of women not only reaches to the classes in which the influence of physical strength is evanescent, but it is derivatively from those classes that the principle has found its footing in our jurisprudence; for it is by those classes that our common law was originally constructed, and has been from time immemorial administered, and in its administration, though modified and controlled by equity jurisdictions, yet essentially and in its general operation maintained. The reasonable presumption seems to be therefore that, both in times long past and more recently, some other ground-work than physical strength must have existed for the laws and customs giving predominance to man over woman. Does this ground-work, whatever it be, exist still, and will it exist always? Is the predominance to be sought in nature's grants to man in perpetuity or in her long leases? It is in the upper classes that nature commonly gives the earliest indications of a

mutable purpose. It is they that first begin to float. For about
two hundred years the Courts of Equity have found means to
protect the property of married women of the upper classes by
the device of marriage settlements, and thereby in some degree
to detract from marital predominance; and in some countries,
especially in the United States and in Canada, the common law
by which the rights of property were denied to married women
has been abrogated by legislation, and in this country there has
been a current of opinion running in the same direction, and
new legislation is in progress. Nor is it at all improbable that
changes affecting man's predominance in marriage will proceed
much faster than they have hitherto and much farther than the
point which has now been reached. But it is precisely this
accelerated movement of innovation and change in public
opinion which is apt to hurry the minds of some philosophers
and project them into larger inferences of subversion to come,
than a reasonable survey of the past and present may be found
to warrant. If a modifying spirit is now at work, and may be
expected to continue at work till much greater improvements
have been made in the relations of the sexes than any yet in
operation or likely to be immediately entertained by the
Legislature, it is nevertheless not to be forgotten that for long
ages, and in all countries, and in all classes of all countries,
law, custom, and opinion have universally sanctioned and
enforced some more or less predominance of man over woman;
and it is reasonable to presume that had there not been a
foundation less unstable than social circumstance for the
predominance to rest upon, – had not the predominance been
supported by some immutable law of nature, – nature's onward
operations would have long ago, in one time or another, in one
country or another, landed the sexes in *legal* equality at least,
and, amongst the classes in which physical strength stands
neutral, in social equality also.

More or less connected with the question how far the
subjection of women is natural, in one sense or another, is the
question whether any such subjection is expedient and just, and
whether in one degree or another it will be so always. And
here, again, I may follow Mr. Mill's example of adducing
political analogies, and revert to my former illustration. If I
have allowed myself to say that the subjection of the Poles to
Russia is natural, using the word in its loose and popular sense,
what I meant to convey was, not certainly that the government

of Russia was good government. The quality of the government was not in question. But from the fact of its being
natural we may infer the possibility that, bad though it be, it
may be better for them than any other that is practicable.
And as to the question whether it is just, we may have no
doubt that it involves much and very cruel injustice, but
whether it is on the whole favourable or unfavourable to
justice will depend on the answer to another question, –
whether there is more injustice perpetrated by Russians upon
Poles than, in the absence of Russians, would be perpetrated
by Poles upon each other; and if so in the past, whether it will
be so in the future, – whether, for example, in the course of
time the cause of justice may not be promoted by the
emancipation of Polish serfs as a result of Russian rule; and
upon that comes the question whether Polish subjection may
not cease, and whether, through the consolidation of classes
or other regenerative processes, the Polish race may not
attain to a fitness for political independence, and through the
fitness to the fruition. And so of the subjection of woman to
man. If it were natural only because women are not at
present all that they should be and might be made, it should
be regarded as good and just only in so far and for so long as
women shall not be fit for independence; and we should be at
liberty to admit that the time might come, or may be now at
our heels, when it may be natural and fit that neither sex
should rule the other, which is Mr. Mill's idea of fitness; or
that woman should rule man, which hitherto does not seem
to be any one's ideal. But if the question is to be determined by
the reference to history and political analogies to which Mr.
Mill invites us, the conclusion seems to be that at which he has
not arrived. For whereas the ground of difference between
nations and organised communities, and even the ground of
difference between races, is manifestly a shifting ground, and
the history of all ages is a history of conquerors and conquered
and of degeneracy in one race and invigoration of another, the
difference of sexes, according to the same universal history,
would seem to be a perennial difference, and the relations of
supremacy and subjection arising out of it to admit of
modification indeed, but not of reversal or overthrow. And if
the historical argument be assumed to show that Poland may
one day be fit for independence, and that independence may
one day conduce, not to anarchy and strife, but to the cause of

justice and to more of happiness for Poland, the same argument
tends to show that that day will never arrive for woman.

The argument from history is, no doubt, as Mr. Mill asserts,
in one sense one-sided. As history contains no record of woman
released from man's control, we cannot form any notion from
history of how she would demean herself, or what would
happen to her, if she were released. And thus, Mr. Mill argues,
we have hitherto no measure of her capabilities. Let her loose,
and then we shall know more about her:

> I consider it presumption in any one to pretend to decide
> what women are or are not, can or cannot be, by natural
> constitution. They have always hitherto been kept, as
> regards spontaneous development, in so unnatural a state
> that their nature cannot but have been greatly distorted and
> disguised; and no one can safely pronounce that if women's
> nature were left to choose its direction as freely as men's, and
> if no artificial bent were given to it except that required by
> the conditions of human society and given to both sexes
> alike, there would be any material difference, or perhaps any
> difference at all, in the character and capacities which would
> unfold themselves.

And again (p. 117) he affirms, not only that in the absence of
opportunities given we cannot know whether women could not
do the same things that men do fully as well on the whole, but
that he 'sees not the smallest reason to doubt it.' It is true that
we cannot know from experience what women would be
capable of should opportunities be given which have not been
given. But what we do know is this, – that the opportunities
which have not been given to women, women have not been
hitherto capable of taking. Opportunities are the result of
capabilities, more than capabilities of opportunities; though
each is in turn, and to a certain extent, the result of the other.

Upon the ground of his supposed equality of capacities Mr.
Mill proceeds to demand for women 'equal justice,' 'equal
rights,' and other equalities, – always as something founded in
nature; and he affirms (p. 79) that 'society in equality is its
normal state.'

Let us listen, however, to a greater philosopher (and few are
they that *are* greater) than even Mr. Mill. 'Intellectus humanus
ex proprietate suâ facile supponit majorem ordinem et
æqualitatem in rebus quam invenit; et cum multa sint in naturâ

monadica et plena imparitatis, tamen affingit parellela et correspondentia et relativa quæ non sunt.'[3] And where in truth shall we find equality to be the condition presumable in the order of nature? Nature renounces equality in races, renounces it in individuals, renounces it both in themselves as they are born into the world and in the fortunes that attend them. Breeds differ, and men of the same breed are by birth unequal in all sorts of attributes, – in stature, in health, in beauty, in understanding, in moral susceptibility, in energy, in passion. Of one man you can affirm little more than that he is not a monkey; of another little less than that he is not an angel. So are they born, and being born, the fate that awaits them is as diverse. One is rich, and his feet are set in a large room from the first; another is poor, but has it in him to become rich; a third inherits, and a fourth achieves, social or political predominance; a fifth becomes intellectually pre-eminent: whilst the multifarious multitude ranges through every variety of fortune allotted by nature to strength or weakness, stupidity or shrewdness; and through every variety also which is tost to the hand of one man or another by the chances of life. And amidst this nature's world of inequality, what is it that is meant by 'equal justice,' and has justice much to do with equality? Mr. Mill will say, no doubt, men are unequal, but let them have equal opportunities, and, freed from all artificial hindrances, be the agents and arbiters of their own destinies. If this be good for mankind, as is quite possible under certain conditions of society, let it be the object of our endeavours accordingly; and if Mr. Mill pleases, let it be called by the name of 'justice;' but equal opportunities to unequal forces will by no means tend to ensure equality of freedom or equality of fruits. Give all opportunities of aggrandisement to wealth, and will not wealth become an instrument of oppression? Give physical force all opportunities, and will it not revel in the pride of power? Remove all hindrances out of the way of intellect, and what tyrant on earth will be more insolent and aggressive? But 'equal justice,' it will be said, means indeed equal opportunities and equal freedom of action to all, but only so far forth as no wrong is done by one free agent to another free agent; that is, it means no more than that the shield of civil and criminal jurisprudence should be thrown over all alike. If this and no

[3] *Novum Organum*, xlv.

other equalisation were meant, though it is a very sorry approximation to real and practical equality, yet there is a strong presumption in favour of it; – stronger, however, in respect of criminal than in respect of civil law; for the right to protection of the person is very large and general in its scope, if not universal, whereas property is the creature of law and expediency. But when we are further called upon to include in equal justice equality of social and political power, a much bolder advance is made into the region of hypothetical expediency, and we are brought amongst the equalities of which all that I will affirm at present is, that 'Nature' and 'Justice' have very little to say to them. Political power, as derived from political franchises, *may* be necessary to women in order to secure their personal protection. May or may not be necessary. Probably any amount of social influence which would suffice to procure the political power, would suffice, without the political power, to procure all the legislation required for the personal protection. And it never should be forgotten that power, in itself and for itself, is not, either in man or woman, a legitimate object of desire; nor is the lust of power at all the more legitimate because in our days that ancient siren so often takes the name and counterfeits the virtues of

The mountain nymph, sweet Liberty.

Men may lawfully woo the siren for access to the nymph; but even men may only do so if they are fitting suitors. And if women demand a political franchise, they should remember that, if demanding it as something to be *enjoyed*, they show themselves *ipso facto* to be unfit for it; inasmuch as it is a function not a fruition, a trust and not a gift, – and a trust to be vested in those only, be they male or female, who are likely to conduce by their exercise of it to the well-being of the beneficiaries; – to the greatest happiness of the greatest number, – if that is the formula most acceptable to Mr. Mill – (always provided that the lesser number are not so tormented as to give suffering a preponderance in the total result). And when Mr. Mill demands the franchise for women on the ground that they are equally competent with men, his inference is, in my apprehension, insufficiently supported. He should extend his ground and say that they are more competent than men, or that (if not more competent on the whole) they have elements of competency which are wanting to men. A constituency identical in competency will do no better for being doubled in number.

It is hard for any one not accustomed to form his opinions by jumping into the air, to come to any assured conclusion as to what sorts of people are competent to exercise political franchises. Theoretically and at first sight, one would say only those few who are qualified by high education and considerable gifts of intelligence to judge of political and legislative questions. Practically we know that the politically wise few are not morally good enough to exercise their judgment disinterestedly for the benefit of the many, unless controlled by the many. It becomes necessary, therefore, to give franchises to large numbers who are wholly incapable of forming a just judgment of their own upon political questions. They are quite as little disinterested as the wise few, and they are not more good; it is their being interested, and their being many, which makes them a desirable element of power. But the interest of large numbers is often opposed to the interest of other large numbers, and also to the interests and just rights of small numbers; and moreover the devotion of large numbers to their own interests is apt to be a blind devotion, tending to the destruction of the interests which they desire to cherish, as well as of those they desire to destroy. What seems expedient therefore, is, not so much that the many should give their attention to political questions and strive to do that which for the most part it is impossible that they should do, – form a just judgment respecting them, – as that they should perceive and acknowledge their own incurable ignorance and incapacity, and seek the guidance of the persons within their reach whom they may have reason to think at once capable and trustworthy. Many can judge of a man who cannot judge of a question; and the presumptuousness of ignorance is less to be anticipated in forming the one judgment than in forming the other. Now, in applying these views to the question of women's eligibility for the suffrage, I think there is a good deal to be said for women's eligibility. Women are, – and I think justly, – generally supposed to have a gift of truer insight into the characters of men than men have; they have for the most part a higher value for goodness in men; and having more humility and a juster sense of their own incompetency to judge of politics and political questions, they may be more confidently expected, first, to seek for the guidance they need, and second, to know where to find it. Possibly they might be more open than men of the same class to what is called corruption; that is, knowing no reason why they should vote for one incomprehensible policy more than another equally incomprehensible, and knowing that *5l.* would enable them to provide medical attendance for a sick child or a less squalid and unwholesome lodging for the family, they would be more ready to indulge their domestic affections and commit one of those statutable offences which, in their eyes, does not wear the appearance of an offence against natural morality. But this I should scarcely regard as any serious evil. On the whole, therefore, if I were given to make wild guesses, (for on such subjects what opinion can be formed which deserves a better name?) I should incline to agree with Mr. Mill as to the expediency of giving the suffrage to women, though I should by no means agree with him as to the grounds for giving it.

The great question which is practically before Parliament and the country at present is the Married Women's Property Bill; and the course taken by the House of Commons last session in passing that Bill, is some evidence that female suffrage is not now indispensable to the vindication of women's rights; though, on the other hand, it may be thought that if female suffrage had been in operation heretofore women's rights would have been vindicated at a much earlier day. What the House of Lords will do with the Bill this coming session remains to be seen. It passed a second reading in that House only a fortnight before the close of the last session, when there was no longer time to refer it to a select committee, but with the understanding that it would be so referred in the session ensuing. Mr. Mill makes no allusion to it in his essay; but his name was on the back of the Bill brought in by Mr. Shaw Lefevre in 1868; he spoke upon it; and if the Bill of 1869 founded upon it should be enacted, some of the most important questions treated in his essay will be disposed of. A careful analysis of the Bill, with a valuable commentary, may be read in an essay by Mr. Herbert Mozley.[4] For my purpose it will be enough to say that the general purport of it is to enact that a woman's property shall not pass from her to her husband merely by her marriage, and that she shall be enabled to

4   *Woman's Work and Woman's Culture*, p. 186.

acquire, as well as to keep, property during coverture, and to hold it free from her husband's control and from liability for her husband's debts, and to spend the proceeds of it, though not to alienate the principal; that a woman shall be entitled also to keep or spend, free from her husband's control, such of her earnings as are made in any occupation carried on separately from her husband; whilst, on the other hand, it is enacted that the wife and not the husband shall be liable for debts contracted by her otherwise than as the husband's agent, and that she shall be liable for such maintenance of her husband and children as shall prevent them from becoming chargeable to the parish. And for the adjustment of any disputes between husband and wife arising out of their respective proprietary obligations and for the determination of any suits brought by either against the other, they are to have recourse to the Court of Chancery or to the County Court, which courts are to have, apparently, a large and somewhat undefined discretion in such matters, subject to the usual appeals to the respective appellate jurisdictions.

This is a measure founded in justice and expediency, and of great magnitude and importance. It was taken charge of in the Lords by Lord Penzance; and the Lord Chancellor and Lord Cairns gave their support to the principle of it; Lord Penzance, however, whilst he maintained the principle of the Bill, maintaining also that the 'paramount authority' of the husband in the household should be supported by law, so long as the household was not broken up and the husband performed his duties and did not use his authority tyrannically. It can scarcely be doubted that a Bill which can boast these authorities in the House of Lords, and the equally high authority of Mr. Russell Gurney in the House of Commons (for to him the charge of it devolved when Mr. Shaw Lefevre took office in the Government), will presently pass into law in its main purport and provisions. To me it appears that it cannot but operate beneficially in every class of society, though in some classes it may not operate largely. In the upper classes it will not perhaps effect much more than marriage settlements for separate use and due testamentary dispositions in favour of married women *might* effect without it; but I believe that the cases are far more numerous than some lawyers in Parliament seem to suppose in which, from one motive or another, or from mere neglect, the needful provisions of this nature are omitted. Mr. Mill alleges

(Commons debates, June 10, 1868), that notwithstanding settlement for separate use of the wife's income, the husband has a right, under the present law, to take it from her as soon as she receives it. If so, it is to be hoped that this Bill will give additional security to the wife's enjoyment of her own, even where settlement for separate use may not have been omitted. But no doubt, so long as husband and wife live together, there must be must difficulty in effecting a division of income and expenditure on the principle of each enjoying, without encroachment, what each owns. Generally speaking, law is too gross an instrumentality to penetrate the economy of households. Still, such a law as that in prospect will give relief, and the courts will know how to administer it in extreme and scandalous cases, if not in others; and it will have a more general operation in declaring a standard and criterion of obligation which cannot but have its effect in all those innumerable cases in which husbands merely fall into unjust and selfish courses because the law now to be abrogated has made such courses customary. For it is needless to say, that a most important operation of law is in giving a beneficial guidance to the operation of customary sentiment:

Mores leges perduxerunt jam in potestatem suam.

How far the new Bill may modify what Lord Penzance calls the 'paramount authority' of the husband, and what others call his 'just' or his 'proper' authority, in cases in which the wife is rich and he is poor, depends upon what views we take of this paramount, or just, or proper authority. If there be a natural predominance of man over woman, and of husband over wife (which I neither affirm nor deny), wives, Mr. Mill would say, will be unable to assume an independence which nature contravenes, for 'what women by nature cannot do,' he tells us (p. 48), 'it is quite superfluous to forbid them from doing;' and if so, the new law may be left to contend against nature in vain, and the just marital authority will hold its own provided the marital authority assumed to be just is no more than that which is natural. And in this I incline to agree; and though, if there be a natural authority of man over woman, there is also an authority scarcely less natural of the rich over the poor, and it is possible to conceive the case of a wealthy wife exercising a tyrannical authority over a destitute husband, yet in the case of husband, as well as in that of wife, pre-nuptial contracts will not be interdicted by the law, and a penniless gentleman, before he ventures to marry an heiress, may require to have a competency settled upon him for his separate use.

Perhaps, after all, the benefits of the law will be found less in facilities afforded for separate use than in those afforded for separation *à mensâ et thoro*. These facilities indeed do not seem to enter into the contemplation of Mr. Mill, inasmuch as they are an escape from difficulties which he scarcely consents to recognise. 'The rule,' he says, 'is simple; whatever would be the husband's or the wife's, if they were not married, should be under their exclusive control during marriage' (p. 86). If we were to look no farther, the simple rule would be in most cases, and in those in which its operation is most required, simply inoperative. The cases of easy-going couples in which no difficulty would occur under the new law are the cases in which no difficulty occurs under the old, and the wife has, if not all she has a right to, yet all she desires. Neither do the cases of the *un*-easy-going in which separate use is provided for by settlement appear to profit largely by the law, unless we look on to the *ultima ratio* of separation or divorce. But Mr. Mill is not disposed to look in that direction; for 'the question of divorce,' he says, 'in the sense of re-marriage, is one into which it is foreign to my purpose to enter' (p. 59). And it would seem to have been equally 'foreign to his purpose' to enter into the question of separation without divorce, for of that question, with all its incidents of custody and maintenance of children and the many complications it presents, he takes small account. Differences may arise, he admits; but they must find their way to a compromise on principles of equal justice, and no need to think of coming to extremities. Some alarmist, scared at the prospect of seeing marital sway abolished, may uplift his voice and tell us that –

His soul aches
To know, when two authorities are up,
Neither supreme, how soon confusion
May enter 'twixt the gap of both, and take
The one by the other.

But Mr. Mill would make short work with his alarms. The difficulty, he seems to think, is solved at once by a reference to the case of a brother and sister living together (Commons debate of 10th June, 1868: *Hansard*, vol. 192, p. 1371) and a partnership in business (*Essay*, p. 71). In all this I cannot concur. It may be 'foreign to Mr. Mill's purpose' to enter into the questions of divorce and separation, with all their brood of disputable problems; but these questions are absolutely vital and essential to the consideration of any scheme for the abrogation of marital authority, and they constitute a large portion of the question concerning conjugal rights of property; nor can the case between man and wife, – or, not to prejudge matters, let us say, wife and man, – be disposed of in a summary way by adducing the anything but analogous cases of brother and sister, or partners in trade. These are associated either from mutual affection or mutual convenience, and when the brother and sister cease to live in harmony, or the partners cease to suit each other's purposes, they can separate. Marriage, if fulfilling its purpose of procreation, is a partnership of a different kind. In the great majority of cases indeed, as Mr. Mill states (p. 83), married people of the higher classes manage matters by mutual arrangement, living in what he calls 'the spirit of a just law of equality,' or what others would call 'the spirit of a mutual and unforced dependence;' but, as all will agree, without any strong pressure of authority; and where this is the case, the analogy of the other partnerships may hold good. But what the law has to contemplate is the numerous minority of cases in which the exercise of authority is indispensable to the arrangements of domestic life. Let the husband be imperious and obstinate, the wife conscientious, resolute and intrepid, and let them take opposite views of some serious questions, – shall the children be sent to this school or that, or to this or that church? Or shall consent be given to the marriage of a daughter not yet of age? On such questions is the wife to be equally entitled with the husband to insist upon having her own way, and is the husband to be equally with the wife entitled to insist upon having his? and if so, what is to be done? For myself, I cannot but feel the force of Dogberry's dictum that 'an two ride of a horse, one must ride behind;' and if so it be, I should lean to the opinion that, unless superiority of judgment, and not merely equality, could be claimed for women, there is no reason for reversing the order of things hitherto customary, and putting the bridle in the hands of the wife, whilst the husband is placed on the pillion.

Nor is it a small portion of authority which, let the law say what it may, circumstances will of itself suffice to devolve upon the wife. Mr. Mill observes (p. 89) that the wife generally takes the management of the household and the bringing up of the children: and if it may be further affirmed that in general the husband has no choice, and must of necessity yield the control of these to his wife, we may do well to remember what a substantial share of power is thereby committed to her hands, and how large a proportion of the matters of common interest will thus fall under her daily direction. Single taken, the acts of authority may seem to be exercised upon trifles; but we are to bear in mind that (in the language of an ethical poet once of unrivalled celebrity, now almost forgotten) –

Small sands the mountain, moments make the year;
And trifles life.[5]

This natural or circumstantial preponderance of the wife in everyday affairs has an inevitable tendency to strengthen her position generally, and, as far as my observation of life enables me to judge, I should say that in the majority of couples, overtly or otherwise, the wife rules. I remember saying so to a very watchful and acute observer of life, who replied that such was her experience also; with this addition, – that for the most part, when it was otherwise, the marriage was not a happy one. In politics the conjunction of physical force with political supremacy is said to produce the worst form of tyranny, because it is in that conjunction that tyranny has nothing to fear. In domestic economies, if the husband tyrannises, there is no help for it. If the wife, the husband *can* rebel.

If, then, the law shall retain in the hands of the husband all the authority, such as it is, he now possesses, excepting only that which is exercised over the wife's property, what change will this exception introduce into conjugal relations in cases in which the wife has property of her own? But little, as I have said already, in the ordinary easy-going cases: but little, also, in the cases of domestic discord in which the wife cannot afford to separate: but possibly a great deal in cases in which the wife is rich enough to maintain herself and children in separation, and the husband is not rich and is disposed to be harsh and tyrannical. For though the law may fall short of such subtle efficacy as would be required to adjust a debtor and creditor account between husband and wife in the details of income and

5 Young's *Satires*.

expenditure so long as the household is one and indivisible, it may nevertheless avail to warn the husband that should he pass certain limits of ill-behaviour it will be competent to his wife to effect a separation, not with the mere alimentary allowance which the Matrimonial Causes Court might award under the existing law, but with all the property that belongs to her; whilst, his own means being by the hypothesis insufficient to the maintenance of the children, she might have it in her power to take them along with her. Such an issue would, no doubt, be matter for adjudication by the Courts; but the law's recognition of her exclusive rights of property could not fail to affect the principles on which the awards in such cases would be founded; and though, if there were faults on both sides, the separating wife might be required to leave some or all of the children with the husband and make provision for them out of her property, the provision, to conform to the principles of the law, would be computed on the basis of mere alimentary allowances.

There is yet another way in which the law might operate to the advantage of a wife rich enough to support herself and her children, and suffering from the ill-behaviour of a poor husband, even when not amounting to legal cruelty. She might induce him to retire upon a pension; and this remedy, if used only in the last resort and upon just and adequate grounds, might not come amiss. But again the ill-behaviour or perversity might be mainly on the wife's side; she might be the tyrant, and he

The rack and light leaf of her termagant blasts.[6]

And further, there may be a desire not only to eliminate him, but also to supplant him. In such cases it is clear that the power vested in the wife of buying out a much-injured but not very valiant and somewhat mercenary husband, would be liable to a good deal of abuse. The old Roman formula of divorce implied that the wife was to take with her what belonged to her, but the words put into the mouth of the husband seem to express that he is rather turning her out of doors, and hurling her goods at her head, than dismissing her with an acknowledgment of her right to them. 'Res tuas tibi habeto; tuas res tibi agito; exi, exi, ocius; vade foras, i foras, mulier, cede domo.' When similar

6   Darley, *Errors of Ecstasie*.

power is given to a wife to turn a peccant husband out of doors
in a like spirit, with his goods – or if he has none, with an
alimentary allowance – there may be no great harm done; but
when the further power is given her, be he peccant or be he
merely pliant, to open the door and beg him to go, taking with
him what will make him quite comfortable, instead of (what
she may have found it convenient to make him) very much the
reverse, a question may reasonably be suggested whether the
moralities of conjugal life will be as much promoted as the
mutual satisfaction of the parties. And it may be worth while to
observe that in the latter days of Rome, when the strict forms
of marriage were generally exchanged for that termed 'usus,'
which gave to the wife, along with separate proprietary rights,
equal rights of repudiation to those possessed by the husband,
what happened as that marriage became a very tenuous tie.
Mr. Lecky[7] cites from St. Jerome a case (an extreme one of
course) of a wife who, marrying a twenty-third husband,
became his twenty-first wife. He does not cite it without a
caution against exaggerating the effects of merely legal
changes, remarking that in a less impure state of public opinion
than existed in Imperial Rome a wide latitude of claiming
divorce might have been allowed to both wife and husband
without serious consequences. And this may be; but no doubt
independent rights of property, even without facilities of
divorce (collusive or other) must afford additional opportunities of separation.

So much for the new legislation as affecting people of
property. It will be capable of doing some harm in certain
cases; but on the whole it will, in my opinion, do a great
amount of good; directly in preventing abuses far worse and far
more numerous than any which it can generate, and indirectly
by giving the sanction and support of law to such sentiments as
ought to prevail respecting the right of women to hold a
position of equality with men in all respects in which nature
and social or domestic circumstance do not make it impossible.

But people of property are not the only people to be
considered. They are indeed the people least to be considered.
The preamble of the Bill of 1868, as originally drawn, pointed
to the wives of the poor as those on whom the existing law
presses with most severity, and who were to be especially

7 *European Morals*, ii. 325.

protected by the proposed change. I fear, however, it is amongst the poor that the law will meet with the greatest practical difficulty in effecting its objects. It is amongst the poor that the element of physical strength contributes so largely to the predominance of the husband, and it is not easy to see how the Court of Chancery or the County Courts could contrive (under § 10 of the Bill) to exempt the earning or small chattels of a wife from the effects of physical force, if the husband should be disposed to exert it; and amongst the poor the husband would in all probability resort to physical force in any case in which the relations between the two were such that the wife would resort to the Courts. Mr. Hastings and Mr. Cyrus Field, in their evidence given to the select committee of the Commons in 1868, adduce American experience to show that no difficulty and no discord is occasioned in families by laws giving wives an exclusive property in all that they earn as well as in all that they own. But in most, if not all, of the States of the Union, there are two variations from the law and the social circumstances of England which very much limit the applicability of American experience as a guide for English legislation. The facilities for divorce and re-marriage are far greater, and far greater also is the ease with which a woman can obtain a living without a man's help. In England the wives of the labouring men could not often avail themselves of separation or divorce even if all possible legal facilities were afforded them: and I am afraid that amongst the poor, if civil jurisdictions are to be of much use, criminal jurisdictions must come in aid of them. And why should they not? it may be said. To answer that, it is necessary to look at the operation of the laws which already exist for the protection of women. What their sufferings are, from brutal husbands of the poorer classes, is adverted to by Mr. Mill (p. 146) in strong language, but in no spirit of exaggeration. The brutalities of which he speaks are frequent; they are atrocious and detestable, and what law can do to abate them law ought to do. But when we come to inquire what it is within the scope and power of legislation to accomplish, we meet with much discouragement. The existing law no doubt might be, and ought to be, so amended as to establish a just standard of penal severity; a Flogging Act should be passed, such as was proposed in the House of Commons some years ago, not without strong indications of a feeling in its favour. But the unhopeful feature of the case is that courts and magistrates are too often as feeble and effeminate as the culprits they have to deal with are savage; so that even the inadequate punishments permitted by the existing law are but rarely inflicted in full measure. The wife, even if in the first impulse of a just anger she brings a charge against the husband, is induced, when that impulse is spent and she considers the consequences to herself and her children, to intercede for him with the magistrate; and whether it be to save the injured wife from after resentment and her and her children from the workhouse, at the expense of other wives for whose protection an exemplary sentence is required; or whether it be as part and lot of the unaccountable imbecility which pervades the administration of our laws against cruelty and violence, the magistrate reduces the often impotent penalty of the law to something even more nugatory than need is. The want of a public prosecutor, which enervates and stultifies our whole system of criminal jurisprudence, is in no class of cases more conspicuous than in this. Such an officer, acting not necessarily at the instance of the wife, but from information derived from police officers or others, would see to the due administration of justice, and to a certain point support and invigorate the more feeble of its ministers; whilst wives would not so often suffer from the vengeance of their husbands, as well as from the crimes which have provoked complaint. And in this way it may be that the institution of a public prosecutor would do more for the protection and well-being of the married women of the poor, than Mr. Russell Gurney's Bill, Mr. Mill's equalisation of rights, or any other of the measures which have been suggested for their special and peculiar advantage.

We are now to pass from the grievances of married women as such, to those of women generally, suffered through legal disability or otherwise. And it would have been convenient if Mr. Mill, or some one of the able and thoughtful essayists whose views are to be found in the volume edited by Mrs. Butler,[8] had treated separately of the disabilities created by law, specifying the particular provisions of common or statute law to which they take exception. And further, in this as in many other cases in which existing law is found fault with, a material advance would be made if the promoters of change

[8] *Woman's Work and Woman's Culture.*

were to reduce their notions to the form of such statute or statutes as they would propose should be enacted. If a man desires to know what he wants, and if he desires to enable others to know what he wants, and if he desires to know also, and to make known, what it is possible that law should give him, the best thing he can do is to draft his Bill.

All trading occupations are already open to single women, and will be open to married women if Mr. Russell Gurney's Bill should become law. Of the learned professions, the Law and the Church are closed against women. Medicine is not absolutely and imperatively closed by law; but under the law the medical schools and a medical board have it in their power to deny what the law renders indispensable. Women are excluded by law from being members of Parliament, magistrates, jurors, mayors, aldermen, or common-councilmen, members of vestries, and guardians of the poor. They are generally excluded by law or custom from holding municipal offices, or offices or employments of trust under the crown.

Now if all legal disabilities were removed, there is room for doubt whether women would occupy themselves much otherwise than they do at present: and whether they would or would not, I see no reason to deprecate the removal of most of these disabilities. It is a sort of case in which custom, when founded in what Philosopher Square calls 'the eternal fitness of things.' can dispense with legal sanctions – custom so founded being stronger than law; and if the custom be *not* founded in the fitness of things, then there would seem to be no good reason why it should be upheld.

As to facts of fitness, it may require some exercise of what may be called practical imagination, so to forecast the career of a woman in those of the learned professions not hitherto attempted by women, as to form a correct judgment of the difficulties she would have to overcome. In the Church we have abundant experience of women, as the wives of clergymen or otherwise, performing some of the more important of a clergyman's duties more effectively than men can perform them. 'Sacerdos per Hic et Hæc olim declinatur,' was said by a poet[9] of the twelfth century of the priest in the ages before he was condemned to celibacy; and since he has been redeemed from celibacy we may say it again. And if a clergyman and his

---

9 Walter de Mapes. He translated from the Latin into French, at the instance of Henry II., the romance of the *Saint Graal*.

wife make, not only one flesh, but not seldom one minister of
the Gospel, I cannot affirm with confidence that there is any
reason in the nature of things – whatever reason there may be
derivable from Scripture – why there should not be a female
clergy. It is hard to say whether some of the ministering
functions for which women are better qualified than men
should not be as highly estimated as the *officiating* duties of
clergymen; and it may be a question whether some of these
even might not be quite as well performed by women of a
high order and an age more then merely mature, as they are
by many of our clergy. About preaching probably more
difficulty would be made. Women's preaching did not find
favour with Dr. Johnson, – 'Sir, a woman's preaching is like a
dog walking on his hind legs. It is not done well, but you are
surprised to find it done at all.' But in Johnson's time learned
or cultivated women were much more rare than they are
now, and they are now more rare than they may in no long
time become, and in the proportion borne to learned and
cultivated men, indeed, than they were 300 years ago.
Nicholas Udall's account of the women of Henry the Eighth's
time (given in his epistle to Queen Katharine) describes a
prevailing female proficiency which is more than we can
quite claim for the present generation, but not more than we
may hope to see attained in the next, when the class of
women who now read more widely than average men of the
same class, may come to read also more deeply. It may then
come to be said once more –

> What a number is there of noble women, especially here in
> this realm of England, yea, and how many in the years of
> tender virginity, not only as well seen, and as familiarly
> traded, in the Latin and Greek tongues as in their own
> mother language, but also both in all kinds of profane
> literature and liberal arts, exacted, studied, and exercised;
> and in the Holy Scriptures and theology so ripe, that they are
> able, aptly, cunningly, and with much grace, either to indite
> or translate into the vulgar tongue for the public instruction
> and edifying of the unlearned multitude! Neither is it now a
> strange thing to hear gentlewomen, instead of most vain
> communication about the moon shining in the water, to use
> grave and substantial talk in Latin or Greek with their
> husbands of godly matters.

Now in women who have attained, or in process of time shall attain, to this measure of knowledge and intelligence, and who shall have ceased from vain communications about the moon, why, it may be said, should the gift of preaching be wanting? and from those who have it, why should the opportunity of employing it be withholden? And even if they should be unable to preach good sermons of their own, is there any reason why they should not preach those of others? Bishop Bull advised young clergymen not to preach sermons of their own writing; and probably there are few hearers of sermons who would not wish that the same advice should be given and taken in the case of very many clergymen, both young and old.

If I am asked, then, why there should not be a female clergy, I repeat that I know of no reason *in the nature of things* why not. But, on the other hand, I am far from confidently maintaining that there ought to be a female clergy. I am not convinced that I can understand the nature of things in matters hitherto unattempted and untried. Custom and customary sentiment is strongly against it. I am very far from being disposed to be servile to custom:

What custom wills in all things should we do 't,
The dust on antique Time would lie unswept,
And mountainous error be too highly heaped
For truth to overpeer –

But old and unbroken custom is, as far as it goes, a presumption in favour of what it supports; not only because old custom may be assumed to have proceeded out of a fitness (fugacious possibly, but not impossibly permanent); but also because it makes a fitness where there was none. Old custom is the parent of adaptations and conformities, often of an enduring, sometimes even of an hereditary character. A generation of flax-spinners in Belgium who can count no forerunners, competes at a disadvantage with the last of successive generations in Lancashire; for want of the hereditary hand to manipulate. The minds of men have their transmitted aptitudes as well as their hands; and this teaches us that some old customs should be rather left to be undermined than sought to be overthrown. To speak 'as one having authority,' belongs, in the present generation, to man rather than to woman. A long time must elapse and a change of opinion on the matter in question be slowly brought about (if it can be brought about), before any change of law can be contemplated.

Mr. Mill does not mention the Church as a career to be thrown open to women. Perhaps he does not think it worthy of them. He does mention the law; whereas I, on my part, am disposed to think, that this is the one of the learned professions which is unworthy of women; and also that there is a special unfitness on the part of women to undertake it. It was called by Serjeant Maynard, '*ars bablativa*.' If it were so, it would be quite as little suited to highly educated women as to intellectual men. But it is not so, and it is from another point of view that I object to it. Mr. Mill affirms (p. 95) that if he can show that women should be admitted to public functions, it ought to be granted that they are admissible to all other occupations. But when he has to meet objections to 'girls in their teens,' and 'young wives of two or three and twenty,' he says these are not the persons in question, but rather 'widows, or wives of forty or fifty' (p. 185). But I would ask Mr. Mill how a widow or a wife of forty or fifty is to jump into practice at the bar without having been brought up to the bar from her early girlhood? 'Commencez par le commencement, Belier, mon ami,' and let us in the first place follow the small foot of our law pupil to the chambers of the Special Pleader, who is her tutor, and see what happens. There we behold her seated,

> Among the blest, the chosen few
> (Blest if their happiness they knew),
> Who for three hundred guineas paid
> To some great master of the trade,
> Have, at his rooms, by special favour,
> His leave to use their best endeavour,
> By drawing pleas from nine till four
> To earn him twice three hundred more;
> And after dinner may repair
> To 'foresaid rooms, and then and there,
> Have 'foresaid leave, from five to ten,
> To draw the 'foresaid pleas again.[10]

At ten o'clock at night, therefore, after a day spent with a company of assiduous young gentlemen, distinguished by that modesty and backwardness which guarantees success at the

---

10 Anstey, *Pleader's Guide.*

196 The Subjection of Women

bar, we are to trace the small footstep back through Holborn or the Strand to her confiding parents, or her solitary lodgings, as the case may be. A year or two having been so passed without adventures, and the young lady having kept her terms at the Temple or Lincoln's Inn, she hires convenient chambers and half a clerk, and receives attorneys and others who may have occasion to transact business with her. Then come the circuits and the attendance in courts, civil and criminal, where she acquires a daily familiarity with all the villanies that are done under the sun, and all the vices that mix themselves up with indictable offences or lead to litigation. 'Touch not, taste not, handle not,' may have been the admonition conveyed to her mother or her grandmother when they were girls, and remembered even when they were 'widows or wives of forty or fifty;' but it is the business of our learned friend to handle everything, making the most or the least of each atrocious or scandalous offence, according to the part she is called upon to take in attacking or defending it. Mr. Mill (p. 117[11]) 'sees not the smallest reason to doubt' that she would perform her task fully as well as a man; and therefore we may expect to see her in due season mount the bench (whence, unless by that time a feminine or emasculated majority in Parliament shall have abolished punishment by death), we may hear her, after duly exchanging her wig for the black cap, sentence a prisoner at the bar to be taken to the place whence he came, and be hanged by the neck until he is dead. Looking at this career, in its several steps and stages, from one end of it to the other, I am of opinion that a good girl would rather herself be hanged by the neck than undertake it.

Of the learned professions there remains medicine. In this some experiments have been already made, and more are in progress; and I think they ought to have a fair trial, and that the Act of 1858, and any other obstructive provisions of law, should be so amended as not to empower public medical

---

[11] I quote the passage in which the general proposition is contained, of which I make here a specific application. 'Like the French compared with the English, the Irish with the Swiss, the Greeks or Italians compared with the German races, so women compared with men may be found on the average to do the same things, with some variety in the particular kind of excellence. But that they would do them fully as well on the whole if their education and cultivation were adapted to correcting, instead of aggravating, the infirmities incident to their temperament I see not the smallest reason to doubt.'

authorities to refuse the right to practise to women whose qualifications are the same as those which entitle men to practise. In some branches of practice, female practitioners, if competent – and I see no reason why they should not be competent when duly instructed – would be manifestly preferable to make. In other branches, anatomical studies, and the necessity of dissection, would be stumbling-blocks on the threshold; and there may be some difficulties – shown however, in the essay of Miss Gex Blake,[12] not to have been insurmountable in other ages and countries, and which, it may be hoped, will not be found wholly so in ours – in the way of opening medical schools to female pupils. No one, it is true, would desire to see girls of our time explore such fields of physiology as were treated by Abella and Trottula in the middle ages (if the work ascribed to the latter was really hers); and whatever limits should be assigned to lecturers and teachers, the mixing of male and female pupils would seem to be, in our time and country at least, undesirable. In our medical schools those of the students whose nature is not its own prophylactic are said to take a taint of hardness and coarseness in the crude season of their early professional training which it requires some years of maturer life and the humanities of their calling to correct. On the other hand, however, it may be said that feminine nature, if spared all unnecessary contact with masculine in the process, is in itself so much less corruptible in this kind, that it may be better fitted for the trials to be encountered; and though most women will probably shrink from such trials, there may be not a few with pure minds and brave hearts who will not; and if a new vocation shall be provided for these, and one of an order and quality so high and beneficent, a great object will be gained for mankind. But at first, and unless and until medical schools exclusively female can be constituted, the difficulties to be met with must be real and formidable; and when we find Miss Gex Blake making light of them, we cannot but think that she attributes to women generally some qualities, some powers, and some immunities which are exceptional and rare, if not peculiar to herself. Those women who can write as she has written may be able to command the respect which she commanded from the young students in medical schools,

12   *Woman's Work and Woman's Culture*, p. 114.

whether English or foreign. But the women who can write as she has written are assuredly not many.

Leaving the learned professions we come next to employments in the public service. Mr. Mill would have women to be considered eligible for all such employments, from the cabinet minister's to the clerk's. And, of course, he would have them to be eligible for seats in Parliament.

Now as to clerkships and employments in the public service of that class and kind, before the Government is called upon to give girls and women appointments in public offices, it would be well to inquire why they are not employed in similar capacities in the counting-houses of bankers or merchants or the offices of railway companies. It is not, I think, because they are considered incompetent to the transaction of the business usually transacted by clerks. They are employed by retail dealers; and they do the book-keeping of shops, if not as well as men, yet well enough. I can only account for their exclusion by ascribing it to the inconvenience of mixing the sexes in the transaction of such business as is to be transacted in rooms, not, like shops, open to public view; and to the reluctance of employers to assume the serious responsibility of looking after girls and women in matters of conduct and character. Men are left to take care of themselves; the care they do take is often not much; but if girls were left to take as little, the consequences would be what the world considers worse.

If the inconvenience of mixing the sexes is a sufficient reason for excluding women from the counting-houses of merchants and bankers, it is a reason more than sufficient for their exclusion from Government offices. The discipline of Government offices is necessarily much more lax than that of counting-houses. The clerk employed by the Government holds his office in these days, not so much during good behaviour, as during what is not extravagantly bad behaviour; for the misconduct must be flagrant and distinctly provable to induce heads of departments to face the difficulties attending a dismissal – difficulties possibly to include a grievous sacrifice of public interests by wasting the time of the House of Commons. Members of that House will sometimes inflict such a sacrifice on very slender grounds; and if they will do so in favour of a male delinquent who pretends that he has been hardly used, much more, and with much more chivalrous pertinacity, would they do so in favour of a female delinquent. Such being the lions in the path of the public employer, the private employer, on the contrary, has only to say, 'You do not suit me: go elsewhere.'

As we proceed upward in the scale of social rank and civil employments, difficulties increase; and the position of women called upon to exercise authority over men, and of men called upon to render obedience, presents new elements of incongruity. In shopkeeping life, men serve under women, as well as women under men; in domestic life, men-servants obey ladies: but it may nevertheless be a question whether ladies could conveniently exercise authority over gentlemen, or gentlemen over ladies. Distinctions of class may be said to be conventional distinctions; but conventional distinctions are real distinctions. Under the operation of natural laws controlling the sensitivo-rational imagination of man, conventional distinctions have their substantial and inevitable incidents; and of these it is but a juvenile philosophy that would refuse to take account. Should I be asked why, if a lady can exercise authority over her footman, a female Secretary of the Treasury should not exercise authority over the clerks in that department, I answer that, not only difference of education, but distance in social position, gives facilities in the one case which are wanting in the other; and this distance constitutes the irrelevancy of the example of queens adduced by Mr. Mill to show that civil authority can be fitly vested in women. If I am asked why, conversely, the gentleman filling the office of Secretary to the Treasury should not have young ladies under him as junior, and old ladies as senior clerks, the answer is the same: proximity of social position generates relations between ladies and gentlemen which are incompatible with the assumption of official authority by either sex over the other.

Seats in Parliament involve incompatibilities quite as forbidding. Mr. Mill says, 'If the political system of this country is such as to exclude unfit men, it will equally exclude unfit women' (p. 97). As the political system of the country is not, and is not likely to be, such as to exclude unfit men, it is hardly necessary to inquiry whether Mr. Mill is right in saying that, if it were, it would exclude unfit women; and the more pertinent inquiry is, whether unfit women would not be a worse element than unfit men; and whether the admission of the unfit of both sexes would not aggravate the unfitness of the unfit members of each. The rough treatment with which man meets man in debate could not be employed by man meeting woman, let the woman be ever so unfit; and if it were, the probability is that the woman would cry. The interference of the Speaker, if a man, would not be exercised towards women with the freedom with which it is exercised towards men, and yet the liberty of speech indulged by women in debate would probably be much larger than that usually permitted to men.

Having come to the end of his argument in favour of admitting women to posts and employments from which they are excluded, Mr. Mill is met by some questions as to how they prosper in some of the higher employments from which they are *not* excluded – in sciences, arts and literature. He admits that in these kinds no production entitled to the first rank has been the work of a woman; and his endeavour is to account for this 'without supposing that women are naturally incapable of producing them' (p. 126). A series of causes are assigned for this state of facts; but from beginning to end of the series we have to ask what, if not natural incapabilities, are the causes of those causes. It is only three generations since women have begun to bestir themselves (p. 127). Their inferiority in science and philosophy is from want of originality (p. 128). Their want of originality is from want of knowledge to bring them to the point from which originality takes its start, and their want of knowledge is from want of education (pp. 128, 130, 136). Their inferiority in literature is owing to men having created a literature before women wrote, so that women became imitators of men as the Romans of the Greeks (p. 132). Their inferiority in the fine arts is because they have not pursued them professionally (pp. 133–4). They do not desire fame, nor

Scorn delights and live laborious days;

and this is 'only the natural result of their circumstances,' and society has so ordered things (pp. 140–1). Throughout this array of reasons we have to ask at every step, why is it thus? What are the reasons of those reasons? Why did not women go to work sooner? why did they not find their way to education and knowledge and originality? why did they let men create a literature, and not take care to be in at the creation? why have they not pursued the fine arts professionally instead of superficially as amateurs? Why should society, which is male and female, have placed its one moiety more than its other equally capable moiety in circumstances unfavourable to lofty aims? Surely the one cause causative of all these proximate causes is not to be found in man's superior strength of body; and yet, from one end to the other of Mr. Mill's treatise, dig and delve as we may, no other root of doctrine is to be reached.

And here I come to a curious evolution of Mr. Mill's in his contention for the claims of women. He rebukes with scorn the 'silly panegyrics' on the superior moral nature of women offered by those who depreciate their intellectual nature, and he instructs us that such empty compliments must provoke a 'bitter smile from every woman of spirit;' seeing that there is 'no other situation in life in which it is the established order, and considered quite natural and suitable, that the better should obey the worse' (pp. 142-3). I hardly know by what spirit 'a woman of spirit' should be said to be animated, who should resent the opinion that women are morally superior to men, even when entertained by a person who ventures to think that they are intellectually unequal. For myself, though I do not positively deny the intellectual equality, I see some reason to doubt it; and as I might easily be betrayed into the panegyric in question (if an estimate ascribing a specific superiority is to be styled a panegyric), I feel as if I might at any moment be confronted by the formidable 'woman of spirit,' and withered by her smile. But, in truth, the difference between Mr. Mill and me has a deeper source than any mere difference in our estimates of the intellects and capabilities of women. His language, which seems so strange at first sight, is the language of indignation at those usages and doctrines by which he conceives that women suffer the loss of independence; and the deeper difference between him and me is in our respective views of the nature and value of the independence they lose. In taking stock of the benefits to ensue on redeeming women from subjection, he says:- 'It would be a grievous under-statement of the case to omit the most direct benefit of all, the unspeakable gain in private happiness to the liberated half of the species. . . . After the primary necessities of food and raiment, freedom is the first and strongest want of human nature . . . the freedom of action of the individual – the liberty of each to govern his conduct by his own feelings of duty, and by such laws and social restraints as his own conscience can subscribe to. . . . He who would rightly appreciate the worth of personal independence as an element of happiness, should consider the

value he himself puts upon it as an ingredient of his own. . . .
Let him rest assured that whatever he feels on this point,
women feel in a fully equal degree' (pp. 178-9). I desire to ask;
– first, is this a just estimate of the value of independence to
men; secondly, is it a just estimate of its value to women; and
thirdly, whether it be so or not, is it well that it should be so?
Freedom and independence are not one, but diverse in kind and
quality. One kind of freedom, which has its value no doubt in
our eyes, is that of a man who is free to sell his independence;
and many are the men who sell it in large measure for a small
price, – not to provide themselves with 'the primary necessities
of food and raiment,' but to provide 'le superflu, chose si
nécessaire,' – very secondary necessities indeed. Another much
valued freedom and independence, is that which relates to
politics and civil organisation, and this has its uses in their
construction, control, and conservation; and very noble uses
they are, and yet the consequences thence proceeding are
mixed. Mr. Mill says (p. 182), that 'the love of power and the
love of liberty are in eternal antagonism,' and that 'when there
is least liberty, the passion for power is the most ardent and
unscrupulous.' If he means the antagonism whereby the love of
power in one man is controlled and suppressed by the love of
liberty in another, I agree with him. But if he means (and this
is, I think, what he does mean), that the man loving liberty for
himself, does not also love power over others, I totally differ
from him. And as of individual men, so of classes and
combinations of men. In my judgment, the love of liberty is in
almost all men, and in absolutely all classes and combinations
of men, liable to pass into the love of power, to become
blended with it, and ultimately, if no correction shall be met
with, to be absorbed by it. I have been accustomed to think
that there is no corruption of the passions to which human
nature is more subject than to this.

But civil freedom, even when itself uncorrupted, is far from
being one and the same with personal independence: the
former is a poor possession in comparison with the latter; and
the former is far from being in all its consequences and
concomitants propitious to the latter. Personal independence is
a high moral and spiritual attribute, – like other such
attributes, in some measure subject to circumstances, and
capable of being impaired; and it is, I think, a mistake to
suppose that civil freedom, conferring equal rights and equal

opportunities of advancement on all men, does thereby cherish and promote in each man this precious possession of an independence seated in the heart. What it does promote is ambition, the mother of restless desires and disquieting apprehensions, and the very step-mother of independence, pursuing it 'novercalibus odiis.' He whose natural wants are satisfied as he is, and to whom no opportunities of rising present themselves, if his lot be moderately easy, will be contented with it; whereas he who sees a path ascending from summit to summit always before him, will be tempted to pass his life in striving and struggling, and through uneasy aspirations to forfeit the true independence which walks hand in hand with contentment.

And again, 'The only school of moral sentiment,' says Mr. Mill, 'is society between equals' (79). If it were so, there would be no such thing as a school of moral sentiment; for, as I have observed already, there is no such thing as equality. But if there were such a thing and such a school, there are some of the moral sentiments which would not be taught in it, even if there were not some of the more or less immoral sentiments which would. 'Let not the strong man despise the weak; and let the weak see that he reverence the strong.' That injunction is contained in the 'False Gospels,'[13] but it would not have been unworthy of a place in the true. Perhaps, however, all that Mr. Mill means is equality in the eye of the law. This there may be, and there ought to be, and in the main in this country there is; and where there is not, the effect is much the same; for the spirit out of which the legal equality has issued is sure to operate more powerfully in society than the law itself can operate, and there will be pretty nearly all the social equality that nature will permit (which is not much), and the school of moral sentiment will be nature's school and not Mr. Mill's. For, in truth, nature, which has made men differ from women, and has also made them differ from each other – differ in age, differ in health, in animal spirits, in energy, in personal attractiveness and in intellect, has provided such a school of moral sentiment as could never be found in relations of equality. And nature furthermore, inasmuch as she has given men an imagination susceptible of impressions from birth, rank, wealth, pomp, and circumstance, has provided yet

13   *First Epis. Clement*, xvii. 34.

another school of moral sentiment through social and adventitious inequalities. These are said to be artificial because their derivation from nature is less direct than some other inequalities; but this makes but little difference; for, as in the case of Perdita's 'streaked gilli-flower' –

> O'er that art
> Which, you say, adds to nature, is an art
> That nature makes –

And what is it that is taught in these schools? Not only patience, forbearance, humility, charity, generosity; but, I will say also, if Mr. Mill will allow me, personal independence. There is in truth, no purer independence than that of the man who, being contented with his own lot, is contented also to recognise superiority in another, be it of what is inborn, or be it of what is social and extrinsic; and there is nothing that strikes at the root of personal independence more than the jealousies of plebeian pride. We have this truth constantly before our eyes in our own country, for men's fear of being accounted by others of less importance than they account themselves, is the counterpart of the hope to rise above equals and to reach the level of superiors; and these hopes and fears are the necessary growth of our free institutions; and thus freedom, with all its progeny of virtues, is the parent of one vice, and that a parricidal vice: for the pride which is begotten of freedom preys upon its vitals. 'The proud man, who is the poor man, braggeth outwardly but beggeth inwardly,' says St. Jerome; and those who set most store by their independence are commonly those by whom independence is unknown; and who, moreover – by an inhibition issuing from their own nature and dispositions – let them rise to what position they may, can by no possibility achieve it. They are, and always must be, in want and in fear. Thus it is that free political institutions, whilst they may be relied upon to make a nation great and rich, and may be expected in some ulterior result, let us hope, to make it, what is more important, good and happy, yet in the meantime and on some natures, perhaps on many, have a mixed operation, not more equivocal in relation to any of the virtues than to that of personal independence. The most perfect liberty of action and development may indeed

Of inward slave make outward free –[14]

but that outward freedom is but a low step on the ladder of our
upward progress; and it may be well, by way of counteraction
to some accompanying influences of merely civil freedom, that
the female half of human kind should be placed in a position
more favourable than that of men for preserving the nobler and
purer independence in which many are born, but which, in this
country at least, not so many as one would desire are enabled
to carry with them through the struggles of an active and eager
life.

It is more than a quarter of a century since I have been out of
England, and the continent as it is now and as Mr. Mill knows
it, must present social aspects other than those with which I
have been acquainted; but when I knew it, the looks, manners
and deportment of the middle classes in Germany and Italy
seemed to express more of independence (in its natural
combination with courtesy and contentment) than those of my
own countrymen. Unequal classes met upon more equal
terms.This I was disposed to attribute, partly no doubt to a
temperament through which happiness was sufficient in itself
and advancement in life was no great object, but partly also to
the few openings upward in the social scale making some sorts
of advancement impracticable and *therefore* not an object at
all. Perhaps no indication of the condition and character of a
people is more significant than the human aspect of a street. It
expressed to my eyes, abroad ease and independence, at home
care and haste. When I look in the faces of men and in the faces
of women, I seem to recognise a difference of the like purport
in favour of the latter.

I will end as I began, with some notice of the general tone
and tenour of Mr. Mill's essay. I have spoken of the large
measure in which matter of opinion is represented as matter of
indubitable truth, ascribing it to the art of the advocate
renouncing for a season the exercise of philosophic circumspec-
tion. But perhaps I should have allowed something also for the
ardour of the man impelling the philosopher to overleap
scientific restraints. And in this ardour I seem to recognise what
is not new to me, except as what was old becomes new after
many years – that incandescent philosophy so characteristic of

[14]   *Paradise Regained.*

Mr. Mill's school of philosophers, when I had the never to be forgotten privilege and delight of meeting them, some forty or five and forty years ago, face to face in debate. I find in undecaying energy after all this efflux of years the vigour of the intellectual athlete, the logical subtlety and the gift of luminous exposition by which the school was distinguished; and along with these, I find traces yet left of a still happier gift which belonged to these philosophers then, and which it might have been supposed would have faded away out of sight when their youth was past. Their felicity was that they knew not to doubt. Whilst other minds wandered in a purgatory of perplexities, a paradise of certainties was theirs. I envied and admired the clearness, the intrepidity, the bright and imperious decisiveness with which some of them delivered themselves of whatever doctrines they taught. Yet delighted and dazzled as I was, I sometimes felt that my faith in their doctrines would have been more if theirs had been less. And whilst I surrender no scintilla of my old admiration, the other feeling has rather grown upon me; I appreciate more and more that element of justness in opinion which consists in gradations of confidence or diffidence; and when opinions are flashed upon me without these pencillings of light and shade, I feel that there is something wanting to place them in the first rank of authority.

THE SUBJECTION OF WOMEN
[Matthew Browne]

The Subjection of Women. by John Stuart Mill. London:
Longmans.

To any one who regards the genius and character of Mr. Mill
with such serious homage as the writer of these lines, it is a task
of peculiar difficulty, and also of considerable pain, to express,
and especially to express in public, strong though qualified
dissent from his opinions upon an important question. In the
present instance the difficulty is certainly not lessened by the
fact that the dissentient person heartily agrees with a large
portion of what the author has written upon that question, and
would most likely be found, in practice, on the same lines of
action with him. There is yet another difficulty. Mr. Mill –
brought up at home under the care of his illustrious father, I
believe, and not in a public school[1] – has preserved, in spite of
extensive contact with the world, that exquisite bloom, I was
going to say blush, of the sense of justice which is so painfully
rare a qualification for discussions such as his upon "The
Subjection of Women." To write but a word against any
serious utterances of a man who possesses this precious and
exceptional sensibility, and suffuses with it every page he
writes, and every sentence he speaks, appears almost a crime.
But, earnestly believing that Mr. Mill, now almost venerable
by his years, and certainly occupying by his achievements a
place second to that of no living man, has actually not seen
some things which in this matter it was vitally important to see,
I ask leave with sincere and even deep-seated pain, to make a
few comments upon his last book. One of the warmest and
ablest of his students, a well-known disciple of Bentham, has
said that this volume is written with less than Mr. Mill's usual

---

[1] That there may be no mistake about my meaning here, I take leave to say
that I think education in a large school, though favourable to the cultivation
of the sense of social "fairness," does tend to take the bloom off the sense of
justice.

"candour" – at least upon one point, namely, that of the intellectual equality of men and women. Whatever force was intended to belong to the word "candour" in this situation, it certainly does appear to me that the essay is written with less than its author's usual temperance. Not that most of the allowances made in the course of this *plaidoyer* are not, strictly speaking, adequate in themselves, but that you have to look narrowly for them, and that when you have found them they are bare. Mr. Mill would say, as in fact he distinctly implies, that he is not bound to more; standing in the position of an advocate for the losing and oppressed side in a desperate case. Be it so. Those who do not think the case so desperate, and, above all, those who fancy that the side taken by Mr. Mill is going ahead too fast for its own interests, may fairly seek to supply any qualifications they think needful. Let me be permitted to hope that what follows may not be altogether the less fitted for its purpose that it is a little desultory.

I. The point into which the public discussion of women's rights tends to run up, is that of their claim to the suffrage. In political, as in all other matters, I hold that the bare rights of men and women, considered as separate human beings, are of necessity equal. Nor does it appear anything less than absurd to introduce into the question any consequences that may follow from ecclesiastical speculations about what is called the *unitas carnis*. I believe with Mr. Mill, that civil society must be based upon the assumption of equal rights all round, and that neither the morality of power, nor that of chivalry, nor that of convenience, but that of justice is here our ultimate. It is absurd to maintain, as Dr. Horace Bushnell does, that the right of women to political power is a *mere* question of expediency. Excluding the point of direct injury, no human being can justly be called upon by another human being to part with one fraction of his liberty of action, except upon his own consent. But in civil society we all agree to part with some portions of our liberty of action, simply in consideration of a greater common good in which every one shares. All this implies that every member of the community may justly demand some voice in the making of the laws by which he is to be bound – what voice, or what kind of voice, is another question. How are women in a different position, abstractly, from men in this particular? Really I can see no difference whatever. But surely Mr. Mill would be the last man to deny that considerations of divine expediency must carry weight in social and political practice. Representative government is, in my opinion, only a very humble step forward in the path towards true self-government; and considering the gross ignorance of most women, the fact that they are numerically the majority, and the fact that they now are (as they always, in my opinion, will be) "intellectually' the "inferiors" of men, I can well understand the dismay with which the majority of men flinch from the bare idea of giving them votes. There are many more considerations besides those which I have mentioned; for instance, the peace of families; the greater openness of average women to bribery in the shape of "influence;" and, not least, the very serious consideration that they may be, *as they have been, and are, to some extent*, made in obscure ways the instruments of bribery of the least resistible kind. Nobody can possibly hold higher opinions of the correctness of the majority of women than the writer of these lines; but if the suffrage were immediately granted to them, I should expect – society being what it is in other respects – that this particular change would be followed in certain circles by particularly intricate forms of collusion and corruption. As to those "other respects," I feel and think with Mr. Mill about most of them, but we cannot suddenly control them, and must guard ourselves as we can. If the advocates of female suffrage will for the present be content with the admission that women are as much entitled to political power as men, and as free to seek it by any kind of advocacy as men to seek any other right, – but that the how and the when are questions of public expediency involved in a still higher question, which is even now knocking at the door, namely, that of reconstituting political self-government upon a basis other than merely "representative," *cadit quæstio*, for Mr. Mill, and the ladies, and the humble unit, myself, are heartily agreed. Let no one say that this admission is just offering a pinch of the empty air – it is made sincerely, and would, in such a reconstruction of civil government as many thinkers have in their minds and believe to be not very far off, cover all that women want. Indeed, this reconstruction could not be made without giving them a share of political power.

II. While we are upon this question we can scarcely overlook the fact that some of the women's advocates – and, I fear, Mr. Mill, amongst the number – are, to say the least, very near to raising a false point in relation to certain differences made by the progress of civilization. It seems quite impossible to deny that the ultimate right of control, in other words the power, must rest with that side which takes the responsibility and risk of protecting the other. It is a right of martial law seldom to be seen in full flower; but can it be excluded? It belongs to "the *penetralia* of the constitution;" but can we help, or should we try to help, its natural reactions? Now, we are constantly being told that the progress of social order has changed the old regimen in this particular, and that man has now lost the position which, in former times, it might have been plausibly said nature had assigned to him. But how is that made out? I cannot see. Civil society still rests upon a basis of force. There is more or less of order, but who guards it? The soldier, the policeman. "If you do so-and-so, we will shoot, stab, hang, fine, or imprison you." That is the last resort. And so long as it remains true, that the average man is twice as strong as the average woman, it will remain true that every woman who pays taxes, or has taxes paid for her, is as much protected by masculine force as if she had a knight told off and sworn in her behalf.

The physical force of a mature man, as tested by the dynamometer (I am now thinking of the results of some experiments of Quetelet) is emphatically more than double that of a woman. Is all this to be altered? Mary Wolstonecroft could and did frankly admit that the mere difference in what is called "physical" power must for ever make a difference, to the advantage of the man, in the effective force of the two sexes; and it seems no more than a simply honest admission. But in some of the later forms of the advocacy of the Left, we find cases thrust forward of women who make mighty Alpine ascents, and nurses who go through more fatigue than a London physician in full practice. But all this proves nothing. Certain women may do these things, but, before we draw any decisive inference from the facts, we must look into all the connotations, and consider what appears to be sacrificed (if anything) as well as what appears to be gained. Nobody desires that women should be weak, and there must be much variety within whatever limits are supposed; but half-a-dozen Amazons or epicene beings prove no more than half-a-dozen infant prodigies. Did such matters lie at all within the compass of the will, I should say that it is the first duty of a woman to be lovely. *If* a woman must either be ignorant of history, for example, or acquire a knowledge of history at the expense of a set lip and a bloodshot eye, we men boldly declare that we shall greatly prefer the ignorance to the ugliness. I know very well the outcry that some people will make over this, and the fine things that will be said about civilization, progress, culture, and what-not. But our answer is ready, and we are inexorable in this matter. I do not care a straw for "civilization," when the question is of antecedent matters; of the primitive strata of life. Here we fall back upon ideals unaltered hitherto, all history and biography being witness – and unalterable for ever, as I believe; and we say that we can no more spare the influence of female loveliness from our lives than we can spare that of hills and stars and seas. We are not entitled, in my opinion, to restrict liberty of action, whether in woman or in man, in order to seek to compel conformity to any ideal we may hold, however well verified it may be; but we *are* entitled to look with jealousy upon whatever seems ever so remotely to threaten those ideals which are dearest and which lie closest to all that we hold most lofty and most precious in our lives.

III. This brings us, by a natural gradient, to another point; or rather, we have already touched it. Mr. Mill seems – I say *seems* with emphasis, because he can hardly mean it – to think that the chief check possessed by a woman upon the arbitrary power of her husband lies in what he calls the "power of the scold, or the shrewish sanction." I know full well that Mr. Mill will agree – at least I cannot bear to doubt that he would agree with what I am about to say; but the point is far too much kept in the background in these discussion. The normal power of a woman is something far different. It consists in being what Milton calls being "loving and *prevalent*;" because, in fact, as Adam told the archangel guest, all fair things else appear "mean, or in her summed up:" –

"Neither her outside, form'd so fair, nor aught
In procreation, common to all kinds,
(Though higher of the genial bed by far
And with mysterious reverence I deem,)
So much delights me as those graceful acts,
Those thousand decencies, that daily flow
From all her words and actions, mix'd with love,
And sweet compliance, which declare unfeign'd
Union of mind, or in us both one soul;

Harmony to behold in wedded pair,
More grateful than harmonious sound to the ear."

How a man affects a woman, no man can do more than
remotely guess; but if a man has ever in his life felt, he had
better die at once than ever lose the feeling that the – what
phrase shall I use? – that the luminosity or *aura* of the woman is
a part, and the loftiest and sweetest part, of

"The presence that disturbs us with the joy
Of elevated thoughts; a sense sublime
Of something far more deeply interfused,
Whose dwelling is the light of setting suns,
And the round ocean, and the living air,
And the blue sky, and in the mind of man:
A motion and a spirit that impels
All thinking things, all objects of all thought,
And rolls through all things –"

I say it is scarcely possible to doubt that Mr. Mill and some of
the advocates on the Left would feel with me in those matters;
but, at the same time, it is hard to understand how a man who
does so feel could write what occurs in page 133 of Mr. Mill's
book:– "I believe there will [eventually] not prove to be any
natural tendencies common to women and distinguishing their
genius from that of men:" hard to understand, because a
peculiar set of qualities would seem naturally, not to say
necessarily, bound up in the woman's power of thus affecting
the man.

IV. Upon the passage quoted I might observe that it appears
hardly consistent with some other portions of the volume; for
example, with the position which I understand Mr. Mill to take
up, that women have peculiar faculties for governing. Confin-
ing the expression of opinion to literature as a test of the
relative powers and qualifies of the two sexes does not shift the
question an inch. But how *can* any man look even the most
unwomanly woman in the face, and hold the opinion in
question? Every woman is not a wife or mother, and no
woman is bound to be either; indeed, a good many women
drift into marriage who have no vocation for either the
conjugal or the maternal life. But, after all, the distinctive
peculiarity of the woman is that she is capable of wifehood and
motherhood; and it has been said, with I believe perfect truth,

that the addition in her case of the delicate organism which confers the capacity, is virtually endowing her with a second brain, heart, and conscience. This point has been overwrought, in his usual efflorescent way, by Michelet, but it is stated with sacred moderation and much force by M. Ernest Legouvé, in his "Histoire Morale des Femmes" – a book that was handed to me by a living woman of genius of the highest character; which I purposely mention before adding that it would be a happy thing if every intelligent man and woman in Britain had read it. It is well known that some American ladies, not wholly unworthy of respect, however we may shrink from some of their procedure, have maintained that the additional complex endowment in question makes the woman, by all analogy, the superior being. However, that is not the question; and I speak not of added power, but of immense inscrutable differentiation. That this exists is staringly true, even of the healthiest and strongest woman. How *can* any one consider the immense physical differences – the unspeakable physical contrasts between a man and a woman, and then write as if there were no "sex in souls?" It does not so much surprise me, when women of a certain order do it; but that men who have been husbands and fathers should do it, does, I confess, stagger me.

It is almost necessary in these discussions for a man to disclaim any personal reason for believing in what is called the intellectual inferiority of woman; and I fully believe that no contested question of a mixed character is completely discussed until the woman has contributed to its discussion her proper peculiar wisdom; while on moral and spiritual questions the suggestive power of the normal woman is indefinitely greater than that of the man. It is, indeed, sad folly to talk of the superior virtue of women as some persons do, for, when allowance has been made for conventional exaggeration, it is still either ignorance or dulness not to recognise, frankly and fearlessly, the fact that each sex has its own peculiar moral difficulties (to be overcome, not succumbed to); and that on one side, a peculiar difficulty does, in the majority of cases, arise from the natural distinctions which make that side the initiating and pursuing side. We are all grateful for any word enforcing the duty of purity, but it would save some mischief if one or two lady-writers, and one or two men of high character and ability, but very ill-posted up in facts, would leave facts alone. I have now in my possession some writings of a most able and excellent man, in which the estimate of the *facts* was brought to me as a *mauvaise plaisanterie*, and that by a man whose estimate of the *duty* was as high as his or as mine. But if we do not believe in the superior *merit* of our sisters, yet on the other hand, it is to the woman that, in the intercourse of love, the sacred function or moral and spiritual impregnation especially belongs, all experience being witness; and a womanly woman, however inferior she may be in culture and bare intelligence, can instantly bring to bear upon a subject a peculiar, tender wisdom that is so utterly *sui generis*, that it seems impossible not to look upon it as bound up with the whole circle of the points in which a woman differs from a man.

In dealing with the general question of the "intellectual inferiority" of woman, I have already observed that one of Mr. Mill's most ardent disciples (a well-known barrister and publicist) finds him less "candid" than usual. Mr. Mill always means to be nobly candid; but here he beats me. To begin with, if women are "subjected," so that they have less than their natural share of culture, how did this result come about? Surely, from an immense complication of causes in which they themselves must count; not because a man has a larger biceps and twice the lumbar force. No human being can strike the balance and exactly divide whatever blame there is in the matter. But, again, supposing difference of culture and opportunity has made all the difference; and, again, supposing women are in future – as I devoutly hope, and I have done my humble best, during many years, to help them to it – to have better culture, and freedom of vocation; supposing all this, what is to happen? The men are now, *ex hypothesi*, in advance of the women. Well, are the men to stand still *now*, while the women alone go ahead? Or are the men still to move onwards with all the benefit of a reaction from the improved culture of the women? And if the latter, which seems, to say the least, rather likely, at what point are our sisters to overtake us in the race?

In dealing with the achievements of women in the higher walks of art, Mr. Mill strikes me as being far from satisfactory. That while women have shown, in music and the drama, executive ability at least equal, and perhaps superior to that of men, while, nevertheless, they have never shown high original capacity in either, is a fact so striking that it might well have claimed more of his attention than it has apparently been able to secure. Two or three (so many?) comedies by women keep the stage; but where is there any considerable dramatic work by a woman? As to music, Mr. Mill suggests that women have done as good musical work, *en amateur*, as men. Well, Mrs. Jordan wrote "The Blue Bells of Scotland," and Queen Hortense "Partant pour la Syrie." There is a place in Beethoven's mass in C, where, after a passage of symphony by the horn, the E, which looks as if it were the third of C, is laid hold of, so to speak, by the second violin, and treated as a chord of suspension in B. Mr. Mill's comment upon the difference, in musical powers, between men and women, is that women have been educated only as amateurs, while men have been educated scientifically. I know that I am not putting an exhaustively fair contrast, but will any sane man look me in the face and maintain that *any such* difference as that between the capacity to compose the "Blue Bells of Scotland," and the capacity to compose the sublime passage in Beethoven which I have referred to, is a matter of education? Was Beethoven or was Mozart - was even Gounod or Wallace - other than an "amateur" because he was taught music scientifically; or is not this a case of putting the cart before the horse? Under almost any conceivable conditions Mozart and Beethoven would have been great musicians; and it was their extraordinary capacity which got them the training they received. Mr. Mill, as a man of the world, must know that the incalculable majority of ladies "in society" cannot even read notes at sight. To be able to "transpose," even deliberately, is thought quite an "accomplishment;" while most "musical" men can do it at a glance - without thinking about it, in fact. Now, ladies in society have ample leisure, deny it who may; they are taught music at great pains and expense; the book of musical knowledge is open to them; and yet not one in a thousand of them is an *unintelligent* amateur. The difficulty with respect to the drama is, to say the least, not less arresting: for women have succeeded in general literature.

But, in fact, the same *kind* of difficulty meets us everywhere in this part of the subject. Mr. Mill claims for women the merit of suggesting to men original ideas which they afterwards work out. Here and there exists a woman who can and does help a man in this way; and a base, ungrateful heart has he who does not acknowledge the help. But I still affirm that the one

startling peculiarity of the typical woman, is want of originative or inventive power. It is nothing new to say – though
Mr. Mill appears, by a quotation from an unpublished work of
some celebrated lady writer, to think it is – that whatever
women do is done at odd times; or that the care of a household
is a great and splendid task. There is an old rhyme which runs –

"From rise of morn to set of sun
Woman's work is never done."

It is true. But, in spite of this, women in the upper ranks have
always had immense leisure as compared with men. And what
have they done with it in the way of "invention" in the true
sense? While half-starved, overworked men – shepherd-boys,
cobblers, book-binders, bond slaves, and what not – have
moved the world, what woman ever "invented" anything, *even
in her own special line*? Which woman was it that "invented" a
needle, a loom, a shuttle, a stocking-frame, a fire-stove, a new
saucepan, a new dish for the table, a new chair, a new baby's
bottle, a new kind of bread, a new sauce, a sewing-machine, or
what not? Have women, as a rule, been the inventors or
initiators in even the early education of the young? In fashion,
however, doubtless the women reign supreme? Quite the
contrary. Shameful to say, it is true also, in female dress, that
the men are the inventors or originators, sometimes behind the
scenes and sometimes openly. So utterly wide of the facts is any
claim of originative or suggesting power for women, that I
assert, on the contrary, that it is rare even unto marvel, to find
a woman who can be driven by any amount of pressure, to
follow the most obviously advantageous initiative set by a man
in her own peculiar walk.

V. In the general spirit of Mr. Mill's work, let it be repeated,
I heartily sympathise. Here is a passage which especially
demands to be quoted:–

"A female slave has (in Christian countries) an admitted
right, and is considered under a moral obligation, to refuse
to her master the last familiarity. Not so the wife; however
brutal a tyrant she may unfortunately be chained to – though
she may know that he hates her, thought it may be his daily
pleasure to torture her, and though she may feel it impossible
not to loathe him – he can claim from her and enforce the
lowest degradation of a human being, that of being made the

instrument of an animal function, contrary to her inclinations."

With the drift of this criticism – addressed as it is to the infamous suit for "restitution of conjugal rights" – I have the profoundest sympathy. But so complex are the reactions and interactions in such matters, and so influential the compensating powers with which nature has armed the woman, that I believe the existing laws, theory, and customs, in these matters bear nearly if not quite as hard on the man as on her. It is all very well to say that the law is so-and-so; but, in fact, owing to ineffaceable natural distinctions, the power of the woman is immense. She has, in fact, though not in law, the custody of her own person nearly as much as the man has the custody of his. The precise particular pointed at is one with which the law does not even pretend to deal (Forster *v.* Forster, 1 Hagg. Cons. 154);[2] however, it may and does (as Mr. Mill and others, among whom I count, think), to the great injury of society and the degradation of the married state, help to foster foolish and injurious customs and brutalities of social opinion, which are worse than law. Whether women do not bring the suit for "restitution of conjugal rights," as it is called – that is, a suit for compelling what cannot be compelled – as often as men, is a question. I am inclined to think they do. On the whole, I feel, and deeply feel, that throughout the book Mr. Mill has forgotten, as too many of the advocates on the Left forget, the immense compensations there are in the powers with which nature has armed the women. Nevertheless, these remarks of mine are addressed solely to the question of *practical* hardship, and I think, as strongly as Mr. Mill does, that the whole scheme of law and custom in these matters is erected on a false basis.

VI. While we are speaking of the degradation of the ideal of marriage (in which I have the honour of being at one with Mr. Mill as to the terms in which it is to be expressed for legal and social purposes), let me be forgiven for a word upon a point as to which some of us stand very far off from him and from some ladies on the same side. We others repudiate with scorn the notion of glorifying anything (but where is that something?) that is merely animal, or of sacrificing the higher to the lower in any department of life. But we also repudiate, with scorn and

2 See also the ludicrous case of Brown *v.* Brown, 1 Hagg. 524.

disgust, the sort of language with which the distinctive peculiarity of the conjugal relation is too frequently spoken of by writers on the Left; and indeed, also, by the majority on the other side. Only here and there some honest, poetic soul speaks the truth. What we complain of is the violent discord which the language in question makes between things which "God hath joined." Why will people persist in treating as naturally unmoral or "animal" that which is, in all normal human experience, deeply moral? Is Fouqué's "Undine" – a story which Sir Walter Scott admired as much as Coleridge did – an "animal" invention? I suppose the pleasure a mother feels in caressing her child is as purely "animal" as anything can be. But, after all, *is* it "animal," or is not all this phrase-mongering mere trash? Can a mother caress her child and, at the same time, harbour cruel and irreverent thoughts? I say no. Her *whole* nature is bettered by that caress. And I will only add the words in which Canon Kingsley describes in "Yeast" the "love" experience of Lancelot Smith's youth:–

> "Love had been to him, practically, ground tabooed and 'carnal.' What was to be expected? Just what happened – if woman's beauty had nothing holy in it, why should his fondness for it? Just what happens every day – that he had to sow his wild oats for himself, and eat the fruit thereof, and the dirt thereof also."

I would give something to see some approach to a more general sense of the "solidarity" of normal human experience in this respect; but I begin to fear the hope is vain. On the Right and on the Left, men, and women too, write of these matters in such terms that, if they were consistent, they ought to be ashamed of their parents, ashamed of the ineffaceable mark of "solidarity" which every human being bears about in his body, and ashamed to look their own children in the face.

Very unwillingly, I must just mention a topic which so readily lends itself to clap-trap, that a writer who respects himself and others may naturally flinch from referring to it against a man like the illustrious author of "The Subjection of Women." Mr. Mill is a wise and good-tempered propagandist, and particularly cautious in "delving" his "approaches" to any fortress which he attacks. But it is easy for any one who reads him frequently and carefully to discern that his policy in the treatment of *this* question is partly influenced by his views on the population question. I shall not do him the injustice of referring to that, except for the purpose of saying that the mass of women are the very last persons among whom his policy in the discussion of their "subjection" is likely to be successful. "Among the barbarians which law and morality have not yet ceased to sanction, surely the most disgusting is the idea that one human being can have a *right* to the person of another." With this expression of opinion, which occurs in the "Political Economy," I heartily agree; but where is the stronghold of this "disgusting barbarism"? Among the women themselves. How many women does Mr. Mill think there are in England who would understand Mr. Browning's "Pompilia?" about as many as he would find able to understand his own picture of the ideal married state. The amount of enlightened, self-respecting sentiment that exists among women upon such matters is, to quote Beatrice, "just so much as you might take upon a knife's point, and choke a daw withal." Here, indeed, I know I am on strong ground, and if it were not for making an enemy with every stroke of my pen, I could, out of my miscellaneous reading, make out a very black book against women – women of culture, novelists, poetesses, and others – in this matter; such a black book of worldliness, conventionality, rootless virtue, artificial "indignation," placid ignorance, and smiling dictation in matters of which they have, from the nature of the case, to let superstition stand for knowledge, as would startle, I do verily believe it, even Mr. Mill out of some of his hopefulness. How women come to be like this is another question; but it would be a very bold man that said, in the face of the evidence I should produce, that the men had made them so.

If advice were not rude, we would, indeed, earnestly beg of women, that they will not allow themselves to be betrayed into blaming men, as men, for their disabilities and the injustice with which they are in some respects treated.[3] They cannot

---

[3] And also, that they would be less perplexing in their appeals. One moment, they demand "work," in tones which make a man exclaim, "Am I God, to kill or make alive, that thou sendest Society to me to recover it of this leprosy?" Next, they cry, "You immoral rascals! We shall starve out your vices directly. With the help of heaven, the police, and the Dialectical Society, we shall cut off the supplies; and then, instead of leaving us poor wall-flowers to pine alone, you will be glad enough to marry us on any terms." But before long they are sniffing the air, and saying, "Go to! We shall decline marriage till you are higher and holier beings." Meanwhile, six

have it both ways. They have been responsible agents from the beginning of the world; they have wielded an immense moral power; they still wield such a power. If a man knocks a woman down, it is something to allege and prove; but a woman, without uttering a quotable word or doing a single provable act, can rouse to fury the latent devil in a man, and sting him with a suffering of which years cannot wipe out the memory. Besides, there are the numerous particulars in which the woman is privileged by exemptions which must, in the nature of things, continue to be granted to her – unless the axis of the globe is altered. Of course, with Pangenesis all things are possible – "we *have* been fishes, and we may be birds – delightful, is it not?" But, for the present, it looks as if we had all been rowing in one boat for thousands of years, making mistakes, and alternately injuring and helping each other. At the present moment, our mutual relations have come up for revision.

And revised they will be. If women in mass were to demand the franchise, I do not see how we could with justice refuse to give it to them; but I devoutly hope they will *not* demand it; and why they should be so anxious to play a part in the solemn farce of representative government by party is a puzzle to some of us men – especially to those of us who never vote at all. Mr. Ruskin says he never votes; I am sure I never do; and what on earth is the difference between Tweedledum and Tweedledee, that people should be so eager to "vote" about it? Under a system of true self-government, it would be a very different matter, and under such a system, as I have said before, the women *must* come in. Not, however, to vote for Mr. Tweedledum or Mr. Tweedledee, but for *laws* themselves.

Holding that we cannot, if pressed, refuse women these unspeakably precious "votes," I would also maintain, in their behalf (as in behalf of men), perfect freedom of vocation and of culture. What my own ideal upon these matters may be is one thing, but I have no right by law, custom, or otherwise, to dictate ideals to any one. Here, as elsewhere, to parody the well-known canon of oratory, the first part of justice is; Hands off! and the second, Hands off! and the third, Hands off!

hundred rude fellows, suffering under the stigma of the sex of Moses, Paul, Plato, Shakspeare, and Garibaldi, stand silent, fronting certain death, while the women are lowered into the boats: and down goes the "Birkenhead."

But this is not a lesson which women in general are quick to learn. Their leaning is strongly towards protectionism, police, and incessant small compulsion. We have lately had to admire their self-sacrifice in addressing public words of disapproval to the tendency of legislation in a certain very unpleasant particular. Passionately sympathising with the indignation of the women in this matter, and willing to help them to the utmost I cannot help saying I think the kind of legislation condemned is precisely after the pattern (I speak of principles) which most women delight in. And it is only too probable that if they had votes, they would immediately add the weight of their superior numbers to the miserable impetus which has for some time past been driving us, and it is now driving us with accelerated force, to a Fool's Paradise of Police under the ignorant tyranny of the Universal Cad.

In the "Political Economy" Mr. Mill refers, in terms such as might be expected from him, to the (shall we call it?) Anti-Malthusian influence of the clergy – of the Roman Catholic clergy in particular among the working classes, over whom he thinks, and with some reason, the other clergy have not much influence. It struck me a little oddly the other day to find him, at a public meeting, accounting for the influence which the clergy have over most women by alleging that they are almost the only class of men who have systemically appealed to women as having souls of their own – or something of that kind – the exact phrase has escaped me. This is a purely fanciful theory: medical men have nearly as much influence over women as their ministers; but scarcely, I suppose, because they treat them as independent spiritual creatures. The truth is, the reasons are very different; and that women as a rule have a superstitious feeling for experts, specialists, and accredited functionaries of every kind, from the clergyman and the doctor down to the policeman. At all events, the clergy of all denominations cannot be accused of teaching women that they are not divinely "subjected" to the men; and what Mr. Mill calls a "disgusting barbarism" they would and do, for the most part, treat as the Archbishop in "Pompilia" treated it when Pompilia fled to him because "he stood for God." And, of course, the Archbishop, not being a man of delicate textual discrimination, and not seeing the difference between stating an ideal, and making a compulsory law, would think himself fully justified by Paul:– Ἡ γυνὴ τοῦ ἰδίου σώματος οὐκ ἐξουσιάζει, ἀλλ' ὁ ἀνήρ· ὁμοίως δὲ καὶ ὁ ἀνὴρ τοῦ ἰδίου σώματος οὐκ ἐξουσιάζει, ἀλλ' ἡ γυνή. If Mr. Mill should see these lines, and if he possesses Canon Kingsley's poems, it is, I would respectfully say, worth his while to turn to the poem on page 61, which I wish had been omitted, beginning –

"Oh, thou hadst been a wife for Shakspeare's self!"

Mr. Mill will find a million women to profess sympathy with that poem for one who will understand his ideal of marriage, or who will see that there is a vast difference between privilege and obligation.

There is one other point, and it is radical. Just as an Experiential thinker *must* be a Utilitarian, so he *must* be a disbeliever in necessary permanence of types. The Experientalists are always saying to the Axiomatic moralists, "You do not understand – we believe in Conscience just as much as you do; only we say it is a growth from a seed, namely, fear of punishment." To this, we, on the other side, make answer (though quite vainly at present), "Yes, gentlemen, we perfectly understand; but we assert that, take Conscience at whatever point of emergence you please, there is something in it *sui generis* which could not be evolved from any such seed." And just so upon the woman's question. The Experientalist is bound to believe that a woman may at some time or other be any mortal thing you please. We, on the other side, say, that we believe we discern the existence of a certain type in Woman, which type is essentially unchangeable. Of course the fact is not directly provable; is only provable by the convergence of certain lines of analogy and indication upon one point. But the convergence being, in our opinion, amply made out, we rest on what we think we see not less certainly than we see the sun in the sky overhead.

THE ELECTORAL DISABILITIES OF WOMEN
[Millicent Garrett Fawcett]

The question of women's suffrage will in a few days again be brought before Parliament. The present, therefore, seems an appropriate time to enumerate as briefly as possible some of the principal objections urged against it, together with what appear to be satisfactory answers to these objections.

It can hardly be too often repeated that the removal of the electoral disabilities of women is not exclusively a woman's question; above all it is not one in which the interests of men and women are opposed. If the extension of political power to women is in accordance with reason and justice, both sexes are equally bound to support the claims of women to the suffrage. If it is in opposition to these, both sexes are equally interested in the withholding of electoral power from women.

It is frequently said that women are sufficiently represented under the present system, and that their interests have always been jealously protected by the legislature. This argument must be very familiar to all who took part in, or remember the great reform agitation which preceded the Reform Bill of 1867. Those who were opposed to an extension of the suffrage were never weary of repeating that working men were quite well represented; that there was no need to give them votes, for their interests were watched over with the most anxious solicitude by noblemen and gentlemen who knew far better than the artisans themselves what was good for the working classes. It is well known that this opinion was not shared by working men. They pointed to the inequality of the law relating to masters and servants, and to the efforts which legislation had made to suppress trade societies. They said, "these laws are unequal and unjust, and they will not be amended until we have some hand in choosing the law-makers." Beside this they said, "we bear a large portion of the taxation of the country; for every pound of tea and sugar we consume we contribute so much to the national revenue, and in common justice we ought to be allowed to exercise a corresponding control over the national expenditure." Every one knows that the struggle for an extension of the suffrage at length terminated; all obstacles were surmounted, and the rights of working men to citizenship were fully recognised. Surely working men, and all who took their part in the great reform agitation, will not cast aside and repudiate the very arguments which they found so useful during that struggle. Let them apply the same arguments to the question of women's suffrage. Are women sufficiently represented? Are there no laws which press unjustly on them? Is that state of the law equitable which renders a married woman incapable of owning or of acquiring property, and which allows her husband to deprive her even of her earnings? Is that law just which gives a married woman no legal right to the guardianship of her own children? If women were virtually represented, would they be excluded from participation in the great educational endowments of the country? Would the door of nearly all lucrative, and, at the same time, honourable employments be shut against them? Finally, using the very same argument which has been so often applied to the working classes, is it right or just that any one should be forced to contribute to the revenue of the country, and, at the same time, debarred from controlling the national expenditure? Either this argument is good for nothing, or it applies to women as forcibly as it does to men.

Another argument sometimes urged against women's suffrage is, that a woman is so easily influenced, that if she had a vote it would practically have the same effect as giving two votes to her nearest male relation, or to her favourite clergyman. This is a very curious argument; it would be a serious thing for men as well as for women if originality were a necessary qualification for the franchise. For instance, the *Times* exercises an extraordinary influence over the political opinions of thousands of people. Now it may be said, following out the argument just quoted, the effect of giving all these people votes is only to multiply a million-fold the voting power of the editor of the *Times*, or the writers of the articles in that journal; therefore all people who take their political views from the *Times* ought to be precluded from exercising the franchise. By carrying out this principle nearly every one would be disfranchised, except the great leaders of political thought, such as Mr. Gladstone, Mr. Disraeli, Mr. Bright, Mr. Mill, Lord Salisbury, and the editors of some of the principal papers.

For there are very few indeed whose political opinions are not biassed by the views of some of these distinguished and able men. But perhaps this objection that women's suffrage would only double the voting power of some men, can best be answered by making way for the next argument, viz., that women are so obstinate that if they had votes endless family discord would ensue. To this it may be replied that a vote is not an opinion but an expression of opinion, so that the same objection would apply to women having any opinions on political subjects. Under the present system women cannot be prevented from having political opinions, or from expressing them; they often even now possess political influence. This being the case, surely it is well that they should have every opportunity of forming just opinions, and that they should feel that a responsibility accompanies the exercise of power. It cannot be expected that women generally will recognise their responsibility until their power is recognised by removing their electoral disabilities. Then as to the argument that husbands and wives of different political opinions would quarrel if the wives had votes, the exclusion of women from the franchise seems a rough and ready way of securing harmony. Suppose, for instance, that in order to secure conjugal harmony on religious matters, a law were passed to prevent all women from going to church. The advocates of such a law might say, "Suppose an Evangelical married a Roman Catholic, what disagreement it would lead to if the husband went off to one place of worship and the wife to another." As a fact, such marriages seldom take place; for it is recognised that women have a right to think for themselves on religious subjects, and there is therefore a strong and most reasonable feeling against marriages between people of opposite religious opinions. Would not the same feeling come into existence against marriages between people of opposite political parties if the political independence of women were recognised? If this feeling were prevalent, I believe a higher harmony than is yet generally known, would gradually pervade domestic life.

   Let us now consider the validity of the fourth objection raised against the enfranchisement of women, viz., "The ideal of domestic life is a miniature despotism, in which there is one supreme head, to whom all other members of the family are subject. This ideal would be destroyed if the quality of women with men were recognised by extending the suffrage to women." It must be at once conceded that if the truth of the premise is granted, the truth of the conclusion must be granted also. Family despotism would receive a deadly blow from the extension of political power to women. But let us inquire how and why men – Englishmen, at least – have come to consider despotic national government immoral, and then let us see whether despotic family government differs essentially in principle from other despotisms. First let us inquire why despotic national government has been so successfully opposed in this country, and why representative government has been set up in its place. It may be briefly said that despotic government has been got rid of in this country because it has been felt to interfere unwarrantably with individual liberty. The leaders of popular rights from the time of Magna Charta to this day have always insisted on the importance of preserving individual liberty. Why has the name "liberty" always had such a magic spell over men? Why has liberty been valued more than life itself by all those whose names make our history glorious? Why have our greatest poets sung the praises of liberty in words that will never be forgotten as long as our language lasts? Is it not because it has been felt, more or less strongly at all times, that man's liberty is essential to the observance of man's duty? Mr. Herbert Spencer has thus analysed the right of mankind to liberty. He says, "If God wills man's happiness, and man's happiness can only be obtained by the exercise of his faculties, then God wills that man should exercise his faculties; that is, it is man's duty to exercise his faculties, for duty means the fulfilment of the divine will. As God wills man's happiness, that line of conduct which produces unhappiness is contrary to His will. Either way then, we find the exercise of the faculties to be God's will and man's duty. But the fulfilment of this duty necessarily supposes freedom of action. Man cannot exercise his faculties without certain scope. He must have liberty to go and to come, to see, to feel, to speak, to work, to get food, raiment, shelter, and to provide for all the needs of his nature. He must be free to do everything which is directly or indirectly requisite for the due satisfaction of every mental and bodily want. Without this he cannot fulfil his duty or God's will. He has divine authority, therefore, for claiming this freedom of action. God intended him to have it; that is, he has a *right* to it. From this conclusion there seems no possibility of escape. Let us repeat the steps by which we arrive at it. God wills man's happiness. Man's happiness can only be produced by the exercise of his faculties. Then God wills that he should exercise his faculties. But to exercise his faculties he must have liberty to do all that his faculties naturally impel him to do. Then God wills that he should have that liberty. Therefore he has a *right* to that liberty." The only limitation to perfect liberty of action is the equal liberty of all. "Liberty is not the right of one, but of all. All are endowed with faculties. All are bound to fulfil the divine will by exercising them. All, therefore, must be free to do those things in which the exercise of them consists. That is, all must have rights to liberty of action. Wherefore we arrive at the general proposition that every one may claim the fullest liberty to exercise his faculties, compatible with the possession of like liberty by every other person." (Social Statics.) Never has the basis of individual liberty been more clearly explained than in this passage. It proves conclusively that despotism being antagonistic to the principle of the "perfect freedom of each, limited only by the like liberty of all," is at variance with the divine will. How then can the ideal of family life be despotism, when despotism is proved to be antagonistic to the divine will? If the importance of recognising the real basis of the rights of man has been dwelt upon at some length, it is not to prove that these rights exist – few in the present day deny that men have some rights – but to show that the "rights of women must stand or fall with those of men; derived as they are from the same authority; involved in the same axiom; demonstrated by the same argument."

Much more could be said in defence of the assertion that despotic family government is very far removed from the ideal state. If space permitted it could be shown that command is blighting to the affections, and that where anything approaching the ideal of domestic happiness at present exists, the subjugation of all members of the family to the husband and father is not enforced. But it is necessary to pass to the consideration of the next objection to the extension of political power to women, viz., that women are intellectually inferior to men. It is unnecessary to enter upon the vexed question whether the mental powers of men and women are equal. It is almost impossible from want of evidence to prove whether they are or not. It may be very interesting as a philosophical discussion, but it is quite irrelevant to the present subject – *i.e.,* whether women ought to have political power. Suppose it could be proved beyond the slightest doubt that on the average the intellectual powers of women were inferior to those of men. If this were fully and satisfactorily established as a fact, it would not furnish the slightest justification for depriving women of electoral power. Suppose it were also proved that the intellectual powers of the inhabitants of the North of England are superior to those of the inhabitants of the South of England. It is often asserted that this is the case. Would any one recognise that as a reason why the inhabitants of the South of England should be deprived of electoral power? Would the people of London be willing to relinquish their right to the franchise if it were proved to demonstration that on the average, and taking them altogether, they were intellectually inferior to the inhabitants of Edinburgh? It is ridiculous to suggest such a thing, and yet this absurdity is exactly similar to what is really urged against allowing women to exercise the franchise. But the question may be looked at from another point of view. It is said that women, on the whole, are not the intellectual equals of men. Whether this is true, I neither affirm nor deny; but even the most ardent asserters of the inferiority of women have never yet said that all women are intellectually inferior to all men. Let us hear what Mr. Spencer has to say on this point. Granting, for the sake of argument, that the intellect of woman is less profound than that of man, he adds, "Let all this be granted, and let us now see what basis such an admission affords to the doctrine that the rights of women are not co-extensive with those of men:–

"I. If rights are to be meted out to the two sexes in the ratio of their respective amounts of intelligence, then must the same system be acted upon in the apportionment of rights between man and man.

"II. In like manner, it will follow, that as there are here and there women of unquestionably greater ability than the average of men, some women ought to have greater rights than some men.

"III. Wherefore, instead of a certain fixed allotment of rights to all males, and another to all females, the hypothesis involves an infinite gradation of rights, irrespective of sex entirely, and sends us once more in search of those unattainable desiderata – a standard, by which to measure capacity, and another by which to measure rights. Not only, however, does the theory this fall to pieces under the mere process of inspection; it is absurd on the very face of it, when freed from the disguise of hackneyed phraseology. For what is it that we mean by rights? Nothing else than freedom to exercise the faculties. And what is the meaning of the assertion that woman is mentally inferior to man? Simply that her faculties are less powerful. What then does the dogma that because woman is mentally inferior to man she has less extensive rights, amount to? Just this, that because woman has weaker faculties than man, she ought not to have like liberty with him to exercise the faculties she has!"

We will now pass to the consideration of another objection to women's suffrage – that the family is woman's proper sphere, and if she entered into politics she would be withdrawn from domestic duties. It may be mentioned in passing – it is a fact not calling for any special importance or regret – that there are some million or so of women in this country without families and without domestic affairs to superintend. The number of women is constantly in excess of the number of men, and so there must always be a certain percentage of women unmarried, and who therefore have no families to be withdrawn from. It is all very well to tell a women that her sphere is to be a wife and a mother, when there must always be a considerable number of women unmarried, owing to the simple fact that there are more women in the world than men. But let us look at the case of women who are married, and see whether the objection that politics would withdraw them from domestic duties, is valid. It would be a great assistance in deciding this question to know the average number of hours in the year which an elector employs in discharging his political duties. Is an hour a week a fair estimate? But surely an elector would not, unless he is engaged in some particular work, such as superintending the registration, or as secretary to a political society; devote as much as an hour a week – no, nor half an hour a week – to duties which the franchise imposes upon him. Then what does this objection, that the right to vote at Parliamentary elections would withdraw women from domestic duties, really come to? Why soon it will be objected that women should not go to church or out for a walk, because so doing withdraws them from their domestic duties. It may, however, be urged that it is not merely the exercise of the franchise, but all that an interest in political questions involves – the reading of newspapers, the attending of meetings, and the like – that would have a mischievous influence in withdrawing women from their domestic duties. But surely the wife and mother of a family ought to be something more than a housekeeper or a nurse, – how will she be able to minister to the mental wants of her husband and her children if she makes the care of their physical comforts the only object of her life? Physical comfort is not to be despised, but if there is no moral and intellectual sympathy between a husband and wife, or between a mother and her children, a permanent and life-long injury is inflicted upon them all, which no amount of physical comfort can in the slightest degree compensate. It is, however, quite erroneous to suppose that an attention to domestic duties and to intellectual pursuits cannot be combined. There is no reason why wives and mothers should not cultivate their minds, and at the same time give proper attention to their domestic affairs. A hundred instances could be given to show that the notion that a woman, in order to manage her house and family well, must devote her whole time and mind to it and do nothing else, is quite incorrect. It cannot, therefore, be maintained that the plea that the franchise would withdraw women from their domestic duties is a valid objection to their enfranchisement.

We now pass to another objection – That the line must be drawn somewhere, and if women had votes they would soon be wanting to enter the House of Commons. The selection of a fit person to serve them in Parliament may safely be left to constituencies. At the present time there is no necessity to pass a law that a man wholly immersed in the conduct of a large business, should not offer himself as a candidate for a seat in Parliament; nor is it necessary to enact that no man of a serious constitutional delicacy should ever have a seat in Parliament. All these things are settled by candidates and constituencies without any legislative interference. As Mr. Mill very justly says, there is no necessity to pass laws to forbid people doing what they cannot do. There is no Act of Parliament needed to enact that none but strong-armed men should be blacksmiths. And so it would prove if all the disabilities of women were swept away. The would-be witty caricatures of sickly women fainting in the House of Commons under the weight of their legislative responsibilities, would lose their brilliancy and point in the cold light of stern reality. No constituency would deliberately choose a representative who would be quite incapable of serving it faithfully and well. All questions about who should or who should not have seats in Parliament may safely be left to constituencies.

Another objection to women's suffrage is that women do not want votes. Notwithstanding the obvious reply that a considerable number of women do want votes, and are continually petitioning Parliament to remove their electoral disabilities, it must be confessed that there is something more formidable in this objection than in any of the others which have been considered. Of course it makes no difference at all so far as abstract justice is concerned; but still, in practical politics, abstract justice does not usually weigh much with statesmen, unless it is accompanied by an urgent and pressing demand for the amelioration of the law. The existance of the Irish Church Establishment was as much opposed to abstract justice in 1769 and in 1869, but disestablishment did not take place until the demand for it was so urgent that it could not longer be disregarded. The demand for the extension of the suffrage to women is daily growing more earnest and more general. The bill now before Parliament has been supported by petitions from every part of the kingdom, signed by many tens of thousands of men and women. In the presence of such facts it cannot be said that there is no demand on the part of women for the suffrage. There is also this very strong argument, which is sometimes overlooked by those who consider that the suffrage should not be extended to women, because the majority of women do not desire to exercise electoral rights. No one proposes that women should be compelled to vote. Any woman who thinks that voting would be unfeminine or injurious to her health, would be quite at liberty to refrain from taking any part in an election. But it seems very unfair that those who do not wish for political power should be enabled to deprive those who do wish for it, of the right to exercise the franchise.

The *Spectator* says that people who do not demand the franchise, would, if they had votes, use them corruptly. I have endeavoured to prove that the franchise is the right of all, not the privilege of a select few. Two hundred years ago Oliver Cromwell, writing to the Governor of Edinburgh Castle, said, "It will be found an unjust and unwise jealousy to deprive a man of his natural liberty on a supposition that he might abuse it. When he doth abuse it – judge."

This sentence seems to indicate precisely two amendments

most urgently required in our electoral system. In the first place, large classes of people are now excluded from the franchise on the supposition that they might abuse it; and in the second place, large classes of people, who are admitted to the franchise, do abuse their freedom, and legislation is almost powerless to visit them with the swift and severe punishment they so justly merit. Surely it would be more in accordance with the principles usually advocated by the *Spectator*, if it used its influence in promoting such an alteration of the law as would facilitate the punishment not only of the bribed, but of the bribers, instead of indulging in what Oliver Cromwell calls the "unjust and unwise jealousy" of depriving people of their natural liberty on the supposition that they might abuse it. The *Spectator* would be the last to say that all workmen ought to be deprived of the right of combination, because some workmen have abused this right. Yet this is a case in which the abuse of power is an actual fact, not a possible fact, such as the abuse on the part of women of the suffrage.

Another objection sometimes urged against women's suffrage is that most women are Conservatives, and that their enfranchisement would consequently have a reactionary influence on politics. But this is an objection, not so much to women's suffrage, as to representative government. Do those who object to the enfranchisement of women, on the ground that they are usually Conservatives, think that all Conservatives ought to be disfranchised? Surely representative institutions require that all differences of opinion should have their due and proportionate weight in the legislature. No class of persons should be excluded on account of their political opinions. What would be thought of a Conservative who gravely asserted that all Dissenters should be disfranchised because they are generally Liberals? It would be almost dangerous even to suggest the hard names which such a misguided person would be called by the very people who oppose women's suffrage because most women are Conservatives. And yet the two cases are exactly parallel, and equally antagonistic to the fundamental principle of representative government. A representative system which excludes half the community from representation surely is a farce. The question ought not to be "How will women vote if they have the franchise?" but, "Is representative government the best form of government that can be devised?" If the answer is in the affirmative, the exclusion of women from electoral rights can in no way be justified.

Sometimes it is said that the indulgence and courtesy with which women are now treated by men, would cease if women exercised all the rights and privileges of citizenship. Let it be granted that women would no longer be treated with exceptional courtesy and indulgence if they had electoral power; and then let us inquire, what this courtesy and this indulgence really amount to. They certainly are not valueless, but let us see of what sort of things they consist. Women are usually assisted in and out of carriages; they take precedence of men in entering and leaving a room; the door also is frequently opened for them; they are helped first at dinner; and they are always permitted to walk on the inside of the pavement. Besides these there are more substantial privileges, such as being allowed to monopolise the seats in a room or a railway carriage in those cases where some of those present are obliged to stand. It would be unwise to underrate these little amenities of social life. They are very harmless, and perhaps even pleasant, in their way; but it must be confessed that their practical value is small indeed, especially if the price paid for them consists of all the rights and privileges of citizenship. If the courtesy of men to women is bought at this price, it must not be forgotten that the sale is compulsory, and can in no case be regarded as a free contract. But would women really lose all the politeness now shown to them if their right to the franchise were recognised? At elections it is not usually the case that those who have votes are treated with the least consideration; but, apart from this, how would the courtesy of every-day life be affected by the extension of the suffrage to women? Some of the mere forms of politeness, which have no practical value, might gradually fall into disuse; but surely true politeness, which is inseparably associated with real kindness of heart, would not suffer any decrease from the extension of suffrage to women.

It is sometimes said that the physique of a woman is so delicate, that she could not stand the excitement of political life. This argument would be more comprehensible if women were entirely debarred from mixing with the outside world; but, as it is, there is nothing to prevent women from sharing the general excitement caused by an election. It is notorious some women do share it. But suppose it were satisfactorily proved that the health of some women would be injured by the excitement caused by taking part in elections, is that a reason why all women should be excluded from political power? The health of many men is frequently injured by excessive political work and excitement. Instances of such cases must occur to every one. The illness from which Mr. Bright is now suffering, and the extreme exhaustion of the Prime Minister at the end of the last session, were both, doubtless, produced by the mental strain attendant on too much political work. But such facts furnish no argument against the exercise of political power by these eminent persons. We all hope that the only practical result of their maladies will be to make them more solicitous of their own health than they have hitherto been. If may safely be left to the inhabitants of a free country to take the necessary precautions for preserving their health; and if any woman found that the excitement of elections endangered either her mind or her body, no Act of Parliament would be required to induce her to withdraw from political strife.

Perhaps the objection to women's suffrage which operates most powerfully with the majority of people is, that the exercise of political power by women is repugnant to the feelings, and quite at variance with a due sense of propriety. In Turkey, a woman who walked out with her face uncovered would be considered to have lost all sense of propriety; her conduct would be highly repugnant to the feelings of the community. In China, a woman who refused to pinch her feet to about a third of their natural size would be looked upon as entirely destitute of female refinement. We censure these customs as ignorant, and the feelings on which they are based as devoid of the sanction of reason. It is therefore clear that it is not enough in order to prove the undesirability of the enfranchisement of women, to say that it is repugnant to the feelings. It must further be inquired to what feelings women's suffrage is repugnant, and whether these feelings are "necessary and eternal," or, "being the result of custom, they are changeable and evanescent." There seems to be little difficulty in proving that these feelings belong to the latter class. In the first place, a feeling that is necessary and eternal must be consistent; and the feeling of repugnance towards the exercise of political power by women is not consistent; for no one feels this repugnance towards the exercise of political power by the Queen. In the second place, it has been previously shown that the equal freedom of all is a necessary pre-requisite of the fulfilment of the Divine will, and that the equal freedom of a part of the community is destroyed if it is deprived of political power; and can it be asserted that the Supreme Being has implanted in man necessary and eternal feelings in opposition to his own will? Again: the state of popular feeling as to what women may and may not do is constantly changing in the same country, and even in the mind of the same individual; the feelings on this subject also differ in different classes of the community; it is consequently quite impossible to say that these feelings are necessary and eternal; they are, therefore, the result of custom, changeable and evanescent, and are destined to be modified by advancing civilisation.

It may be that a great deal of the repugnance which undoubtedly exists against women taking part in politics, arises from the disturbance and disorder which are too often the disgraceful characteristics of elections in this country. The adoption of the ballot and the abolition of nominations which will almost certainly take place before the next dissolution, will in all probability cause elections to be conducted with order and tranquillity. But the danger of women proceeding to polling places under the present system is greatly exaggerated. This is a point on which a small amount of experience is worth a great deal of theorising. At the general elections of 1865 and 1868, I went round to many of the polling places in several large boroughs. On most of these occasions I was accompanied only be a young girl, and no incident whatever took place which could have alarmed or annoyed any one. My experience on this point has always been the same, and it is corroborated by the experience of all ladies with whom I am acquainted, who, like myself, have tested by personal experiment whether it is either unpleasant or unsafe for a woman to go to a polling place. There are surely few men so unmanly as wilfully to annoy a well-conducted woman in the discharge of what she believed to be a public duty.

Many thousands of women have recorded their votes at the poll of the municipal elections. There is frequently quite as much bribery, drunkenness, and excitement at these elections as at the parliamentary elections, and yet I do not remember hearing of any instance in which a woman was subjected to insult or roughness in recording her vote at the municipal elections.

CONDORCET'S PLEA FOR THE CITIZENSHIP
OF WOMEN. A TRANSLATION.[1]
[John Morley, trans.]

It is in the power of habit to familiarise men with the violation
of their natural rights to such a degree that, among those who
have lost them, nobody ever thinks of reclaiming them or
supposes himself to have suffered any wrong. There are even
some of these cases of violation which have escaped philosophers and legislators, when they were devoting themselves with
most zeal to the establishment of the common rights of the
members of the human race, and to the foundation in these
rights, and in them only, of political institutions.

For instance, have they not every one violated the principle
of the equality of rights, in tranquilly depriving the half of the
human race of that of assisting in the making of law; in
excluding women from the right of citizenship? Is there a
stronger proof of the power of habit, even over enlightened
men, than the spectacle of equality of rights being invoked in
favour of three or four hundred men that an absurd prejudice
had deprived of them, and being forgotten in respect of twelve

[1] The pieces which I have here reproduced, with the omission of one or two
sentences of no significance, was published by Condorcet on the 3rd of July,
1790, in the *Journal de la Société de* 1789, and was no doubt intended to
influence the deliberations of the Constituent Assembly, of which he was
not a member. It is to be found in Vol. X. of Condorcet's Works, p. 121 –
Sur l'Admission des Femmes au Droit de Cité.

It is natural that the question of the equal place of women with men in the
rights of citizenship should come into prominence in times of revolution like
'89. The more profound and moral the revolutionary feeling is, the more
certain is the subjection of women to arrest attention. There are at least two
good reasons why this should be so. In such times men are deeply stirred by
a sense of justice; and in such times they feel to an unusual degree the need
of the intelligent co-operation of women. Both conditions are to be met
with in those men of our own day who are most penetrated by social
sentiment, though there is marked difference among them as to the ideal of
the female character, and also as to the precise way in which their action in
public affairs may best make itself felt. The simplest and truest view surely
is that we have no right to deprive women of the opportunity of deciding
both of these questions for themselves. – Editor.

millions of women? For this exclusion not to be an act of tyranny, it would be necessary either to prove that the natural rights of women are not absolutely identical with those of men, or else to show that women are incapable of exercising them.

Now the rights of men result only from this, that men are beings with sensibility, capable of acquiring moral ideas, and of reasoning on these ideas. So women, having these same qualities, have necessarily equal rights. Either no individual of the human race has genuine rights, or else all have the same; and he who votes against the right of another, whatever the religion, colour, or sex of that other, has henceforth abjured his own.

With reference to the other horn of the dilemma, it would be hard to prove that women are incapable of exercising the rights of citizenship. Why should beings to whom pregnancy and passing indispositions are incident, not be able to exercise rights of which nobody ever dreamt of depriving people who have the gout every winter or who easily catch cold? Again, even if we admit in men a superiority of intelligence not the necessary result of difference of education – which is as far as possible from being proved, and which ought to be proved, to enable us to deprive women of a natural right without injustice – this superiority can only consist in two points. It is said that no woman has made an important discovery in science, nor given proofs of genius in art, literature, &c. But, we may presume, the franchise is not to be accorded only to men of genius. It is said, further, that no woman has the same range of knowledge, the same force of understanding, as certain men. But what follows from this, that, except a not very large class of highly enlightened men, there is entire equality between women and the rest of men; that, this small class apart, inferiority and superiority are equally divided between the two sexes? Now, since it would be utterly absurd to confine to this superior class the rights of citizenship and the liability to public functions, why should we exclude women from them, any more than those among men who are inferior to a great number of women?[2]

2 It would be astonishing, if we did not remember the omnipotence of prejudice, how many clever men suppose that they are discussing the justice of giving the franchise to women, by asserting in a variety of forms that past history and present experience prove that men are superior to women. The meaninglessness of their proposition is evident the moment they come to

In short, will anybody contend that women have in intelligence or in heart any qualities that ought to exclude them from the enjoyment of their natural rights? Let us interrogate facts. Elizabeth of England, Maria Theresa, the two Catherines of Russia, proved that it was neither strength of character nor courage of mind that women failed in. Would not the rights of citizens have found a better champion at the States of 1614 in the adopted daughter of Montaigne, than in Councillor Courtin, who believed in sortilege and occult virtues? Was not the Princess des Ursins worth more than Chamillard? Would not the Marquise du Châtelet have composed a dispatch as well as M. Rouillé? Would Madame de Lambert have made laws as absurd and as barbarous as those

quantify it. Surely not *all* men are superior to *all* women; the stupidest man to the ablest woman; one of the good Lord Shaftesbury's male serfs to Georges Sand or George Eliot? It not, then what men are superior to what women? It may be well, as we are at translation, to reproduce the passage in which Plato has dealt with this.

Many women are superior to many women in many things. So there is no function, my friend, says Socrates, proper to those who administer the city, which belongs especially to a woman, because she is a woman, nor to a man because he is a man, but their natures are distributed alike among both creatures, and a woman shares in all functions, as a man shares in all; but in all woman is weaker than man. Shall we then assign all functions to men, and to women none?

I do not follow.

Well, you will agree in this, that one woman has a turn for doctoring, and another has not; that one is musical by constitution, and another unmusical?

Certainly.

And one fond of athletic games and fighting, and another peaceful and not fond of athletics?

True.

Well, and you find women who love knowledge and women who hate it; and women with spirit and women without spirit?

Yes, that is so.

Then there are women with the qualities required for a guardian, and others without them. And this is just the conclusion we came to about men. So the constitution and character of men and women are the same, as far as the guardianship of the city goes; . . . only lighter offices will be imposed on women than on men, on account of the inferior physical strength of the former. Our projects, therefore, were far from being impracticable and visionary, for the law we proposed was conformable to nature, and it is the existing system which is against nature. – (*Republ.*, Bk. v. 455. D . . . 457).

In short, Plato's view was that the best men excel the best women, but that the best women excel all men below the second-best; and that women have as many individual differences of taste and capacity as men have. Mr. Bouverie, however, one should add, does not agree with Socrates and Plato.

of D'Armenonville, against Protestants, thievish servants, smugglers, and negroes? As they cast an eye over the list of those who have been their rulers and law-makers, men have no right to be so proud.

Women are superior to men in the milder and domestic virtues; they know, as well as men, how to love liberty, though they do not share all its advantages; and in republics they have many a time sacrificed themselves for it. They have shown the virtues of citizens as often as accident or civil troubles have brought them on a stage from which among all nations the pride of men had repulsed them.

It has been said that women, notwithstanding much wit, judgment, and a faculty of reasoning carried as far as it has been by subtle dialecticians, have never been guided by what is called reason. This remark is untrue. They are not guided, it is true, by the reason of men, but they are guided by their own. Their interests not being the same by the defect of the laws, and the same things not having for them the same importance as for us, they may without failing in reason, make up their minds on other principles, and aim at a different end. It is not more unreasonable for a woman to take pains about her personal appearance than it was for Demosthenes to take pains with his voice and his gesticulation.

It has been said that women, though better than men, more gentle, more sensitive, less subject to the harsher and more egoistic sort of vices, have not the sentiment of justice; that they obey feeling rather than conscience. This remark is more near being true, but it proves nothing. It is not nature, it is education, it is the manner of social life, which is the cause of this difference. Neither one nor the other has accustomed women to the idea of what is just, but only to the idea of what is amiable. Banished from affairs, from everything that is settled according to rigorous justice and positive laws, the matters with which they occupy themselves are precisely those which are ruled by natural amiability and by feeling. It is hardly fair, therefore, to allege as a reason for continuing to deny women the enjoyment of their natural rights, reasons which only possess a certain amount of substance because women do not enjoy these rights.

If we admitted such arguments against women, we must also deprive of the franchise the part of the people which, devoted to incessant labour, can neither acquire light nor exercise its reason, and soon we should come, step by step, to such a pass as only to permit citizenship in men who had gone through a course of public law. If we admit such principles, we must as a necessary consequence renounce the whole idea of a free constitution. The various aristocracies have only had similar pretexts for foundation or for excuse; the etymology of the word proves it.

You cannot bring forward the subjection of wives to their husbands, because, in the first place, it would be possible at the same time to destroy this tyranny of the civil law; and, in the second, one injustice can never be a reason for perpetrating another.

There only remain two objections to discuss. In truth, they only oppose to the admission of women to the right of citizenship motives of utility, which cannot outweigh a genuine right. The contrary maxim has too often been the excuse and pretext of tyrants; it is in the name of utility that commerce and industry groan in fetters, and that the African remains devoted to slavery; it was in the name of public utility that the Bastile was crowded with prisoners, that censors were appointed over books, that legal procedure was kept secret, that the torture was applied. Still, we will discuss these objections, so as to leave nothing unanswered.

We should have to dread, it is said, the influence of women over men.

We reply, to begin with, that this influence, like every other, is much more to be feared when used in private than in a public discussion; that the influence which may be peculiar to women would lose all the more by this; as, if it extends over more than one individual, it cannot be durable after it is known. Again, as hitherto women have never been admitted in any country to an absolute equality, as their empire has none the less for this existed everywhere, and the lower women have been placed by the laws, the more dangerous it has been, it does not seem as if we ought to have much confidence in this remedy. Is it not probable, on the contrary, that this empire would diminish if women had less interest in maintaining it, if it ceased to be for them the only means of defending themselves and of escaping from oppression? If politeness prevents most men from upholding their opinion against a woman in society, it is a politeness that has a good deal to do with pride; they yield a victory which has no consequences; defeat does not humiliate, because it is regarded as voluntary. Does anybody seriously suppose that it would be the same in a public discussion on an important subject? Does politeness prevent people from pleading a cause in the courts against a woman?

But, we shall be told, this change would be contrary to general utility, because it would draw women away from the tasks that nature seems to have reserved for them.

This objection does not seem very well grounded. Whatever constitution is set up, it is certain that in the existing state of the civilisation of European nations, there will never be more than a very small number of citizens able to occupy themselves with public business. You would not be tearing women away from their housekeeping any more than you tear the labourer from his plough or the artisan from his workshop. In the richer classes, we never see the women surrendering themselves to domestic cares in so continuous a manner that we need be afraid of distracting their attention from them; and a serious occupation would certainly distract women from them much less than the futile tastes to which idleness and bad education condemn them.

The principle cause of this apprehension is the idea that every man admitted to enjoy the franchise thinks henceforth of nothing but governing; which may be true, to a certain extent, at the moment when a constitution is being established. But this stir and agitation could not be permanent. In the same way we must not suppose that, because women might possibly be members of national assemblies, they would on the spot abandon their children, their households, their needle. They would be all the more fit to bring up their children and to form men. It is natural that the woman should suckle her children, and should attend to their first years. Kept to the house by these tasks, and being physically weaker than man, it is natural further that she should lead a more retired and domestic life. So women would be in the same class as the men who are obliged by their position to attend to a business for a certain number of hours. This may be a good reason for not preferring them in the elections, but it cannot be the foundation of a legal exclusion. Gallantry would lose by this change, but domestic manners would gain by that as by every other equality.

Hitherto all known nations have had barbarous or corrupt manners and customs. The only exception that I know of must be made in favour of the Americans of the United States, who are spread in a small number over a large territory. Hitherto, among all nations, legal inequality has existed between men and women; and it would not be hard to prove that in these two phenomena, equally general, the second is one of the principal causes of the first. For inequality necessarily introduces corruption, and is the most common, where it is not the only, cause of it.

It is singular enough that in many countries women should have been counted incapable of every public function, yet worthy of royalty; that in France a woman could have been regent, and that up to 1776 she could not be a *marchande de modes* at Paris; that, in fine, in the elective assemblies of our bailliages, that should have been accorded to a right of the fief which was denied to the right of nature. Several of our noble deputies owe to ladies the honour of sitting among the representatives of the nation. Why, instead of taking away this right from the owners of fiefs, not extend it to all those who have property, who are householders?[3]

3   It is an interesting fact in the history of French opinion upon the position of women, that so far back as 1673 there was published in Paris by a Sieur de P., a little volume – for knowledge and perusal of which I am indebted to Mr. Colvin – entitled "De l'Egalité des Deux Sexes, Discours Physique et Moral, où l'on voit l'importance de se Défaire de Préjugés." The reasons for accepting this equality have never been stated with calmer or more rational force, and the writer, whoever he was, had the courage to maintain the equal fitness of women with men for all offices, including those of Prince, Preacher, and General. "Pour moy," he said (p. 168), "je ne serois pas plus surpris de voir une femme le casque en teste, que de luy voir une Couronne; présider dans un Conseil de Guerre, comme dans celuy d'un Etat; exercer elle-même ses soldats, ranger une armée en bataille, la partager en plusieurs corps, comme elle se divertiroit à le voir faire. L'Art Militaire n'a rien pardessus les autres, dont les femmes sont capables. . . . Une femme peut inventer des stratagèmes pour surprendre l'ennemy, luy mettre le vent, la poussière, le soleil, en face," &c. Joan of Arc, the Countess of Derby, and other women, are cases in point. If it be said that physical strength is inadequate, the doubter may be referred to the well-known passage where Macaulay describes the physical weakness of William III. and his enemy, Luxembourg.

The writer gives a singularly good account of the way in which in primitive times the ideas of male supremacy would be likely to arise. It was, in fact, owing to the operation of Natural Selection. Women, in seasons of pregnancy and lactation, would be less capable than men of carrying on the struggle for subsistence, and would therefore have died out, if they had not been essential to the appetites of their male companions. That the idea of superiority should arise from this was natural enough among barbarians. Its continuance in communities that, like some of those of our own time, have really made partial advances towards high civilisation, is more wonderful. – Editor.

EQUALITY
[James Fitzjames Stephen]

Having tried to show in what sense justice and equality are connected, and in what sense they are independent of each other, I proceed to examine the question of the expediency of equality in some of its more important features.

The doctrine upon this subject which I deny and which I am disposed to think Mr Mill affirmed – though, if he did, it was with somewhat less than his usual transparent vigour and decision – is that equality is in itself always expedient, or, to say the very least, presumably expedient, and that in every case of inequality the burden of proof lies on those who justify its maintenance.

I might cite in proof or illustration of this the whole of his essay on the Subjection of Women, a work from which I dissent from the first sentence to the last, which I will consider on the present occasion only with reference to the particular topic of equality, and as the strongest distinct illustration known to me of what is perhaps one of the strongest, and what appears to me to be by far the most ignoble and mischievous of all the popular feelings of the age.

The object of Mr Mill's essay is to explain the grounds of the opinion that 'the principle which regulates the existing social relations between the two sexes, the legal subordination of one sex to the other, is wrong in itself, and now one of the chief hindrances to human improvement; and that it ought to be replaced by a principle of perfect equality, admitting no power or privilege on the one side, or disability on the other.'

Mr Mill is fully aware of the difficulty of his task. He admits that he is arguing against 'an almost universal opinion,' but he urges that it and the practice founded on it is a relic of a bygone state of things. 'We now live – that is to say, one or two of the most advanced nations of the world now live – in a state in which the law of the strongest seems to be entirely abandoned as the regulating principle of the world's affairs. Nobody professes it, and as regards most of the relations between human beings, nobody is permitted to practise it. . . . This being the ostensible state of things, people flatter themselves that the rule of mere force is ended.' Still they do not know how hard it dies, and in particular they are unaware of the fact that it still regulates the relations between men and women. It is true that the actually existing generation of women do not dislike their position. The consciousness of this haunts Mr Mill throughout the whole of his argument, and embarrasses him at every turn. He is driven to account for it by such assertions as that 'each individual of the subject class is in a chronic state of bribery and intimidation combined,' by reference to the affection which slaves in classical times felt for their masters in many cases, and by other suggestions of the same sort. His great argument against the present state of things is that it is opposed to what he calls 'the modern conviction, the fruit of a thousand years of experience:'

> That things in which the individual is the person directly interested never go right but as they are left to his own discretion, and that any regulation of them by authority except to protect the rights of others is sure to be mischievous . . . The peculiar character of the modern world . . . is that human beings are no longer born to their place in life and chained down by an inexorable bond to the place they are born to, but are free to employ their faculties and such favourable chances as offer, to achieve the lot which may appear to them most desirable. Human society of old was constituted on a very different principle. All were born to a fixed social position, and were mostly kept in it by law or interdicted from any means by which they could emerge from it . . . In consonance with this doctrine it is felt to be an overstepping of the proper bounds of authority to fix beforehand on some general presumption that certain persons are not fit to do certain things. It is now thoroughly known and admitted that if some such presumptions exist no such presumption is infallible . . . Hence we ought not . . . to ordain that to be born a girl instead of a boy shall decide the person's position all through life.

The result is that 'the social subordination of women thus stands out as an isolated fact in modern social institutions.' It is in 'radical opposition' to 'the progressive movement, which is the boast of the modern world.' This fact creates a '*prima facie* presumption' against it, 'far outweighing any which custom and usage could in such circumstances create' in its favour.

I will not follow Mr Mill through the whole of his argument, much of which consists of matter not relevant to my present purpose, and not agreeable to discuss, though many of his assertions provoke reply. There is something - I hardly know what to call it; indecent is too strong a word, but I may say unpleasant in the direction of indecorum - in prolonged and minute discussions about the relations between men and women, and the characteristics of women as such. I will therefore pass over what Mr Mill says on this subject with a mere general expression of dissent from nearly every word he says. The following extracts show the nature of that part of his theory which bears on the question of equality:

> The equality of married persons before the law . . . is the only means of rendering the daily life of mankind in any high sense a school of moral cultivation. Though the truth may not be felt or generally acknowledged for generations to come, the only school of genuine moral sentiment is society between equals. The moral education of mankind has hitherto emanated chiefly from the law of force, and is adapted almost solely to the relations which force creates. In the less advanced states of society, people hardly recognize any relation with their equals. To be an equal is to be an enemy. Society, from its highest place to its lowest, is one long chain, or rather ladder, where every individual is either above or below his nearest neighbour, and wherever he does not command he must obey. Existing moralities accordingly are mainly fitted to a relation of command and obedience. Yet command and obedience are but unfortunate necessities of human life; society in equality is its normal state. Already in modern life, and more and more as it progressively improves, command and obedience become exceptional facts in life, equal association its general rule . . . We have had the morality of submission and the morality of chivalry and generosity; the time is now come for the morality of justice.

In another part of the book this doctrine is stated more fully in a passage of which it will be enough for my purpose to quote a very few lines:

There are many persons for whom it is not enough that the inequality [between the sexes] has no just or legitimate defence; they require to be told what express advantage would be obtained by abolishing it. To which let me first answer, the advantage of having all the most universal and pervading of all human relations regulated by justice instead of injustice. The vast amount of this gain to human nature it is hardly possible by any explanation or illustration to place in a stronger light than it is placed in by the bare statement to any one who attaches a moral meaning to words.

These passages show what Mr Mill's doctrine of equality is, and how it forms the very root, the essence, so to speak, of his theory about the subjection of women. I consider it unsound in every respect. I think that it rests upon an unsound view of history, an unsound view of morals, and a grotesquely distorted view of facts, and I believe that its practical application would be as injurious as its theory is false.

The theory may be shortly restated in the following propositions, which I think are implied in or may be collected from the extracts given above.

(1) Justice requires that all people should live in society as equals.

(2) History shows that human progress has been a progress from a 'law of force' to a condition in which command and obedience become exceptional.

(3) The 'law of the strongest' having in this and one or two other countries been 'entirely abandoned' in all other relations of life, it may be presumed not to apply to the relation between the sexes.

(4) Notorious facts as to the nature of that relation show that in this particular case the presumption is in fact well founded.

I dissent from each of these propositions. First, as to the proposition that justice requires that all people should live in society as equals. I have already shown that this is equivalent to the proposition that it is expedient that all people should live in society as equals. Can this be proved? for it is certainly not a self-evident proposition.

I think that if the rights and duties which laws create are to be generally advantageous, they ought to be adapted to the situation of the persons who enjoy or are subject to them. They ought to recognize both substantial equality and substantial inequality, and they should from time to time be so moulded and altered as always to represent fairly well the existing state of society. Government, in a word, ought to fit society as a man's clothes fit him. To establish by law rights and duties which assume that people are equal when they are not is like trying to make clumsy feet look handsome by the help of tight boots. No doubt it may be necessary to legislate in such a manner as to correct the vices of society or to protect it against special dangers or diseases to which it is liable. Law in this case is analogous to surgery, and the rights and duties imposed by it might be compared to the irons which are sometimes contrived for the purpose of supporting a weak limb or keeping it in some particular position. As a rule, however, it is otherwise. Rights and duties should be so moulded as to clothe, protect, and sustain society in the position which it naturally assumes. The proposition, therefore, that justice demands that people should live in society as equals may be translated thus: 'It is inexpedient that any law should recognize any inequality between human beings.'

This appears to me to involve the assertion, 'There are no inequalities between human beings of sufficient importance to influence the rights and duties which it is expedient to confer upon them.' This proposition I altogether deny. I say that there are many such differences, some of which are more durable and more widely extended than others, and of which some are so marked and so important that unless human nature is radically changed, we cannot even imagine their removal; and of these the differences of age and sex are the most important.

The difference of age is so distinct a case of inequality that even Mr Mill does not object to its recognition. He admits, as every one must, that perhaps a third or more of the average term of human life – and that the portion of it in which the strongest, the most durable, and beyond all comparison the most important impressions are made on human beings, the period in which character is formed – must be passed by every one in a state of submission, dependence, and obedience to orders the objects of which are usually most imperfectly understood by the persons who receive them. Indeed, as I have already pointed out, Mr Mill is disposed rather to exaggerate than to underrate the influence of education and the powers of educators. Is not this a clear case of inequality of the strongest kind, and does it not at all events afford a most instructive precedent in favour of the recognition by law of a marked natural distinction? If children were regarded by law as the equals of adults, the result would be something infinitely worse than barbarism. It would involve a degree of cruelty to the young which can hardly be realized even in imagination. The proceeding, in short, would be so utterly monstrous and irrational that I suppose it never entered into the head of the wildest zealot for equality to propose it.

Upon the practical question all are agreed; but consider the consequences which it involves. It involves the consequence that, so far from being 'unfortunate necessities', command and obedience stand at the very entrance to life, and preside over the most important part of it. It involves the consequence that the exertion of power and constraint is so important and so indispensable in the greatest of all matters, that it is a less evil to invest with it every head of a family indiscriminately, however unfit he may be to exercise it, than to fail to provide for its exercise. It involves the consequence that by mere lapse of time and by following the promptings of passion men acquire over others a position of superiority and of inequality which all nations and ages, the most cultivated as well as the rudest, have done their best to surround with every association of awe and reverence. The title of Father is the one which the best part of the human race have given to God, as being the least inadequate and inappropriate means of indicating the union of love, reverence, and submission. Whoever first gave the command or uttered the maxim, 'Honour thy father and thy mother, that thy days may be long in the land,' had a far better conception of the essential conditions of permanent national existence and prosperity than the author of the motto Liberty, Equality, and Fraternity.

Now, if society and government ought to recognize the inequality of age as the foundation of an inequality of rights of this importance, it appears to me at least equally clear that they ought to recognize the inequality of sex for the same purpose, if it is a real inequality. Is it one? There are some propositions which it is difficult to prove, because they are so plain, and this is one of them. The physical differences between the two sexes affect every part of the human body, from the hair of the head to the soles of the feet, from the size and density of the bones to the texture of the brain and the character of the nervous system. Ingenious people may argue about anything, and Mr Mill does say a great number of things about women which, as I have already observed, I will not discuss; but all the talk in the world will never shake the proposition that men are stronger than women in every shape. They have greater muscular and nervous force, greater intellectual force, greater vigour of character. This general truth, which has been observed under all sorts of circumstances and in every age and country, has also in every age and country led to a division of labour between men and women, the general outline of which is as familiar and as universal as the general outline of the differences between them. These are the facts, and the question is whether the law and public opinion ought to recognize this difference? How it ought to recognize it, what difference it ought to make between men and women as such, is quite another question.

The first point to consider is whether it ought to treat them as equals, although, as I have shown, they are not equals, because men are the stronger. I will take one or two illustrations. Men, no one denies, may, and in some cases ought to be liable to compulsory military service. No one, I suppose, would hesitate to admit, that if we were engaged in a great war it might become necessary, or that if necessary it would be right, to have a conscription both for the land and for the sea service. Ought men and women to be subject to it indiscriminately? If any one says that they ought, I have no more to say, except that he has got into the region at which argument is useless. But if it is admitted that this ought not to be done, an inequality of treatment founded on a radical inequality between the two sexes is admitted, and if this admission is once made, where are you to draw the line? Turn from the case of liability to military service to that of education, which in Germany is rightly regarded as the other great branch of State activity, and the same question presents itself in another shape. Are boys and girls to be educated indiscriminately, and to be instructed in the same things? Are boys to learn to sew, to keep house, and to cook, and are girls to play at cricket, to row, and be drilled like boys? I cannot argue with a person who says Yes. A person who says No admits an inequality between the sexes on which education must be founded, and which it must therefore perpetuate and perhaps increase.

[1]Follow the matter a step further to the vital point of the whole question – marriage. Marriage is one of the subjects with which it is absolutely necessary both for law and morals to deal with in some way or other. All that I need consider in reference to the present purpose is the question whether the laws and moral rules which relate to it should regard it as a contract between equals, or as a contract between a stronger and a weaker person involving subordination for certain purposes on the part of the weaker to the stronger. I say that a law which proceeded on the former and not on the latter of these views would be founded on a totally false assumption, and would involve cruel injustice in the sense of extreme general inexpediency, especially to women. If the parties to a contract of marriage are treated as equals, it is impossible to avoid the inference that marriage, like other partnerships, may be dissolved at pleasure. The advocates of women's rights are exceedingly shy of stating this plainly. Mr. Mill says nothing about it in his book on the Subjection of Women, though in one place he comes very near to saying so, but it is as clear an inference from his principles as anything can possibly be, nor has he ever disavowed it.[2] If this were the law, it would make women the slaves of their husbands. A woman loses the qualities which make her attractive to men much earlier than men lose those which make them attractive to women. The tie between a woman and young children is generally far closer than the tie between them and their father. A woman who is no longer young, and who is the mother of children, would thus be absolutely in her husband's power, in nine cases out of ten, if he might put an end to the marriage when he pleased. This is one inequality in the position of the parties which must be recognized and provided for beforehand if the contract is to be for their common good. A second inequality is this. When a man marries, it is generally because he feels himself established in life. He incurs, no doubt, a good deal of expense, but he does not in any degree impair his means of earning a living. When a woman marries she practically renounces in all but the

---

1 With reference, I suppose, to this passage, which extends to p. 196, Mr Harrison says of me: 'When he talks about marriage, it is in the tone of Petruchio taming the shrew.'

2 A passage near the end of the 'Essay on Liberty' strongly implies the opinion that divorce ought to be permitted at the discretion of the parties. See p. 87, 1st ed.[3]

rarest cases the possibility of undertaking any profession but one, and the possibility of carrying on that one profession in the society of any man but one. Here is a second inequality. It would be easy to mention others of the deepest importance, but these are enough to show that to treat a contract of marriage as a contract between persons who are upon an equality in regard of strength, and power to protect their interest, is to treat it as being what it notoriously is not.

Again, the contract is one which involves subordination and obedience on the part of the weaker party to the stronger. The proof of this is, to my mind, as clear as that of a proposition in Euclid, and it is this:

(1) Marriage is a contract, one of the principal objects of which is the government of a family.

(2) This government must be vested either by law or by contract in the hands of one of the two married persons.

(3) If the arrangement is made by contract, the remedy for breach of it must either be by law or by a dissolution of the partnership at the will of the contracting parties.

(4) Law could give no remedy in such a case. Therefore the only remedy for breach of the contract would be a dissolution of the marriage.

(5) Therefore, if marriage is to be permanent, the government of the family must be put by law and by morals in the hands of the husband, for no one proposes to give it to the wife.

Mr Mill is totally unable to meet this argument, and apparently embraces the alternative that marriage ought to be dissoluble at the pleasure of the parties. After much argument as to contracts which appear to me visionary, his words are these: 'Things never come to an issue of downright power on one side and obedience on the other except where the connection has been altogether a mistake and it would be a blessing to both parties to be relieved from it.'

This appears to me to show a complete misapprehension of the nature of family government and of the sort of cases in which the question of obedience and authority can arise between husband and wife. No one contends that a man ought to have power to order his wife about like a slave and beat her if she disobeys him. Such conduct in the eye of the law would be cruelty and ground for a separation. The question of obedience arises in quite another way. It may, and no doubt often does, arise between the very best and most affectionate married people, and it need no more interfere with their mutual affection than the absolute power of the captain of a ship need interfere with perfect friendship and confidence between himself and his first lieutenant. Take the following set of questions: 'Shall we live on this scale or that? Shall we associate with such and such persons? Shall I, the husband, embark in such an undertaking, and shall we change our place of residence in order that I may do so? Shall we send our son to college? Shall we send our daughters to school or have a governess? For what profession shall we train our sons?' On these and a thousand other such questions the wisest and the most affectionate people might arrive at opposite conclusions. What is to be done in such a case? for something must be done. I say the wife ought to give way. She ought to obey her husband, and carry out the view at which he deliberately arrives, just as, when the captain gives the word to cut away the masts, the lieutenant carries out his orders at once, though he may be a better seaman and may disapprove them. I also say that to regard this as a humiliation, as a wrong, as an evil in itself, is a mark not of spirit and courage, but of a base, unworthy, mutinous disposition – a disposition utterly subversive of all that is most worth having in life. The tacit assumption involved in it is that it is a degradation ever to give up one's own will to the will of another, and to me this appears the root of all evil, the negation of that which renders any combined efforts possible. No case can be specified in which people unite for a common object from making a pair of shoes up to governing an empire in which the power to decide does not rest somewhere; and what is this but command and obedience? Of course the person who for the time being is in command is of all fools the greatest if he deprives himself of the advantage of advice, if he is obstinate in his own opinion, if he does not hear as well as determine; but it is also practically certain that his inclination to hear will be proportioned to the degree of importance which he has been led to attach to the function of determining.

To sum the matter up, it appears to me that all the laws and moral rules by which the relation between the sexes is regulated should proceed upon the principle that their object is to provide for the common good of the two great divisions of mankind who are connected together by the closest and most durable of all bonds, and who can no more have really conflicting interests than the different members of the same body, but who are not and never can be equals in any of the different forms of strength.

This problem law and morals have solved by monogamy, indissoluble marriage on the footing of the obedience of the wife to the husband, and a division of labour with corresponding differences in the matters of conduct, manners, and dress. Substantially this solution appears to me to be right and true; but I freely admit that in many particulars the stronger party has in this, as in other cases, abused his strength, and made rules for his supposed advantage, which in fact are greatly to the injury of both parties. It is needless to say anything in detail of the stupid coarseness of the laws about the effects of marriage on property, laws which might easily be replaced by a general statutory marriage settlement analogous to those which every prudent person makes who has anything to settle. As to acts of violence against women, by all means make the law on this head as severe as it can be made without defeating itself. As to throwing open to women the one or two employments from which they are at present excluded, it is rather a matter of sentiment that of practical importance. I need not revive in this place a trite discussion. My object at present is simply to establish the general proposition that men and women are not equals, and that the laws which affect their relations ought to recognize that fact.

I pass to the examination of the opinion that laws which recognize any sort of inequality between human beings are mere vestiges of the past, against which as such there lies the strongest of all presumptions.

Mr Mill's view as exhibited in the passages above quoted or referred to may, I think, be reduced to these two propositions: (1) History shows that human progress has been a progress from a 'law of force' to a condition in which command and obedience become exceptional. (2) The 'law of the strongest' having in this and one or two other countries, been 'entirely abandoned' in all other relations of life, it may be presumed not to apply to the relations between the sexes.

I think these propositions completely unsound. They appear to me to rest on a mistaken view of history and on a misinterpretation of its facts.

In the first place they involve the assumption that the

progress of society is from bad to good; for to say that it is from good to bad, and that we ought to promote it, would be absurd. No doubt, however, Mr Mill's assumption is that the progress of society is from bad to good; that the changes of the last few centuries in our own and the other leading nations of Western Europe and in the United States have been changes for the better.

This is an enormously wide assumption, and it is one to which I certainly cannot assent, though I do not altogether deny it. I think that the progress has been mixed, partly good and partly bad. I suspect that in many ways it has been a progress from strength to weakness; that people are more sensitive, less enterprising and ambitious, less earnestly desirous to get what they want, and more afraid of pain, both for themselves and others, than they used to be. If this should be so, it appears to me that all other gains, whether in wealth, knowledge, or humanity, afford no equivalent. Strength, in all its forms, is life and manhood. To be less strong is to be less of a man, whatever else you may be. This suspicion prevents me, for one, from feeling any enthusiasm about progress, but I do not undertake to say it is well founded. It is not and it cannot be more than a suspicion, and the fallacies of the imagination in this matter are so obvious and so nearly irresistible that it is impossible for any one to be too much on his guard against giving way to them. The doubt is enough, however, to stop enthusiasm. I do not myself see that our mechanical inventions have increased the general vigour of men's characters, though they have, no doubt, increased enormously our control over nature. The greater part of humanity appears to me to be a mere increase of nervous sensibility in which I feel no satisfaction at all. It is useless to lament or even to blame the inevitable. It is rash to draw general conclusions as to the character of a process extending over centuries from the observations which one man can make in a few years, but it is at least equally rash to rejoice over the inevitable, and to assume that it is good. To observe and to take our part in the changes in which we live is rational; but for my part I will neither bless them at all nor curse them at all, and no one, I think, has a right to do otherwise without showing cause for what he does. The inference applicable to the present subject is that, even if the inequality between men and women is a vestige of the past, and is likely to be destroyed by the same process which has destroyed so many other things, that is no reason for helping the process on. The proper reflection upon its approaching removal may be, The more's the pity. Mr Woodhouse liked his gruel thin, but not too thin. At a certain point of wateriness he would probably have turned off the tap. If Emma had been a disciple of Mr Mill's, she might have remarked, 'Reflect, dear sir, that you are interrupting the stream of progress. Such remains of cohesiveness as are exhibited by the grits which form the substratum of your simple meal are relics of the past, and as such are probably defects in your gruel instead of merits.'

Be this as it may, let us consider the question whether the 'law of force' – the 'law of the strongest' – really has been abandoned? whether if it were abandoned it would tend to produce equality? and whether the general course of events in recent times has tended or does now tend to set it aside? First, and by way of introduction to the other questions, let us consider what it is.

Force is an absolutely essential element of all law whatever. Indeed law is nothing but regulated force subjected to particular conditions and directed towards particular objects. The abolition of the law of force cannot therefore mean the withdrawal of the element of force from law, for that would be the destruction of law altogether.

The general tenor of Mr Mill's argument rather indicates that by the 'law of force' and the 'law of the strongest' he means force unregulated by any law at all. If this was what he meant, he should have said it; but he could not have said it without being at once involved in an obvious contradiction to facts, for the marriage institutions of modern Europe are anything but a case of force unregulated by law. They are cases of laws which regulate in the sternest way the most impetuous of human passions. Can any one doubt that the principles of monogamy and the indissolubility of marriage effectually controlled the most ardent passions of the strongest-willed races in the world during the dark and the middle ages, or that the control so exercised was in its results eminently beneficial to the human race at large and to women in particular? De Miastre claims, and in this case I think justly, great credit for the mediaeval clergy for having upheld these principles, which are the central principles of our version of morals, against the repeated attacks which were made upon them by the passions of kings and nobles in the most violent periods of history.

Assuming, then, that the 'law of force' is a somewhat indefinite expression for the general importance of force, and that Mr Mill means to assert that force tends to lose its importance, I proceed to his whole conception of the theory of equality and its history.

It is no doubt perfectly true that in all the institutions of the nations which principally interest us, and in particular in such of their institutions as have to do with law and government, there is a constant tendency to the rejection of distinctions and to the simplification of laws. This is due to a variety of causes. In the first place the societies in question have a tendency to increase. The different kingdoms into which our own and the other great European nations were subdivided in the early stages of our history gradually ran into each other. The growth of wealth, and changes in the habits of life proceeding from an infinite number of causes, not only rendered old institutions unsuitable for later times, but in many cases made them unintelligible. Thus, for instance, the word murder, which for centuries has been the name of a crime, was, it seems, originally the name of a fine laid upon a township in which a person unknown was found slain, unless the legal presumption that the unknown man was a Dane could be disproved by positive testimony that he was an Englishman, by a proceeding called a 'presentment of Englishry.' The strange distinction introduced in favour of the Danes, and maintained in favour of the French, was not finally removed till the fourteenth year of Edward III. By that time the presentment of Englishry had become unmeaning and was abolished, and the name of the fine had passed into the name of the crime in respect of which the fine was imposed.

This was one case out of a multitude of the growth of equality, by the rejection of a distinction between the murders of men of different races which had become senseless. Probably every part of the institutions of every nation in the world would afford illustrations of the same principle. The history of the Roman law from the days of the Twelve Tables to the time of Justinian is little else than one continued illustration of it. Another, and one of the utmost importance, is afforded by a process which Mr Mill refers to in a passage quoted above about the distinction which exists between the present and the former arrangements of society for the purpose of assigning to men their position in life. In former times, Mr Mill tells us, 'all were born to a fixed social position, and were mostly kept in it by law or interdicted from any means by which they could emerge from it.' Sir Henry Maine refers to, and to a certain extent gives the theory of, this matter in a passage which he sums up by saying, 'The movement of the progressive societies has hitherto been a movement from status to contract' – a movement, that is, from a condition of things in which the relations between man and man are determined by membership of a family or of a tribe, or of a conquering or conquered race, towards a condition of things in which they depend upon contract. This is no doubt quite true, and to Sir Henry Maine's account of the matter, which is as interesting as it is ingenious, I have no objection to make. I will only observe upon it that in this, as in other cases, he confines himself to the investigation of or to speculations about matters of fact; and neither says nor, as it seems to me, assumes, as Mr. Mill always does, that to show that the course of events has in fact led from A to B, and appears to be in the direction of C, proves that B is better than A, and that C is better than B.

The question with which I have to deal is whether these facts authorize Mr Mill's two doctrines: namely, first, the doctrine that the law of the strongest, or the law of force, has been abandoned in these days – an assertion which, I think, must, for the reasons already assigned, be taken to mean that force tends to be less and less important in human affairs; and, secondly, the doctrine that this abandonment of the law of force is equivalent to the growth of equality. Both of these doctrines I deny; and I deny that the facts which I have admitted tend even to prove them.

As to the first, I say that all that is proved by the fact that status, to use Sir Henry Maine's expression, tends to be replaced by contract, is that force changes its form. Society rests ultimately upon force in these days, just as much as it did in the wildest and most stormy periods of history. Compare Scotland in the fourteenth century with Scotland in the nineteenth century. In the fourteenth century the whole country was a scene of wild confusion, of which one of the most learned of Scott's novels (though it was written after his genius had received its fatal blow), 'The Fair Maid of Perth,' gives a striking picture. 'My name,' said one of the characters, 'is the Devil's Dick of Hellgarth, well known in Annandale for a gentle Johnstone. I follow the stout Laird of Wamphray, who rides with his kinsman, the redoubted Lord of Johnstone, who is banded with the doughty Earl of Douglas; and the Earl, and the Lord, and the laird, and I, the esquire, fly our hawks where we find our game, and ask no man whose ground we ride over.' Every page of the book is full of the feuds of Highland and Lowland, Douglas and March, burghers and nobles, Clan Chattan and Clan Quhele. The first impression on comparing this spirited picture with the Scotland which we all know – the Scotland of quiet industry, farming, commerce, and amusement, is that the fourteenth century was entirely subject to the law of force, and that Scotland in the nineteenth century has ceased to be the theatre of force at all. Look a little deeper and this impression is as false, not to say as childish, as the supposition that a clumsy rowboat, manned by a quarrelsome crew, who can neither keep time with their oars, nor resist the temptation to fight among themselves, displays force, and that an ocean steamer which will carry a townful of people to the end of the earth at the rate of three hundred miles a day so smoothly that during the greater part of the time they are unconscious of any motion or effort whatever, displays none. The force which goes to govern the Scotland of these days is to the force employed for the same purpose in the fourteenth century what the force of a line-of-battle ship is to the force of an individual prize-fighter. The reason why it works so quietly is that no one doubts either its existence, or its direction, or its crushing superiority to any individual resistance which could be offered to it. The force of the chain of champions of whom the Devil's Dick was the last link is now stored up in the vast mass of peaceable and rational men, who, in case of need, would support the law, and from them it is drawn off as required. It can be defied only on the smallest possible scale, and by taking it at a disadvantage. A criminal may overpower an isolated policeman just as a pigmy might with his whole weight hold down the last joint of the little finger of a giant's left hand, if the hand were in a suitable position; but deliberate individual resistance to the law of the land for mere private advantage is in these days an impossibility which no one ever thinks of attempting. Force not only reigns, but in most matters it reigns without dispute, but it does not follow that it has ceased to exist.

This proposition is true, not merely in its general and abstract shape, but also of every relation of life in detail. Nowhere is it more strikingly illustrated than in the relation of marriage. Mr Mill says: 'I readily admit that numbers of married people, even under the present law (in the higher classes of England probably a great majority), live in the spirit of a just law of equality. Laws never would be improved if there were not numerous persons whose moral sentiments were better than the existing laws.' This is an admission that most marriages under the existing laws are happy. The reason, says Mr Mill, is because the moral tone of particular classes is superior to the law. I says that it is because the law is good, and the people in question obey it. I go beyond Mr Mill in his opinion about marriages, I should say that in all classes of life they are much more often happy than otherwise; but I say that is because as a general rule both husbands and wives keep the solemn promises which they made at their marriage, including the wife's promise to obey her husband. Surely the natural inference to draw from the fact that an institution works well is that it is founded on true principles, and answers its purpose. The administration of justice in this country is singularly pure. The inference is, not that the judges are superior to the law, but that the law in which they are trained is favourable to the pure administration of justice.

Mr Mill is not quite consistent upon this head, for he tells us distinctly that if the family in its best forms is a school of sympathy and tenderness, 'it is still oftener, as respects its chief, a school of wilfulness, overbearingness, unbounded self-indulgence, and a double-dyed and idealized selfishness, of which sacrifice itself is only a particular form;' the individual happiness of the wife and children 'being immolated in every shape to his [the head of the family's] smallest preferences.' 'What better,' he asks, 'is to be looked for under the existing form of the institution?' If this is at all like the truth, I cannot understand how marriage can be or ever can have been anything but an odious tyranny and school of every kind of vice; nor can I reconcile such statements with the one just quoted as to the general happiness of marriage. Certainly the higher classes of society in this country are not less strict in their views as to the duties of married life than their inferiors. Few ladies would like to be told that they were disobedient wives. Few gentlemen would feel it otherwise than a reproach to learn that they were not masters in their own homes; but how can this be, if authority on the one side and obedience on the other are fundamentally immoral? Mr Mill's theory involves the absurd consequence that good fruit grows on a bad tree. Mine involves the natural consequence that a good institution produces good results. The real reason why the marriages of sensible and well-educated people in all ranks of life are happy, is that people know their respective places, and act accordingly. The power exists and is exercised, but as the right to exercise it is undisputed, and as its exercise is unresisted, it acts smoothly, and the parties concerned are seldom unpleasantly reminded of its existence.

An exact parallel to the case of married life, is to be found in the common case of hospitality. You go into a handsome, well-appointed house, full of well-behaved people. You observe that one of the company exerts himself in every possible way to promote the enjoyment and to provide for the amusement or occupation of the rest, and that he in all cases studiously though unostentatiously takes, in a certain sense, the lowest place. You are told that this man has an undoubted legal right to order all the rest out of his house at a moment's notice – say in a storm in the middle of the night – to forbid them to touch an article of furniture, to open a book, or to eat a crumb of bread:[3] and this appears harsh; yet if he were deprived of that right, if the presence of his guests rendered its existence doubtful for a moment in any particular, not one of them would cross his doors; matters go well, not because the master of the house has no powers, but because no one questions them, and he wishes to use them for the general comfort of the society.

To say that the law of force is abandoned because force is

---

3   Mrs Fawcett (who wrote a pamphlet on this chapter) considered that she has answered this by showing that a man who exercised this right would not only act in a very brutal manner, but expose himself to social penalties by so acting. This is as true as it is irrelevant. It is the only remark of Mrs Fawcett's which I think it necessary to notice, and I notice it only as an illustration of what she understands by argument.

regular, unopposed, and beneficially exercised, is to say that day and night are now such well-established institutions that the sun and moon are mere superfluities.

It should be observed that though marriage is the most important of all contracts, it is far from being the only one which confers upon one of the parties authority over the other. Nearly every contract does so. A man passes his life in a Government office. He contracts to serve the public on certain terms. Is there here no authority on the part of the employer over the employed? Dismissal from such a post would be as severe a punishment, in most cases, as could be inflicted on a man, a far more severe punishment than a short term of imprisonment or a heavy fine unaccompanied by dismissal. The power of a French Minister of the Interior over an immense multitude of subordinates is as real and quite as formidable as the power of a feudal lord over his vassals ever was. It is true that it is founded on contract and not on status. In the one case the man was born to a certain position, and in the other he entered into it by agreement, but that makes very little real difference between the two cases. In each case there is a stronger and a weaker position, and in each the weaker is subject to the authority of the stronger.

The truth is that the change above referred to, from status to contract, is very far indeed from being universally favourable to equality. I will not speculate on the nature of the change itself. It may be the best and most glorious of all conceivable states of society that all the relations between man and man should be resolved into the single relation of the earning and paying of wages in various forms; but whether this is so or not, it is perfectly certain that the result of the arrangement is to produce not equality but inequality in its harshest and least sympathetic form. The process is this. Society is converted into one immense machine, the powers of which are all concentrated into one body, which is called the public force. It consists of a legislative and an executive body backed up in case of need by soldiers and policemen. The direction in which this force is to act is ascertained by laws which apply with continually increasing precision and inflexibility to all sorts of cases. Each person is left to make use of these laws for his own purposes in his own way. They may be reduced to these four:

(1) Thou shalt not commit crimes. (2) Thou shalt not inflict wrong. (3) Thou shalt perform thy contracts. (4) Thou and thine may keep whatever you can get. To say that such a state of society is favourable to equality, that it tends to supersede obedience and command, that it has superseded force, and the like, sounds more like a poor kind of irony than anything else. What equality is there between the rich and the poor, between the strong and the weak, between the good and the bad? In particular, what equality is there between the well-born and well-bred man, the son of a good, careful, prudent, prosperous parent, who has transmitted to him a healthy mind and body, and given him a careful education; and the ill-born, ill-bred man whose parents had nothing to teach which was not better unlearned, and nothing to transmit which would not have been better uninherited. It is quite true that in these days we have not much titular inequality. It is quite true that we have succeeded in cutting political power into very little bits, which with our usual hymns of triumph we are continually mincing, till it seems not unlikely that many people may come to think that a single man's share of it is not worth having at all. But with all this, real substantial inequalities in every respect, inequalities of wealth, inequalities of talent, of education, of sentiment, and of religious belief, and therefore inequalities in the most binding of all obligations, never were so great as they are at this moment. I doubt much whether the power of particular persons over their neighbours has ever in any age of the world been so well defined and so easily and safely exerted as it is at present. If in old times a slave was inattentive, his master might no doubt have him maimed or put to death or flogged; but he had to consider that in doing so he was damaging his own property; that when the slave had been flogged he would still continue to be his slave; and that the flogging might make him mischievous or revengeful, and so forth. If a modern servant misconducts himself, he can be turned out of the house on the spot, and another can be hired as easily as you would call a cab. To refuse the dismissed person a character may very like be equivalent to sentencing him to months of suffering and to a permanent fall in the social scale. Such punishments are inflicted without appeal, without reflection, without the smallest disturbance of the smooth surface of ordinary life.

The older mode of organizing society has, like other things, been made the subject of much romantic exaggeration, but it is clear that it had a side which was favourable to poverty and weakness, though it produced its inequalities, as our own social maxims do. To try to make men equal by altering social arrangements is like trying to make the cards of equal value by shuffling the pack. Men are fundamentally unequal, and this inequality will show itself, arrange society as you like. If the object were to secure the greatest amount of equality, the way to do it would be by establishing a system of distinctions, a social hierarchy corresponding as nearly as possible to the real distinctions between men, and by making the members of each class equal among themselves. Something by no means unlike this has actually been done by the caste system in India, and the result is that Hindoo society, though in some ways elastic and possessed of a considerable power of assimilating new ideas, is stable and conservative to a degree utterly unknown and hardly even imaginable in Europe. If we were possessed of any test by which men could be marshalled according to their intrinsic differences with unfailing accuracy, we should really obtain the repose, the absence of conscious and painful restraint, the calm play of unresisted and admitted force which people appear to expect from the establishment of what they call equality. The establishment of even this ideal state of things would leave some of the most important of social problems unsolved, but it is almost an identical proposition that it would afford not merely the best but the only full solution of the great problem of harmonizing self-interest with the interests of the public at large. A nation in which every one held the position for which he was best fitted, and in which every one was aware of that fact, would be a nation in which every man's life would be passed in doing that which would be at once most agreeable to himself and most beneficial to his neighbours, and such a nation would have solved at all events several of the great problems of life.

It is needless to insist on the plain fact that such an ideal is unattainable; but the maintenance of broad and well-marked distinctions which really exist at a given time and place is a step towards it. The distinctions of age and sex are universal. Distinctions of race are at given times and places most important, and the fact that they have been exaggerated and abused is no reason for denying their existence. Distinctions of wealth and of the education and other qualities which are associated with the acquisition and retention of wealth are no less real. Such distinctions will continue to exist and to produce inequalities of every description, whether or not they are recognized by law, and whether or not they are permitted to affect the distribution of political authority. Leave them to find their own level by unrestricted competition, and they will display themselves in their most naked and their harshest form.

Let us suppose, to take a single illustration, that men and women are made as equal as law can make them, and that public opinion followed the law. Let us suppose that marriage became a mere partnership dissoluble like another; that women were expected to earn their living just like men; that the notion of anything like protection due from the one sex to the other was thoroughly rooted out; that men's manners to women became identical with their manners to men; that the cheerful concessions to acknowledged weakness, the obligation to do for women a thousand things which it would be insulting to offer to do for a man, which we inherit from a different order of ideas, were totally exploded; and what would be the result? The result would be that women would become men's slaves and drudges, that they would be made to feel their weakness and to accept its consequences to the very utmost. Submission and protection are correlative. Withdraw the one and the other is lost, and force will assert itself a hundred times more harshly through the law of contract than ever it did through the law of status. Disguise it how you will, it is force in one shape or another which determines the relations between human beings. It is far less harsh when it is subjected to the provisions of a general law made with reference to broad general principles than when it acts through a contract, the terms of which are settled by individuals according to their own judgment. The terms of the marriage relation as settled by the law and religion of Europe are an illustration, of course on an infinitely wider and more important scale, of the very principle which in our own days has led to the prohibition of the employment of little children in certain classes of factories and of women in coalpits.

To recapitulate, I think that equality has no special connection with justice, except in the narrow sense of judicial impartiality; that it cannot be affirmed to be expedient in the most important relations of social life; and that history does not warrant the assertion that for a great length of time there has been a continual progress in the direction of the removal of all distinctions between man and man, though it does warrant the assertion that the form in which men's natural inequalities display themselves and produce their results changes from one generation to another, and tends to operate rather through contracts made by individuals than through laws made by public authority for the purpose of fixing the relations between human beings.

FEMALE SUFFRAGE[1]
[Goldwin Smith]

Mr. Forsyth's bill for removing the Electoral Disabilities of
Women, the second reading of which is at hand, has received
less attention than the subject deserves. The Residuum was
enfranchised for the sake of its vote by the leaders of a party
which for a series of years had been denouncing any extension
of the suffrage, even to the most intelligent artisans, on the
ground that it would place political power in unfit hands. An
analogous stroke of strategy, it seems, is now meditated by the
same tacticians in the case of Female Suffrage, the motion in
favour of which is brought forward by one of their supporters,
and has already received the adhesion of their chief. The very
foundations of Society are touched when Party tampers with
the relations of the sexes.

In England the proposal at present is to give the suffrage only
to unmarried women being householders. But the drawing of
this hard-and-fast line is at the outset contested by the
champions of Women's Rights; and it seems impossible that the
distinction should be maintained. The lodger-franchise is
evidently the vanishing point of the feudal connection between
political privilege and the possession of houses or land. The
suffrage will become personal in England, as it has elsewhere.
If a property qualification remains, it will be one embracing all
kinds of property; money settled on a married woman for her
separate use, as well as the house or lodgings occupied by a
widow or a spinster. In the counties already, married women
have qualifications in the form of land settled to their separate
use; and the notion that a spinster in lodgings is specially
entitled to the suffrage as the head of a household, is one of
those pieces of metaphysic in which the politicians who affect
to scorn anything metaphysical are apt themselves unwarily to
indulge. If the present motion is carried, the votes of the female

---

[1] A few paragraphs in this paper have already appeared in a Transatlantic
periodical.

householders, with that system of election pledges which is now enabling minorities, and even small minorities, to control national legislation, will form the crowbar by which the next barrier will be speedily forced.

Marriage itself, as it raises the position of a woman in the eyes of all but the very radical section of the Woman's Right party, could hardly be treated as politically penal. And yet an Act conferring the suffrage on married women would probably be the most momentous step that could be taken by any legislature, since it would declare the family not to be a political unit, and for the first time authorize a wife, and make it in certain cases her duty as a citizen, to act publicly in opposition to her husband. Those at least who hold the family to be worth as much as the state will think twice before they concur in such a change.

With the right of electing must ultimately go the right of being elected. The contempt with which the candidature of Mrs. Victoria Woodhull for the Presidency was received by some of the advocates of Female Suffrage in America only showed that they had not considered the consequences of their own principles. Surely she who gives the mandate is competent herself to carry it. Under the parliamentary system, whatever the forms and phrases may be, the constituencies are the supreme arbiters of the national policy, and decide not only who shall be the legislators, but what shall be the course of legislation. They have long virtually appointed the Ministers, and now they appoint them actually. Twice the Government has been changed by a plebiscite, and on the second occasion the Budget was submitted to the constituencies as directly as ever it was to the House of Commons. There may be some repugnance, natural or traditional, to be overcome in admitting women to seats in Parliament; but there is also some repugnance to be overcome in throwing them into the turmoil of contested elections, in which, as soon as Female Suffrage is carried, some ladies will unquestionably claim their part.

There are members of Parliament who shrink from the step which they are now urged to take, but who fancy that they have no choice left them because the municipal franchise has already been conceded. The municipal franchise was no doubt intended to be the thin end of the wedge. Nevertheless there is a wide step between this and the national franchise; between allowing female influence to prevail in the disposition of school rates, or other local rates, and allowing it to prevail in the supreme government of the country. To see that it is so, we have only to imagine the foreign policy of England determined by the women, while that of other countries is determined by the men; and this in the age of Bismarck.

The writer of this paper himself once signed a petition for Female Household Suffrage got up by Mr. Mill. He has always been for enlarging the number of active citizens as much as possible, and widening the basis of government, in accordance with the maxim, which seems to him the sum of political philosophy, "That is the best form of government which doth most actuate and dispose all parts and members of the commonwealth to the common good." He had not, when he signed the petition, seen the public life of women in the United States. But he was led to reconsider what he had done, and prevented from going further, by finding that the movement was received with mistrust by some of the best and most sensibly women of his acquaintance, who feared that their most valuable privileges, and the deepest sources of their happiness, were being jeopardized to gratify the political aspirations of a few of their sex. For the authority of Mr. Mill, in all cases where his judgment was unclouded, the writer felt and still feels great respect. But since that time, Mr. Mill's autobiography has appeared, and has revealed the history of his extraordinary and almost portentous education, the singular circumstances of his marriage, his hallucination (for it surely can be called nothing less) as to the unparalleled genius of his wife, and peculiarities of character and temperament such as could not fail to prevent him from fully appreciating the power of influences which, whatever our philosophy may say, reign and will continue to reign supreme over questions of this kind. To him marriage was a union of two philosophers in the pursuit of truth; and in his work on the position and destiny of women, not only does he scarcely think of children, but sex and its influences seem hardly to be present to his mind. Of the distinctive excellence and beauty of the female character it does not appear that he had formed any idea, though he dilates on the special qualities of the female mind.

Mr. Mill has allowed us to see that his opinions as to the political position of women were formed early in his life, probably before he had studied history rationally, perhaps before the rational study of history had even come into existence. The consequence, with all deference to his great name be it said, is that his historical presentment of the case is fundamentally unsound. He and his disciples represent the lot of the woman as having always been determined by the will of the man, who, according to them, has willed that she should be the slave, and that he should be her master and her tyrant. "Society, both in this (the case of marriage) and other cases, has preferred to attain its object by foul rather than by fair means; but this is the only case in which it has substantially persisted in them even to the present day." This is Mr. Mill's fundamental assumption; and from it, as every rational student of history is now aware, conclusions utterly erroneous as well as injurious to humanity must flow. The lot of the woman has not been determined by the will of the man, at least in any considerable degree. The lot both of the man and the woman has been determined from age to age by circumstances over which the will of neither of them had much control, and which neither could be blamed for accepting or failing to reverse. Mr. Mill, and those who with him assume that the man has always willed that he should himself enjoy political rights, and that the woman should be his slave, forget that it is only in a few countries that man does enjoy political rights; and that, even in those few countries, freedom is the birth almost of yesterday. It may probably be said that the number of men who have really and freely exercised the suffrage up to the present time is not much greater than the number of those who have in different ages, and in various ways, laid down their lives or made personal sacrifices of other kinds in bringing the suffrage into existence.

In the early stages of civilization the family was socially and legally as well as politically a unit. Its head represented the whole household before the tribe, the state, and all persons and bodies without; while within he exercised absolute power over all the members, male as well as female, over his sons as well as over his wife and daughters. On the death of the head of a family his eldest son stepped into his place, and became the representative and protector of the whole household, including the widow of the deceased chief. This system, long retained in conservative Rome, was there the source of the national respect for authority, and, by an expansion of feeling from the family to the community, of the patriotism which produced and sustained Roman greatness. But its traces lingered far down in history. It was not male tyranny that authorized a Tudor queen to send members of the royal household to the Tower by her personal authority as the mistress of the family, without regard to the common law against arbitrary imprisonment. Such a constitution was essential to the existence of the family in primitive times; without it, the germs of nations and of humanity would have perished. To suppose that it was devised by the male sex for the gratification of their own tyrannical propensities would be most absurd. It was at least as much a necessity to the primitive woman as it was to the primitive man. It is still a necessity to woman in the countries where the primitive type of society remains. What would be the fate of a female Bedouin, if she were suddenly invested with Woman's Rights and emancipated from the protection of her husband?

That the present relation of women to their husbands literally has its origin in slavery, and is a hideous relic of that system, is a theory which Mr. Mill sets forth in language such as, if it could sink into the hearts of those to whom it is addressed, would turn all affection to bitterness, and divide every household against itself. Yet this theory is without historical foundation. It seems, indeed, like a figure of inventive heedlessly converted into history. Even in the most primitive times, and those in which the subjection of the women was most complete, the wife was clearly distinguished from the slave. The lot of Sarah is different from that of Hagar; the authority of Hector over Andromache is absolute, yet no one can confound her position with that of her handmaidens. The Roman matron who sent her slave to be crucified, the Southern matron who was the fierce supporter of slavery, were not themselves slaves. Whatever may now be obsolete in the relations of husband and wife is not a relic of slavery, but of primitive marriage, and may be regarded as at worst an arrangement once indispensable which has survived its hour. Where real slavery has existed, it has extended to both sexes, and it has ceased for both at the same time. Even the Oriental seclusion of women, perhaps the worst condition in which the sex has ever been, has its root, not in the slave-owning propensity so much as in jealousy, a passion which, though extravagant and detestable in its excessive manifestation, is not without an element of affection. The most beautiful building in the East is that in which Shah Jehan rests by the side of Nourmahal.

If the calm and philosophic nature of Mr. Mill is ever betrayed into violence, it is in his denunciations of the present institution of marriage. He depicts it as a despotism full of mutual degradation, and fruitful of no virtues or affections except the debased virtues and the miserable affections of the master and the slave. The grossest and most degrading terms of Oriental slavery are used to designate the relations of husband and wife throughout the whole book. A husband who desires his wife's love is merely seeking "to have, in the woman most nearly connected with him, not a forced slave, but a willing one – not a slave merely, but a favourite." Husbands have therefore "put everything in practice to enslave the minds of their wives." If a wife is intensely attached to her husband, "exactly as much may be said of domestic slavery." "It is part of the irony of life that the strongest feelings of devoted gratitude of which human nature seems to be susceptible are called forth in human beings towards those who, having the power entirely to crush their earthly existence, voluntarily refrain from using their power." Even children are only links in the chain of bondage. By the affections of women "are meant the only ones they are allowed to have – those to the men with whom they are connected, or to the children who constitute an additional and indefeasible tie between them and a man." The Jesuit is an object of sympathy because he is the enemy of the domestic tyrant, and it is assumed that the husband can have no motive but the love of undivided tyranny for objecting to being superseded by an intriguing interloper in his wife's affections. As though a wife would regard with complacency, say a female spiritualist, installed beside her hearth. It is impossible to doubt that Mr. Mill's views, in writing such passages, were coloured by the incidents of his life. But it is by circulating his book and propagating his notions that the petitions in favour of Female Suffrage have been obtained.

The anomalies in the property law affecting married women, to which remedial legislation has recently been directed, are like whatever is obsolete in the relations between the sexes generally, not deliberate iniquities, but survivals. They are relics of feudalism, or of still more primitive institutions incorporated by feudalism; and while the system to which they belonged existed, they were indispensable parts of it, and must have been so regarded by both sexes alike. And any one who is tolerably well informed ought to be ashamed to represent them as the contrivances of male injustice. It is not on one sex only that the relics of feudalism have borne hard.

The exclusion of women from professions is cited as another proof of constant and immemorial injustice. But what woman asked or wished to be admitted to a profession fifty or even five and twenty years ago? What woman till quite recently would have been ready to renounce marriage and maternity in order that she might devote herself to law, medicine, or commercial pursuits? The fact is, the demand is connected with an abnormal and possibly transient state of things. The expensiveness of living, in a country where the fashion is set by millionaires, combined with the overcrowded condition of the very callings to which women are demanding admission, has put extraordinary difficulties in the way of marriage. Many women are thus left without an object in life, and they naturally try to open for themselves some new career. The utmost sympathy is due to them, and every facility ought in justice to be afforded them; though unhappily the addition of fresh competitors for subsistence to a crowd in which literally famine has already been at work, will be as far as possible from removing the real root of the evil; to say nothing of the risk which a woman must run in committing herself irrevocably to a precarious calling and closing against herself the gate of domestic life. But the demand, as has been already said, is of yesterday, and probably in its serious form is as yet confined to the countries in which the special impediments to early marriages exist. In the United States it is not easy to distinguish the serious demand from a passion for emulating the male sex which has undoubtedly taken possession of some of the women there, as it took possession of women under the Roman empire, who began to play the gladiator when other excitements were exhausted. With regard to the profession of law, indeed, so far as it is concerned with the administration of justice, there is, and, while human emotions retain their force, always will be, a reason, independent of the question of demand, for excluding women, at least for excluding one of the two sexes. The influence of a pretty advocate appealing to a jury, perhaps in behalf of a client of her own sex, would not have seemed to Mr. Mill at all dangerous to the integrity of public justice; but most people, and especially those who have seen anything of sentimental causes in the United States, will probably be of a different opinion.

What has been said as to the professions is equally true of the universities, which, in fact, were schools of the professions. A few years ago, what English girl would have consented to leave her home and mingle with male students? What English girl would have thought it possible that she could go through the whole of the medical course with male companions of her studies? Even now, what is the amount of settled belief in the right, as it is termed, of "co-education?" What would be said to a young man if he presented himself in the name of that right at the door of Vassar, or any female college? Without arraigning the past, those whose duty it is may consider, with the deliberation which they deserve, the two distinct questions, whether it is desirable that the education of both sexes shall be the same, and whether it is desirable that the young men and the young women of the wealthier classes shall be educated together in the same universities. Beneath the first probably lies the still deeper question whether it is good for humanity that woman, who has hitherto been the helpmate and the complement, should become, as the leaders in the Woman's Right movement in the United States evidently desire, the rival and competitor of man. Both she cannot be; and it is by no means clear that, in deciding which she shall be, the aspirations of the leaders of this movement coincide with the interests of the sex.[2]

If the education of women has hitherto been defective, so has that of men. We are not going to do our best to improve both. Surely no accomplishment in the acquisition of which woman has been condemned to spend her time could well be less useful than that of writing Greek and Latin verses. That the comparative absence of works of creative genius among women is due entirely to the social tyranny which has excluded, or is supposed to have excluded, them from literary and scientific careers, cannot be said to be self-evident. The case of music, often cited, seems to suggest that there is another cause, and that the career of intellectual ambition is in most cases not likely to be happier than that of domestic affection, though this is no reason why the experiment should not be fairly tried. Perhaps the intellectual disabilities under which women have laboured, even in the past, have been somewhat

---

[2] The question of Female Education is not here discussed. But the arbiters of that question will do well to bear in mind that the happiness of most women materially depends on their having healthy children; and that children are not likely to be healthy if the brains of both parents are severely tasked.

exaggerated. If Shelley was a child to Mrs. Mill, as Mr. Mill says, no "social disabilities" hindered Mrs. Mill from publishing poems which would have eclipsed Shelley. The writer once heard an American lecturer of great eminence confidently ascribe the licentiousness of English fiction in the early part of the last century to the exclusion of women from literary life. The lecturer forgot that the most popular novelist of that period, and certainly not the least licentious, was Mrs. Aphra Behn. And this lady's name suggests the remark that as the relations of the sexes have been the most intimate conceivable, the action of character has been reciprocal, and the level of moral ideas and sentiments for both pretty much the same.

Mr. Mill, seeing that the man is the stronger, seems to assume that the relations between man and woman must always have been regulated simply by the law of the strongest. But strength is not tyranny. The protector must always be stronger than the person under his protection. A mother is overwhelmingly superior in strength to her infant child, and the child is completely at her mercy. The very highest conception that humanity has ever formed, whether it be founded in reality or not, is that of power losing itself in affection. This may be said without lapsing into what has been called the religion of inhumanity. St. Paul (who on any hypothesis is an authoritative expositor of the morality which became that of Christendom) preaches Fraternity plainly, and even passionately enough. He affirms with the utmost breadth the essential equality of the sexes, and their necessary relations to each other as the two halves of humanity. Yet he no less distinctly ratifies the unity of the family, the authority of its head, and the female need of personal government; a need which, when it is natural, has nothing in it more degrading than the need of protection.

The "Revolt of Woman" is the name given to the movement by a female writer in America, who, by the way, claims, in virtue of "superior complexity of organization," not only political equality, but absolute supremacy over man. But, in this revolt, to what do the insurgents appeal? To their own strength, or to the justice and affection of man?

The main factors of the relation between the sexes have hitherto been, and probably still are, natural affection – the man's need of a helpmate, the woman's need of a protector and provider, especially when she becomes a mother, and the common interest of parents in their children. One of these factors must be withdrawn, or greatly reduced in importance, to warrant us in concluding that a fundamental change in the relation is about to take place. Mr. Mill hardly notices any one of the four, and he treats the natural relation which arises from them as a purely artificial structure, like a paper constitution or an Act of Parliament, which legislatures can modify or abolish at their pleasure.

It has no doubt been far from a satisfactory world to either sex; but unless we attach a factitious value to public life and to the exercise of public professions, it will be very difficult to prove that it has been more unsatisfactory for one sex than the other. If the woman has had her sorrows at home, the man has had his wars and his rough struggles with nature abroad, and with the sweat of his brow he has reclaimed the earth, and made it a habitation for his partner as well as for himself. If the woman has had her disabilities, she has also had her privileges. War has spared her; for if in primitive times she was made a slave, this was better, in the days before sentiment at least, than being massacred. And her privileges have been connected with her disabilities. If she had made war by her vote, she could not have claimed special respect as a neutral, nor will she able to claim special respect as a neutral if she makes war by her vote hereafter.

In the United States the privileges of women may be said to extend to impunity, not only for ordinary outrage, but for murder. A poisoner, whose guilt has been proved by overwhelming evidence, is let off because she is a woman; there is a sentimental scene between her and her advocate in court, and afterwards she appears as a public lecturer. The whisky crusade shows that women are practically above the law. Rioting, and injury to the property of tradesmen, when committed by the privileged sex, are hailed as a new and beneficent agency in public life; and because the German population, being less sentimental, asserts the principles of legality and decency, the women are said to have suffered martyrdom. So far from the American family being the despotism which Mr. Mill describes, the want of domestic authority lies at the root of all that is worst in the politics of the United States. If the women ask for the suffrage, say some American publicists, they must have it; and in the same way everything that a child cries for is apt to be given it, without reflection as to the consequences of the indulgence.

There is therefore no reason for setting the sexes by the ears, or giving to any change which it may be just and expedient to make the aspect of a revolt. We may discuss on his own merits the question whether female suffrage would be a good thing for the whole community. The interest of the whole community must be the test. As to natural rights, they must be sought by those who desire them, not in communities, but in the primeval woods, where the available rights of women will be small.

The question whether female suffrage on an extended scale is good for the whole community is probably identical, practically speaking, with the question whether it is good for us to have free institutions or not. Absolute monarchy is founded on personal loyalty. Free institutions are founded on the love of liberty, or, to speak more properly, on the preference of legal to personal government. But the love of liberty and the desire of being governed by law alone appear to be characteristically male. The female need of protection, of which, so long as women remain physically weak, and so long as they are mothers, it will be impossible to get rid, is apparently accompanied by a preference for personal government, which finds its proper satisfaction in the family, but which gives an almost uniform bias to the political sentiments of women. The account commonly accepted of the reactionary tendency which all admit to be generally characteristic of the sex, is that they are priest-ridden. No doubt many of them are priest-ridden, and female suffrage would give a vast increase of power to the clergy. But the cause is probably deeper and more permanent, being, in fact, the sentiment inherent in the female temperament, which again is formed by the normal functions and circumstances of the sex. And if this is the case, to give women the franchise is simply to give them the power of putting an end, actually and virtually, to all franchises together. It may not be easy to say beforehand exactly what course the demolition of free institutions by female suffrage would take. In the United States probably some woman's favourite would be elected President, and re-elected till his power became personal, and perhaps dynastic. But there can be little doubt that in all cases, if power were put into the hands of the women, free government, and with it liberty of opinion, would fall.

In France, it is morally certain that at the present moment, if votes were given to the women, the first result would be the restoration to power of the Bourbons, with their reactionary priesthood, and the destruction of all that has been gained by the national agonies of the last century. The next result would be a religious crusade against German Protestantism and Italian freedom.

But would the men submit? Would they, in compliance with the edict of the women, and in obedience to a woman's government, haul down the tricolor, hoist the white flag, bow their necks to the yoke of Reaction, and march against the victors of Sedan in a cause which they detest? This question points to another serious consideration. It is true that law is much stronger now than it was in primitive or feudal times, and a woman is more under its protection and less under the private protection of her husband and her kinsmen. But law, after all, though the fact may be rough and unwelcome, rests at bottom on the force of the community, and the force of the community is male. No woman can imagine that her sex can execute, or in the case of rebellion re-assert, the law; for that they must look entirely to the men. The men would be conscious of this, and if any law were made exclusively in the interest of the women, and in contradiction to the male sense of justice, they would refuse to carry it into effect. In the United States there have been intimations, on the part of the women, of a desire to make a very lavish use of capital punishment, untrammelled by the technical rules of evidence, for offences or supposed offences against the sex. The men would, of course, refuse execution; law would be set at defiance, and government would be overturned. But the bad effects of the public consciousness that executive force – the rude but indispensable basis of law – had been partly removed, and that the law was being made by those who had not power to carry it into effect, would not be limited to manifest instances of the influence of sex in legislation. In cases where, as in Jamaica, an elective government has rested on two races, equal, legally speaking, in political power, but of which one was evidently inferior in real force to the other, reverence for law has been weak, and the result has been disastrous. There can be little doubt that, as soon as the Federal bayonets are removed, there will be another case of the same kind in the Southern States; laws made by negro majorities will be set at defiance by the stronger race. To personal despotism or class domination civilization can put an end, but it cannot eliminate force.

It is very likely that in England, the women, to reform drunken husbands, would vote for extreme prohibitory measures against liquor; but the difficulty of carrying such legislation into effect, great as it is already, could hardly fail to be much increased by the feeling that it was the act of the women, and the consequence would probably be contempt, and perhaps open defiance, of the law. Female legislation with regard to education in the interest of clerical ascendancy, would be apt to be attended by the same effects.

Elective government, with the liberty of opinion and the power of progress which are its concomitants, has been brought into existence by the most terrible throes of humanity. When perfected and firmly established, it will, as we hope, and have good grounds for believing, give to reason and justice an ascendancy which they have never had before in human affairs, and increase the happiness of all by making private interest subordinate to the public good. But its condition, if we look at the world as a whole, is still exceedingly precarious. All the powers of class interest, of sybaritism, of superstition, are arrayed against it, and have vast forces at their command, including the great standing armies of Europe, while they find accomplices in the lassitude, the alarm, the discouragement caused by the revolutionary storms which, unhappily, are almost inevitable attendants upon the birth of a new order of things. Its existence having been so far a struggle, and an assertion at the sword's point, of principles, just in themselves, but needing qualification to make them available as the foundations of a polity, it is full of defects, to remedy which, so as to make it the deliberate expression of public reason, clear of sectional interest and passion, is now the great aim of political thought and effort. Those to whose hands it is committed at this crisis are trustees for posterity of a heritage bought by ages of effort and torrents of blood; and they are bound to allow neither their own ambition nor that of any one else, if they can help it, to imperial the safety of their trust. That women would be likely to vote for one set of aspirants to political office rather than for the opposite set, would be a very bad reason for withholding from them the suffrage even for a day; but that they would probably overturn the institutions on which the hopes of the world rest, is as good a reason as there can be for withholding anything from anybody. When free institutions are firmly established in Europe, the question of Female

Suffrage may perhaps be raised with less peril, so far as political interests are concerned; but to take a female vote on their fate at present, would be as suicidal as it would have been to take a female vote on the issues between Charles the First and the Parliament in the middle of the Civil War.

So far as elective government has succeeded, women in general have fully reaped the benefit of the improvements, moral and material, which it has produced. They are mistaken if they imagine that they fared better under the form of government which, in France and elsewhere, if they had the power, their sentiment would lead them to restore. They were not exempt from the misery and starvation brought into every home by the ambitious wars and the general misrule of the monarchies or even from the cruelty of their criminal laws. Down to the last days of the monarchy in France women as well as men were broken alive upon the wheel for theft.

It is needless to say that any discussion of the relative excellence, intellectual or moral, of the two moieties of humanity would be equally barren and irrelevant. The only question is as to the proper spheres of the man and woman; and assuredly, by unsexing women, we would do no homage to their sex.

It is alleged that female influence would mitigate the violence of party politics. But what ground have we, in reason or experience, for believing that women, if introduced into the political arena, would be less violent than men? Hitherto they have been free from political vices, because they have generally taken no part in politics, just as home has been an asylum from political rancour, because political division has not been introduced between man and wife. But the chances are, that, being more excitable, and having, with more warmth and generosity of temperament, less power of self-control, women would, when once engaged in party struggles, be not less but more violent than men. All our experience, in fact, points this way. In the Reign of Terror, and in the revolt of the Commune, the women notoriously rivalled the men in fury and atrocity. The same was the case in the late American Civil War. What has been the effect of public life on the character of the women who have thrown themselves into it in the United States can be doubted by no human being; and our experience of female agitations in this country seems to tell pretty much the same tale. That party politics require mitigation, and perhaps something more, may be readily admitted; but we are not likely to make the caldron boil less fiercely by flinging into it female character and Home.

That Home would escape disturbance it is surely difficult to believe. We are told that a difference of religion between man and wife does not produce unhappiness. The fact may be doubted when the difference is strong. But religion is an affair of the other world; and it does not, at all events it need not, bring people into direct, much less into public collision in this world. A man and his wife taking opposite sides in politics would be brought into direct and public collision, especially if they happened to be active politicians, about a subject of the most exciting kind. Would the harmony of most households bear the strain? Would not a husband who cared for his own happiness be apt to say that if his wife wanted it she might have the vote, but that there should be only one vote between them?

Men are not good housekeepers, and there need not be anything disparaging in saying that women, as a rule, are not likely to be good politicians. Most of them, after all, will be married, and their sphere will be one in which they do not directly feel the effects of good or bad government, which are directly felt by the man who goes forth to labour, and the practical sense of which, more than anything else, forms the political wisdom, such as it is, of the great mass of mankind. Nor would there be anything, generally speaking, to balance the judgment, as it is balanced in men by the variety of practical needs and considerations. Even with male constituencies, particular questions are apt to become too predominant, and to lead to the exaction of tyrannical pledges and to narrow ostracism of conscientious public men. But with Female Suffrage there would probably be always a woman's question, of a kind appealing to sentiment, such as the question of the Contagious Diseases Act, which demagogues would take care to provide, and which would swallow up every other question, and make a clean sweep of all public men who might refuse to take the woman's pledge. With Female Suffrage, the question of the Contagious Diseases Act would probably have made a clean sweep at the last general election of all the best servants of the State.

Mr. Mill had persuaded himself that great capacity for government had been displayed by women, and that there was urgent necessity for bringing them into the management of the

State. But he can hardly be serious when he cites as an instance of female rule a constitutional queen whose excellence consists in never doing any act of government except under the guidance of her Ministers. The queens regnant or consort, before our monarchy became constitutional, who may be said to have wielded power, are the Empress-Queen Matilda, Eleanor the wife of Henry II., Isabella the wife of Edward II., Margaret of Anjou, Mary, Elizabeth, and Henrietta Maria. Not much can be made of this list, when it is considered that both Margaret of Anjou and Henrietta Maria were, by their temper, principal causes of civil wars, and that the statesmanship of Elizabeth has totally collapsed between Mr. Froude's first volume and his last, while her feminine relations with Leicester and other favourites have contracted a much more ominous complexion in a political as well as in a moral point of view. On the other hand, it is probable that Eleanor the wife of Edward I., and certain that Caroline the wife of George II., rendered, in a womanly way, high services to the State. Mr. Mill says, from his experience at the India Office, that the queens in India are better than the kings. But the reason is obvious. British protection has suspended the operation of the rude checks on the vices of Indian despots, and a woman brought up in the zenana, though she cannot possibly be a good ruler, may well be better than a hog or a tiger.

Neither the cases of queens, however, nor those of female regents of the Netherlands, to which Mr. Mill gives so strange a turn (as though Charles V. and Philip II. had preferred females on account of their ability to male members of the house), are in point. They all belong to the hereditary system, under which these ladies were called to power by birth or appointment, and surrounded by counsellors from whose policy it is scarcely possible to distinguish that of the sovereign. Under the elective system, women would have to make their own way to seats in Parliament and to office by the same means as male politicians, by canvassing, stumping, wrestling with competitors in debate; and the female character would be exposed to influences entirely different from those which operated on Isabella of Castile.

Without pressing the argument against "Premiers in the family way" too far, it may safely be said that the women who would best represent their sex, and whose opinions would be worth most, would be generally excluded from public life by conjugal and maternal duty. Success with popular constituencies would probably fall to the lot, not of the grave matrons and spinsters whom Mr. Mill evidently has in view, but of dashing adventuresses, whose methods of captivating their constituents would often be by no means identical with legislative wisdom, or calculated to increase our veneration for their sex.

Mr. Mill is the real father of the whole movement; the arguments of its other champions are mere reproductions of his. Whatever biased his mind, therefore, ought to be carefully noted; and again it must be said that he was possessed by an illusion – an illusion beautiful and touching, but still an illusion – as to the political genius of his wife. He has given us the means of judging of her speculative powers, and even they, it is evident, were not extraordinarily high.

That there are women eminently capable of understanding and discussing political questions nobody will deny. These will find a sphere in the press, through which many men exercise a power which makes it a matter of indifference whether they have a vote or not. But it by no means follows that it is expedient to put political power into the hands of the whole sex; much less that it is expedient to do so at a moment when it is morally certain that they would use their power to cancel a good deal of what has been done in their interest, as well as in that of their partners, by the efforts of the last two hundred years.

Some supporters of the movement flatter themselves that women would always vote for peace, and that Female Suffrage would consequently be a short method of ridding the world of war and standing armies. Such experience as we have hardly warrants this anticipation. Female Sovereigns, as a rule, have not been eminently pacific. It would be difficult to find four contemporary male rulers who made more wars than Catherine the Second of Russia, Maria Theresa, Madame de Pompadour (who ruled France in the name of her lover), and the Termagant, as Carlyle calls her, of Spain. It is widely believed that the late Empress of the French, inspired by her Jesuits, was a principal mover in the attack on Germany. Those who know the Southern States say that the women there are far more ready to renew the Civil War than the men. The most effective check on war is, to use the American phrase, that every one should do his own fighting. But this check cannot be applied to women, who will be comparatively irresponsible in voting for war. A woman, in fact, can never be a full citizen in countries where, as in Germany, it is part of a citizen's duty to bear arms.

Finally, it is said that there are certain specific grievances under which women labour, and which call for immediate redress, but of which redress cannot be had unless women are empowered to extort it from their husbands and brothers at the polls. Of course if there is wrong, and wrong to half humanity, which cannot be righted in any other way, we must at once accept Female Suffrage, whatever perils it may entail.

In the United States the grievance of which most is heard is the tyrannical stringency of the marriage tie, which, it is alleged, gives a man property in a woman, and unduly interferes with the freedom and genuineness of affection. Some of the language used is more startling than this, and if reproduced might unfairly prejudice the case. But male legislatures in the United States have already carried the liberty of divorce so far, that the next step would be the total abolition of marriage and the destruction of the family. The women themselves have now, it is said, begun to draw back. They have probably become aware that liberty of divorce must be reciprocal, that marriage is pre-eminently a restraint placed on the passions of the man in the interest of the woman. That a woman loses her charms more easily than she loses her need of a protector, and that to the children divorce is moral and social ruin. Mr. Mill demands for the "slave" the privilege of changing her master; he forgets that he would at the same time give the master the privilege of changing his slave.

The question, of which more is heard here, as to the right of women to the control of their own property, was one the importance of which was not likely to be fully perceived while comparatively few women earned their own bread. However, now that it is perceived, the British legislature has at least gone so far in removing anomalies that it need not despair of seeing itself do complete justice. In the United States, male legislatures, so far from being unwilling, display almost an exaggerated propensity to sever the interest of the wife from that of the husband. An eminent American jurist told the writer that he knew a case in which a woman was compelling her husband to work for her as a hired labourer, and another in which a woman had accomplished a divorce by simply shutting the door of the house, which was her own property, in her husband's face. After all, it must be remembered that the man remains responsible for the maintenance of the woman and her children, and that the analogy of a commercial partnership, which is in vogue with the champions of Woman's Right in the United States, is very far from holding good; commercial justice between themselves and their husbands is not what the women really want. It must be remembered, too, that the male has by nature certain advantages over the female which no legislature on earth can annul; and that it is necessary in the interest of both sexes, but especially in the interest of women, to render the restraint of marriage acceptable, not only to persons of cultivated sensibility, but to ordinary men. If the ideal of marriage which floats in the pages of Mr. Mill were actually embodied in legislation, and the husband were stripped of all conjugal rights, and left with nothing but the responsibility of maintaining the family, it is at least possible that the result among the coarser masses of mankind might be the increase of license and the consequence degradation of women.

It is commonly said in the United States by the Woman's Right party, that women are under-paid for their labour, and a vague hope is held out that this might be set right by female legislation. In most fields of industry women are new-comers, and on all new-comers old custom is apt at first to bear hard. Female singers, pianoforte players, novelists, painters, milliners, are not underpaid. If female clerks and school-mistresses are paid less than male clerks and school-masters, this may be partly because continuance in the calling is an element of value, the women are taken off by marriage. That a New-Yorker will persist, out of regard for the aristocracy of sex, in paying a man a high price for his labour when he can get the work done as well for less money by a woman is not much to be apprehended. But that legislatures, male or female, could equalize wages, few will be credulous enough to believe, though it is possible that the attempt might be made.

As to domestic cruelty, if it can be stopped by any extension of the criminal law, there is surely not the slightest reason for believing that male legislatures are unwilling to perform that duty; thought of course, criminal legislation in this case, as in all others, to be effective, must keep terms with reason and justice. In fact, in this matter, women are probably better in the present hands than they would be in their own. The source of these infamies and horrors in ninety-nine cases out of a hundred is drink; and if the member for Marylebone, instead of tampering with the relations between the sexes, will turn his mind to the improvement and extension of the legislation commenced under the late Government against intemperance, he will deserve in the highest degree the gratitude of women in general, and especially of those who have the greatest claim to our sympathy.

The case of women is not that of an unenfranchised class, the interest of which is distinct from that of the enfranchised. The great mass of them are completely identified in interest with their husbands, while even those who are not married can hardly be said to form a class, or to have any common interest, other than mere sex, which is liable to be unfairly affected by class legislation. There is, therefore, no reason why Parliament should not do justice in any practical question relative to the rights of women which may be brought before it, as it has already done justice in several such questions, without invoking upon itself the coercion of Female Suffrage.

WOMAN SUFFRAGE – A REPLY
[J. E. Cairnes]

The recent utterance of Mr. Goldwin Smith against Woman
Suffrage has been for many friends of the cause, it may be
confessed, a painful surprise. It seemed strange and almost
portentous that the voice which had been so often, so boldly,
and so eloquently raised on behalf of liberal principles, should
suddenly be heard issuing from the Conservative camp, in
opposition to a measure which many Liberals regard as
amongst the most important of pending reforms. No one,
however, who has read Mr. Smith's essay will have any doubt
that the opinions expressed in it – urged as they are with all his
characteristic energy – are as genuine and sincere as anything
he has ever written on the Liberal side. Whether he has made
any converts to his views amongst the supporters of the
movement he has attacked, is more than I can say; but as one of
those who have not been convinced by his reasonings, I wish to
state in what they seem to me to be unsatisfactory, and why,
having given them my best consideration, I still remain in my
former state of mind.

There is one portion of Mr. Smith's remarks into which, I
may as well say here at the outset, I do not propose to follow
him. I refer to what he has said of Mr. Mill's relations with his
wife, and of his estimate of her mental powers. These are
points respecting which, in my opinion, the data do not exist,
at least within reach of the general public, for forming a
trustworthy opinion. They are, moreover, absolutely irrelevant
to the practical controversy, which should be decided, as Mr.
Smith himself in his essay confesses, "on its merits", "the
interest of the whole community" being the test, and not by
what people may think as to the life and opinions of any
individual, however eminent. Further, their discussion cannot
but inflict the keenest pain on more than one living person,
who, from the nature of the case, are precluded from defending
those whom they hold dear. To employ such arguments,

therefore, is to use poisoned shafts; and I should have thought that Mr. Goldwin Smith would be about the last man living to resort to such modes of warfare.

Nor is this the only topic introduced by Mr. Smith into this discussion, which might, if not with advantage, at least without detriment to his argument, have been omitted. In his criticism of Mr. Mill's view of the historical origin of the present disabilities of women, there is much, the connection of which with the practical question now before the English public it is not very easy to discern. When indeed Mr. Mill first took the question up, the discussion of this aspect of the case was imperatively demanded; because the thing then to be done was, not simply to find arguments to prove the expediency of admitting women to the suffrage, but first of all, and most difficult of all, to gain a hearing for his cause – to make some impression on the solid mass of prejudice that was arrayed against any consideration of the subject; and this could only be done by showing the factitious nature of the existing relation of the sexes. Accordingly, Mr. Mill addressed himself to this task, and in his work on the 'Subjection of Women' deduced their disabilities from that primitive condition of the human race in which man employed his superior physical strength to coerce woman to his will. Such being the origin of the subjection of women, the disabilities complained of Mr. Mill regarded as, in ethnological phrase, "survivals" from a state of society in which physical force was supreme. To this explanation Mr. Smith demurs, and contends that the "lot of the woman has not been determined by the will of the man, at least in any considerable degree." According to him it had its origin in those circumstances which made it expedient, on public grounds, that in the early stages of civilization the family should be socially, legally, and politically a unit. Into this portion of the controversy, however, I cannot see that there would be any advantage in entering. Whether Mr. Mill was right or wrong in his view of the historical question, he was at all events eminently successful in the purpose for which he introduced the discussion. He has secured a hearing for the cause of woman, so effectually, that we may now at least feel confident that it will not be ultimately decided on other grounds than those of reason and justice. Nor does it in truth matter whether in approaching the question of woman suffrage we adopt Mr. Mill's or Mr. Smith's theory. Both alike regard the existing disabilities of women as "survivals" – Mr. Mill, as survivals from a very early period in which physical force was supreme; Mr. Smith, as survivals from the state of things which produced the peculiar constitution of the patriarchal family; but both as survivals, and therefore as belonging to a condition of life which has passed away. The point is thus of purely archæological interest, while the real question now before the public is, not as to the origin of woman's disabilities, but as to their present expediency; "the interest of the whole community," to borrow once more Mr. Smith's language, being "the test."

In the Bill lately before Parliament the intention of the framers, as the reader is aware, was to confer the suffrage on widows and spinsters only; married women having been expressly excluded from its operation. Mr. Smith, in entering on the discussion, is naturally anxious to deal with the question in its broadest form, and accordingly declines to be bound by this limited conception of it. He may be perfectly justified in this course; but the reasons given by him for extending the scope of the controversy are by no means convincing. To say that "marriage could hardly be treated as politically penal, is to put the argument for his view into a neat phrase; but Englishmen have not hitherto been much governed by phrases, and I hope they are not now going to begin to be. The political disqualification which attaches to the military and naval services, as well as to some branches of the civil service, might also be described as a "penal" incident of those honourable callings, but it is nevertheless maintained; and I have no doubt that if people come to believe that it is advantageous to give the suffrage to widows and spinsters, but disadvantageous to extend it to married women, they will set epigrams at defiance, and draw in Mr. Forsyth's Bill. Again, I deny altogether that there is anything in the logic of the case that would compel those who have given the suffrage to women, to take the further step of admitting them to Parliament. "Surely," says Mr. Smith, "she who gives the mandate is competent herself to carry" – on the principle, I suppose, that

"Who drives fat oxen should himself be fat."

But granting, for argument's sake, that she is competent to carry *her own* mandate, it still does not follow that she is competent to carry the mandates of *other people*; and this is what the right to a seat in Parliament means. Indeed it is only quite lately that the law has ceased to distinguish between the right to vote and the right to be elected;[1] and if the distinction no longer exists, its abolition has been due, not in the least to a desire for logical consistency, but simply to the fact that the qualification required by the law for a seat in Parliament was found in practice ineffective for its purpose and in other ways mischievous. If it prove on full examination that the character and circumstances of women are such as to render their admission to Parliament unadvisable on public grounds, those who are in favour of giving them the suffrage will be perfectly within their right in taking their stand at this point, and in refusing to grant them the larger concession. For my own part, as I do not believe that any detriment would come from including married women with others in the grant of the suffrage, or from the admission of women to Parliament, I am quite willing to argue the question on the broader ground on which Mr. Smith desires to place it.[2]

The most important argument advanced by Mr. Smith against the policy under consideration is contained in the following passages:– "The question whether female suffrage on an extended scale is good for the whole community is probably identical, practically speaking, with the question whether it is good for us to have free institutions or not. Absolute monarchy is founded on personal loyalty. Free institutions are founded on the love of liberty, or, to speak more properly, on the preference of legal to personal government. But the love of liberty and the desire of being governed by law alone appear to be characteristically male" (p. 145). From this position Mr. Smith concludes that "to give women the franchise is simply to give them the power of putting an end actually and virtually to all franchises together." "It may not be easy," he allows, "to say

[1] In the case of clergymen, as well as in other cases, the distinction is still maintained.

[2] I cannot, however, go the length that Mr. Smith appears inclined to go in one passage, where he argues, or seems to argue, that all who are in favour of woman suffrage are bound by their own principles to vote, under all circumstances, for woman candidates. He would scarcely, I presume, contend that all who are in favour of Catholic Emancipation are bound, when a Catholic offers himself, to vote for one; and, similarly, that those who favour Jewish Emancipation are bound, when they can, to vote for Jews; but, unless he is prepared to go this length, on what ground does he hold that the advocates of woman suffrage in America must, "if they had considered the consequences of their own principles," have voted for Mrs. Victoria Woodhull?

beforehand what course the demolition of free institutions by female suffrage would take." "But," he holds, "there can be little doubt that in all cases, if power were put into the hands of the women, free government, and with it liberty of opinion would fall."

It cannot be denied that the consequences here indicated as likely to follow from the extension of the suffrage to women are sufficiently serious; and we may admit that a better reason could not easily be imagined for withholding anything from anybody than that its concession "would probably overturn the institutions on which the hopes of the world rest." But the greatness of a fear does not prove that it rests on solid grounds; and when we come to examine the grounds of Mr. Smith's dark forebodings, we find them about as substantial as the stuff that dreams are made of. "The female need of protection," he says, "of which, so long as women remain physically weak, and so long as they are mothers, it will be impossible to get rid, is apparently accompanied by a preference for personal government." "Women are priest-ridden;" but this does not go to the root of the "reactionary tendency characteristic of the sex." The effect of those physical and physiological peculiarities is, Mr. Smith thinks, to give "an almost uniform bias to the political sentiments of women;" this bias being opposed to law and liberty, and in favour of personal government; so that women may be trusted, whenever an opportunity offers, to act *en masse* for the destruction of free institutions.

Women in these passages are spoken of as if, so to speak, *in vacuo*: it is not to the women of any particular country or age that the description applies, but to woman in the abstract. In conformity with this, the illustrations which follow are taken by Mr. Smith from various ages and countries – I should have said with tolerable impartiality, if it were not that, strangely enough, scarcely any reference is made to the women of modern England. And yet it is the women of modern England whose case is in issue. Now this is a point of some importance; because it is quite possible, at least as I regard it – not being a believer in "natural rights," – that the suffrage may be as good a thing for women in certain stages of social progress, as for men, but a bad thing for both where the social conditions are different. This being so, it is not obvious how Mr. Smith helps the intelligent discussion of the question by taking his examples at random from ancient Rome, Italy, France, and the United

States, England in the seventeenth century – in a work, from any source where he can find cases to suit his purpose, but without the least reference to the special circumstances of each case. I have no desire to restrict unduly the range of the discussion; but I think that, when examples are taken from foreign countries, and still more when they are taken from former ages, with a view to prejudice the claims of English-women to the franchise, some attempt should be made to show that the cases cited are really pertinent to the question in hand.

Turning, then to the persons and country immediately concerned, let us consider how far the state of things here affords any support to Mr. Smith's speculations. I will not attempt to deny that there may be priest-ridden women in England, possibly in considerable numbers; nor will I dispute what some well-informed persons have asserted, that the passing of a woman suffrage bill would not improbably, at all events for a time, give an accession of political influence to the clergy. But granting this, and even conceding, for the sake of argument, Mr. Smith's theory as to the natural bias of the female mind, we are still a long way off from the terrible catastrophe that his fears portend. "Female suffrage, " he says, "would give a vast increase of power to the clergy;" but we have still to ask if the English clergy, Church and Nonconform-ist, are, as a body, ready to join in a crusade against free institutions. I am quite unable to discover what the grounds are for such a supposition; but if this cannot be assumed, then their influence would not be exercised in the direction Mr. Smith apprehends, and his fears for free institutions are groundless. Even if we were to make the extravagant supposition that the clergy are to a man in favour of personal government and absolutism, there would still be husbands, fathers, and brothers, whose appeals on behalf of free government would not surely pass altogether unheeded. Is it being over sanguine to assume that at the worst a sufficient number of women would be kept back from the polls to leave the victory with the cause that is "characteristically male?"

In short, we have only to attempt to realize the several conditions, *all of which would need to be fulfilled before the catastrophe which Mr. Smith dreads could ever be approached*, in order to perceive the extravagant improbability, if not intrinsic absurdity, of his apprehensions. But instead of attempting to follow further the possible consequences of social and political combinations which are never likely to have any existence outside Mr. Smith's fancy, let us consider for a moment the theory he has advanced as to the mental constitution of women, which lies at the bottom of the whole speculation. Women, it seems, are so constituted by nature as to be incapable of the "love of liberty, and the desire of being governed by law;" and this results from a "sentiment inherent in the female temperament," "formed by the normal functions and circumstances of the sex." Now if this be so – if the sentiments of women with regard to government and political institutions are thus determined by physiological causes too powerful to be modified by education and experience, then those sentiments would in all countries and under all conditions of society be essentially the same. But is this the fact? On the contrary, is it not matter of common remark that the whole attitude of women towards politics is strikingly different in different countries; that it is one thing in England, another in the United States, something different from either in France and Italy, and something different from all in Turkey and the East? and, not to travel beyond the range of the present controversy, do we not find within the United Kingdom almost every variety of political opinion prevailing amongst women, according to the circumstances of their education and social surroundings? It may be true that the interest taken by women in politics has hitherto been in general somewhat languid; that, as a body, they are less alive than men to the advantages of political liberty and of legal government. But is not this precisely what was to be expected, supposing their political opinions to be subject to the same influences which determine the political opinions of men? As a rule they have from the beginning of things been excluded from politics; their whole education has been contrived, one might say, with the deliberate purpose of giving to their sentiments an entirely different bent; home and private life have been inculcated on them as the only proper sphere for their ambition; yet in spite of these disadvantages, by merely mixing in society with men who take an interest in politics, a very great number of women have come to share that interest, while there are some, as Mr. Smith admits – I will add a rapidly increasing number – "eminently capable of understanding and discussing political questions." Can it be said that of the women who in this country take an interest in politics the bias of their political sentiments is uniformly in one direction, and this – the direction of personal government and absolutism? I can only say, if this be Mr. Smith's experience, it is singularly different from mine. No doubt there are women in abundance who care nothing for politics, and who would be quite content to live under any government which offered a fair promise of peace and security; but may not precisely the same be said of no inconsiderable number of men even in England? Would it not be easy to find men enough, and these by no means among the residuum, who take no interest at all in politics, and who, so far as they are concerned, would be willing to hand over the destinies of the human race to-morrow to a Cæsar, or to any one else who, they had reason to believe, would maintain the rights of property, and keep their own precious persons safe? This state of feeling amongst some men is not considered to prove that men in general are unfitted by nature for the functions of citizenship under a free government; and when we meet exactly the same phenomenon amongst women, why are we to deduce from it a conclusion which in the case of men we should repudiate.

In short, the patent facts of experience in this country (and if here or anywhere the facts are as I have stated them, they suffice to dispose of Mr. Smiths' theory) are consistent with one supposition and with one supposition only – the existence in women of political capabilities which may be developed in almost any direction, according to the nature of the influences brought to bear upon them. It may very well be that, when experience has furnished us with sufficient data for observation, a something will prove to be discernible in the political opinions of the two sexes in the nature of a characteristic quality; but at present conjecture upon this subject is manifestly premature; and Mr. Smith's arrow, apparently shot at a venture, we may confidently say, has not hit the mark. The love of liberty and the desire of being governed by law are feelings which have as yet been developed in but a very small proportion of men; they have been developed in a still smaller proportion of women, but the difference is not greater than the difference in the education and circumstances of the two sexes is amply sufficient for account for.

Mr. Smith having thoroughly frightened himself by the chimeras his imagination had conjured up as the probable result of giving the suffrage to women, puts the question:– "But would the men submit?" and he resorts to an ingenious, though perhaps questionable, speculation on the ultimate sanctions of law, to show that they would not. If the laws passed by women were such as men disapproved of, "the men," he says, "would, of course, refuse execution; law would be set at defiance, and government would be overturned" (p. 146). When, therefore, "the female vote" came to be taken "on the fate of free institutions," and the decree for their abolition went forth, it seems that, after all, it would prove mere *brutum fulmen*. The consummation would never take place; and the institutions on which the hopes of the world rest would remain erect, unharmed amid the impotent feminine rage surging around, much (if one may venture on the profane illustration) like one of those gin palaces in the United States that has held its ground against the psalmody of the whisky crusaders. One would have thought that this reflection would have brought some solace to Mr. Smith's soul; but, strange to say, he regards it as an aggravation of the impending evils; and would apparently be better pleased if, in the supposed contingency, men in general should exhibit the same implicit subserviency which, he tells us, has been shown by a man, somewhere in the United States, who, under his wife's compulsion, is in the habit of working for her as a hired labourer – a fact, by the way, not very happily illustrating his theory of the ultimate sanctions of law.

In truth this portion of Mr. Smith's argument – and it is in a logical sense the very heart of his case, in such sort, that, this part failing, the whole collapses – is so utterly – I will not say, weak – but so utterly unlike the sort of argument ordinarily to be found in his political writings, that it is difficult to resist the impression that it does not represent the real grounds of his conviction, but is rather a theory excogitated after conviction to satisfy that intellectual craving which an opinion formed on other grounds than reason invariably produces. And this impression is confirmed, if not reduced to certainty, as we continue the perusal of his essay. In an early passage Mr. Smith had told us that he "himself once signed a petition for female household suffrage got up by Mr. Mill;" adding that, when he signed it, he "had not seen the public life of women in the United States." Further on he gives us an account of this public life as he conceives it; and I have no doubt that we have here disclosed to us the real source, if not of his present opinions on woman suffrage, at least of the intensity with which they are held. In the United States, he says, "a passion for emulating the male sex has undoubtedly taken possession of some of the women, as it took possession of women under the Roman empire, who began to play the gladiator when other excitements were exhausted." It seems further that there are women in the United States who claim, "in virtue of 'superior complexity of organization,' not only political equality but absolute supremacy over man, of whom one has given to the movement the name of the 'Revolt of Woman.' " Again, "in the United States the privileges of women may be said to extend to impunity, not only for ordinary outrage, but for murder. The poisoner whose guilt has been proved by overwhelming evidence, is let off because she is a woman; there is a sentimental scene between her and her advocate in court, and afterwards she appears as a public lecturer.[3] The Whisky Crusade shows that women are practically above the law." Once more, it appears that "in the United States the grievance of which most is heard is the tyrannical stringency of the marriage tie . . . Some of the language used . . . if reproduced might unfairly prejudice the case." Already "male legislatures in the United States have carried the liberty of divorce so far, that the next step would be the total abolition of marriage and the destruction of the family;" and this is followed by a story of "a

[3] Mr. Smith gives neither dates nor places; but there can be little doubt that in the allusion in the text two distinct transactions are confounded: the inference suggested, moreover, is such as the facts by no means warrant. "The prisoner whose guilt has been proved by overwhelming evidence," but who "is let off," must, I think, refer to the case of a woman tried some time ago in one of the eastern cities, I think Baltimore. It is true she was "let off," but, as an American barrister informs me, with perfect propriety; the evidence against her not being sufficient to sustain the charge. In this case there was no sentimental scene in court, and no appearance afterwards as a public lecturer. These latter incidents belong to a case which occurred in San Francisco, in which a woman, Laura Fair by name, was tried, not for poisoning, but for shooting her paramour in the open street, and was acquitted in the face of the most conclusive evidence. The advocate, however, as I am informed, was passive in "the sentimental scene," and afterwards sued the lady for his fees. It is true, too, that she appeared shortly afterwards as a public lecturer; but Mr. Smith omits to add – what is surely pertinent to the question in hand – that she was hooted by the audience from the platform, and found it prudent to leave the town without delay. No one who knows anything of the United States would regard San Francisco as a typical American city; it is rather an extreme example of all that is most pronounced in American rowdyism; yet even in San Francisco we find that popular feeling on the immunity of women from penalties for crime is something very different from what Mr. Smith represents it.

woman who accomplished a divorce by simply shutting the door of the house, which was her own property, in her husband's face." It would be easy, had I space at my command, to add to these extracts; but the foregoing will suffice. One is led to ask what is the bearing of such statements, assuming the facts to be all correctly given, upon the question of woman suffrage? Mr. Smith has not troubled himself to point this out – apparently has never considered it; but finds it simply to throw in such sensational allusions here and there as a sort of garnishing for his argument, trusting no doubt that they will produce upon the minds of his readers the same impression which they have evidently made upon his own. The case seems to be this:– Mr. Smith's finer susceptibilities have been rudely shocked by the antics of a sort of Mænad sisterhood holding their revels here and there in the vast territory of the United States; and a state of mind has supervened which leads him to regard with disfavour any cause with which these women happen to be associated. Woman suffrage, unfortunately, is one of those causes; and therefore Mr. Smith is opposed to woman suffrage.

Now to let one's opinions be formed in this way is not to be guided by experience, as some people would have us believe. Let not any one suppose that Mr. Smith has any such solid support for the views advanced in his essay. Woman suffrage has nowhere yet, out of Utah, been tried in the United States; whereas we in England have witnessed its working at least in our municipal and school-board elections. In point of experience, therefore, we who have remained at home have the advantage of Mr. Smith. His sojourn in America, however, has brought to his notice the sort of women – or, more properly, *a* sort of women – who contrive to make themselves conspicuous in the United States in social and political agitations. It may be allowed that, as depicted by him, they are not a gracious band; though hardly less attractive than some of the male politicians who figure at Caucuses, Rings, and other political gatherings in the same country. Is Mr. Smith, in disgust at this latter product of American institutions prepared to abolish male suffrage, and with it representative government – to abolish it not merely in the United States, but here and everywhere? for to this length does his argument against woman suffrage, drawn from analogous manifestations on the part of some American women, carry him.

As I have said, Mr. Smith has not pointed out the bearing of his sensational allusions on the question of woman suffrage. If he intended them to support his case he was undoubtedly prudent in not doing so. Let us consider one or two of them in connection with the question at issue. We are told, for example, that "in the United States the privileges of women may be said to extend to impunity, not only for ordinary outrage, but for murder;" and then comes the story of the poisoner which I have examined in a note. Further on he says, "if the women ask for the suffrage, say some American publicists, they must have it; and in the same way, everything that a child cries for is apt to be given it without reflection as to the consequences of the indulgence." Now, assuming (what I am by no means disposed to admit) that the state of feeling towards women in the United States is such as these remarks suggest, it is to be observed in the first place that it is a state of feeling which has grown up, not under a female, but under an exclusively male, suffrage, and it is not easy to believe that the extension of the suffrage to women could make it worse. In the next place, the feeling in question is merely an exaggeration of that sickly sentimentalism regarding woman and all that concerns her which has come down to us from times of chivalry, and which has hitherto been fostered by the careful exclusion of women from political life, as well as from the great majority of useful and rational occupations. In the United States, a portion of the women appear, from Mr. Smith's account, to have suddenly broken loose from many of these restraints; and the use they are making of their freedom appears to be about as wise and edifying as the use which men commonly make of political freedom when it has been suddenly conferred upon them after centuries of servitude. The sentiment deserves all the scorn that Mr. Smith pours upon it; but the corrective for it, if it exists, is not to be found in a continuance of the state of things which produced it, but in opening to women those spheres of action from which they have been hitherto debarred, and in subjecting them to the free and bracing air of equality, alike in rights and in responsibilities, with men.

And this consideration furnishes the answer to another of Mr. Smith's arguments. He considers that the admission of women to the suffrage, instead of mitigating, is likely to aggravate the violence of political strife, and in support of this view refers to the Reign of Terror, the revolt of the Commune, and the American Civil War. I must own this latter reference has taken me by surprise. I have never heard before that the women of the United States during the Civil War "notoriously rivalled the men in fury and atrocity." I remember some very great atrocities committed during that war; for example, the massacre at Fort Pillow, the treatment of prisoners of war in some of the Southern military hospitals, the attempts to burn down some of the public buildings and hotels in New York; but these were all committed by men, and I have never heard of similar acts committed or attempted by American women. If Mr. Smith knows of any such, he ought to enlighten the world by stating them, or else withdraw his injurious assertion. On the other hand I have heard, and I imagine so must Mr. Smith, of the magnificent devotion to their country shown by the women of the Northern States in organizing and working hospital corps, and in actual services rendered to the wounded on the field, mitigating thus the hardships and horrors of war in a manner to reflect honour on their country and on their sex. As to the women of the Reign of Terror and the Commune, they were, at all events, not worse than the men; and the shocking crimes committed by both, so far as they are not purely mythical are, no doubt, referable to the same causes – the tremendous excitement of the time, the wild doctrines current, and, above all, the absolute inexperience in political affairs of those to whom power, for the moment, fell.

Again, what is the bearing of Mr. Smith's statements regarding the great freedom of divorce existing in some of the States of the Union? "Male legislatures," it seems, "have already carried the liberty of divorce so far that the next step would be the total abolition of marriage and the destruction of the family." Does it follow from this that female, or rather mixed, legislatures would go further in the same direction? for this seems to be the drift of this portion of Mr. Smith's remarks. In an earlier part of his essay he had told us that it was inherent in the nature of women to be subservient to the clergy: he now suggests that, if admitted to the suffrage, they would probably enact the abrogation of the marriage tie. Perhaps he sees his way to reconciling these two opinions, but it is not obvious on the surface; any more than it is easy to reconcile the latter with what he tells us, a few lines lower down, that women have a far deeper interest in maintaining the stringency of the marriage tie than men. If so, then, one naturally asks, why will they not use their influence to maintain it? Are they such imbeciles as not to discern their interest in so important a matter, or, discerning it, to throw their weight into the scale adverse to the most vital concerns? Here again Mr. Smith answers himself:– he tells us, "the women themselves [I presume the Mænads] have now, it is said, begun to draw back."

I now turn to a side of the question on which Mr. Smith lays very great stress, and of which I am not in the least disposed to underrate the importance – the extension of the suffrage to married women. I do not yield to Mr. Smith, or to any one, in the firmness of my conviction that the family is at the bottom of our existing civilization, and I should, for my part, regard as dearly purchased any gain in material or political well-being which should introduce a jar or weakness into this pivot of our social system. But I believe that to open political life to women, far from being fraught with the disastrous consequences Mr. Smith anticipates, would, taking things in their entire scope, be productive of quite opposite effects. If I were asked to name the principal element of weakness in the family as things now stand, I should have no hesitation in pointing to the want of sufficient subjects of common interest between man and woman. It is owing to this that matrimonial engagements are entered into so rarely on the basis of any broad intellectual sympathy, such as might furnish some security for lasting affection, and so often at the bidding of impulses and fancies that do not outlive the honeymoon; and it is owing to the same cause that so very large a proportion of the lives of most husbands and wives are spent practically apart, with little or no knowledge on the part of either of the objects or aims that engross the greater portion of the other's thoughts and energies. That under such circumstances the marriage tie is, on the whole, maintained as well as it is, seems rather matter for wonder; and to argue that the introduction of a new source of very profound common interest for husband and wife must of necessity weaken the bond, is, in my opinion, to evince a singular inability to appreciate the real dangers now besetting the institution. It is true, no doubt, that every new subject of common interest for husband and wife, must, from the nature of the case, constitute also a new possible occasion for disagreement; but if this is to be accounted a good reason for excluding women from politics, they might with equal justice be excluded from literature, from the fine arts, from everything in which men also take an interest – above all from religion. The value of these several pursuits as bonds and cements of married life is just in proportion to the degree of common interest which husbands and wives take in them, and just in the same proportion also is the possible danger that they may become the grounds of dissension. Mr. Smith is greatly scandalized at the prospect of a man and his wife taking opposite sides in politics. I cannot see that it would be at all more scandalous than that a man and his wife should take opposite sides in religion – going, for example, every Sunday to different places of worship, where each hears the creed of the other denounced as soul-destroying and damnable. It will serve to throw light upon the present problem if we consider for a moment how it happens that this latter spectacle is on the whole so rarely presented; and that, even where the event occurs, it is so frequently found consistent with tolerable harmony in married life. The explanation, I have no doubt, is of this kind: where difference of religion consists with matrimonial happiness, it will generally be found that one or both of the partners do not take a very deep interest in the creeds they profess; while, on the other hand, where people do feel strongly on religion, they generally take care, in forming matrimonial alliances, to consort with those who, on fundamental points, are of the same opinion with themselves. Now it seems to me that this may serve to illustrate for us what will be the practical working of politics in respect to married life when women begin to receive a political education, or at least to learn as much about politics, and take as much or as little interest in them as men do. A number only too large of men and women will probably continue for long enough to take but small interest in public affairs, and these will marry, as they do now, with little reference to each other's political opinions; but the danger of discord from politics under such circumstances would be infinitesimal. The only cases in which this danger would become serious would be when both husband and wife were strong politicians. Here, no doubt, there would be danger; though no greater, I think, than when two persons of strong but opposite religious convictions enter into marriage. Mr. Smith seems to think that, because "religion is an affair of the other world," it is less likely than politics to be an occasion of strife. This is probable enough when people do not believe in another world; but when they do, and believe also that the fate of people there will depend on what they believe in this, I cannot see the wisdom of his remark. Some of the worst and cruellest wars that have ever been waged have been religious wars; and so notoriously is religion an engenderer of strife, that it is now scarcely good manners to moot a religious question in private society, where politics are quite freely and amicably discussed. If persons of genuine but different religious opinions can contrive to get on together in married life, they would certainly not be likely to be severed by political differences, however strongly their opinions might be held. But, however this may be, my argument is that, in practice, such cases would very rarely occur. When politics became a subject of interest alike for men and women, it would very soon become a principal consideration in determining matrimonial alliances. Even now this is the case to some extent, and it will no doubt become more and more so as the political education of women advances. Mr. Smith's question, therefore, "Would the harmony of most households bear the strain?" may be answered by saying that in very few households would there be any strain to bear; while in most - at least in those in which politics were intelligently cultivated - home life, no longer the vapid thing it is so often now, would acquire a new element of interest, and the family would be held together by powerful sympathies that now lie undeveloped.

Mr. Smith seems to think that, if women are only excluded from the suffrage, the harmony of married life can never be endangered by politics; but this is to attribute to the mere right of voting a degree of efficacy which I, for one, am not disposed to allow to it. If women only come to take an interest in politics - it matters not whether they have the suffrage or not - all the danger that can arise from the suffrage to married life will be already incurred. It is not the giving of a vote every four or five years that constitutes the danger, if danger there be; but the habitual mental attitude of husband and wife towards each other. Those, therefore, who share Mr. Smith's apprehensions on the present subject, ought clearly to take their stand against the suffrage movement very much higher up. They ought to oppose every extension of female education which may reasonably be expected to lead women to take an interest in politics. The intelligent study of history should, in the first place, be rigidly proscribed. Political economy would be excluded as a matter of course; and, along with it, that large and increasing class of studies embraced under the name 'social.' Every one of these, intelligently cultivated, leads inevitably, where faculty is not wanting, to an interest in contemporary politics; and if women are to be shut out from this field of ideas, lest purchase they should adopt opinions which should not be those of their future husbands, their education ought at once to be truncated by this large segment. Mr. Smith indeed suggests that women who are capable of discussing political questions "will find a sphere in the press." Does he then suppose that there would be less danger to the harmony of married life from women writing in the press – writing leaders, perhaps, for strong party papers – than from tendering a vote at the polls every four or five years? Besides, the suggestion falls utterly short of the requirements of the case. The number of women who are capable, or who desire, to find a sphere in the press are never likely to be more than a handful: the numbers who desire a liberal education, in the best and broadest sense of that word, and who are or may become quite fitted to form sound opinions on political questions, are already to be numbered by thousands, perhaps I might say by tens of thousands: what their numbers will become in another generation, I will not pretend to conjecture. Mr. Smith's suggestion, therefore, though graciously meant, is hardly to the purpose. Plainly nothing short of lopping off from the education of women some of the most important branches of human knowledge will meet the difficulty.

I must, before concluding, refer briefly (for my space is all but exhausted) to an aspect of the case touched on at the opening of these remarks – the probability of the admission of women to Parliament as a consequence of giving them the suffrage. As I have already pointed out, the latter concession by no means necessarily involves the former; so that it is quite open to those who are in favour of women suffrage to decline, or if they see fit to do so, to concede the latter privilege. For my own part, however, I desire to say frankly that I am in favour of removing, not only this, but all legal impediments whatever, to the freest choice by women of a career whether in political or in civil life. It is not that I look forward to women taking advantage, in any very large degree, of the new fields of activity that would thus be opened to them; for I am not of Mr. Smith's opinion that women can be 'unsexed' by acts of parliament. I believe that all the substantial reasons of convenience, natural aptitude, and taste, which, in the division of labour between men and women, make it desirable that women should, as a rule, take charge of the domestic half of the world's work, and men of that which is transacted out of doors, will, whatever laws we may pass, remain in their full force, and will keep the general distribution of occupations between the sexes, even under the freest competition, in the main not very different from what it now is. Still, though this, as I believe, will be the rule, there will no doubt be numerous exceptions to it; and why should there not be? If some women find it suitable to their circumstances and to their natural talents or taste to embrace careers now open only to men, why should they be debarred from turning their abilities to the best account? If they make mistakes, as very possibly at first many will, and adopt unsuitable occupations, they will discover their mistakes, as men do now, by experience, and their failure will serve as a warning to others. If, on the other hand, they prove successful in their ventures, their success can only be a gain for themselves and for society at large. All this would hold true, even though the alternative of marriage and domestic life were really open to every woman in the country. But it is a fact of very great importance as regards the practical aspect of this question that no inconsiderable number of women in this country pass, and cannot but pass, their lives unmarried. Mr. Smith, indeed, regards this as connected "with an abnormal and possibly transient state of things." For my part I regard it as a perfectly normal phenomenon in such a country as England, and, therefore, as likely to endure. In any case, while it lasts, the exclusion of women from professional and other careers is something more than a theoretical injustice. It is a real and substantial wrong, involving penury and all its consequences, inflicted on a large number of persons, whose only crime is their sex, and who only ask to be permitted to earn a livelihood by making themselves useful to their fellow-creatures. The claim to be admitted to Parliament, indeed, if it should be advanced (which it has not yet been), would stand on somewhat different ground. Exclusion of this case would not mean exclusion from the means of earning a livelihood, and therefore the reasons in favour of the claim are undoubtedly less strong than those which may be urged in favour of opening professional and industrial careers; but why should women not be allowed the fullest and freest use of their faculties in any walk of life, whether lucrative or otherwise, in which any competent portion of the community may think it expedient to employ them? At all events the onus of proof lies with those who would resist such a claim; and if the opponents have nothing better to urge than the fatuous jokes which have hitherto been the staple of their argument, but from which Mr. Smith has had the good taste to abstain, the case against women is certainly not a strong one. Whether many women, if the opportunity offered, would be ambitious of a parliamentary career; or whether in this case, they would find many constituencies disposed to elect them, are questions, the consideration of which may perhaps be left, without disadvantage, to a future day.